RETRIBUTION, JUSTICE, AND THERAPY

PALLAS PAPERBACKS

Pallas Paperbacks Series is a natural outgrowth of Reidel's scholarly publishing activities in the humanities, social sciences, and hard sciences. It is designed to accommodate original works in specialized fields which, by nature of their broader applicability, deserve a larger audience and lower price than the standard academic hardback. Also to be included are books which have become modern classics in their fields, but have not yet benefitted from appearing in a more accessible edition.

Volumes appearing in Pallas will be promoted collectively and individually to appropriate markets. Since quality and low price are the two major objectives of this program, it is expected that the series will soon establish itself in campus bookstores and other suitable outlets.

PALLAS titles in print:

1. Wolff, *Surrender and Catch*
2. Fraser, *Thermodynamics in Geology*
3. Goodman, *The Structure of Appearance*
4. Schlesinger, *Religion and Scientific Method*
5. Aune, *Reason and Action*
6. Rosenberg, *Linguistic Representation*
7. Ruse, *Sociobiology: Sense or Nonsense?*
8. Loux, *Substance and Attribute*
9. Ihde, *Technics and Praxis*
10. Simon, *Models of Discovery*
11. Murphy, *Retribution, Justice, and Therapy*

Photograph by Sean Murphy

JEFFRIE G. MURPHY

A PALLAS PAPERBACK / 11

JEFFRIE G. MURPHY
University of Arizona, Tucson, Arizona

RETRIBUTION, JUSTICE, AND THERAPY

Essays in the Philosophy of Law

D. REIDEL PUBLISHING COMPANY

DORDRECHT : HOLLAND / BOSTON : U.S.A.

LONDON : ENGLAND

Library of Congress Cataloging in Publication Data

Murphy, Jeffrie G.
　　Retribution, Justice, and Therapy

　　(Philosophical studies series in philosophy ; v. 16)
　　Includes indexes
　　1.　Law–Philosophy–Addresses, Essays, Lectures.
　　2.　Justice–Addresses, Essays, Lectures.　3.　Punish-
ment–Addresses, Essays, and Lectures.　I.　Title.
K246.M87　　　340.1　　　79–15903
ISBN 90–277–0998–X
ISBN 90–277–0999–8 pbk. (Pallas edition)

Publishing by D. Reidel Publishing Company,
P.O. Box 17, Dordrecht, Holland

Sold and distributed in the U.S.A., Canada, and Mexico
by D. Reidel Publishing Company, Inc.
Lincoln Building, 160 Old Derby Street, Hingham,
Mass. 02043, U.S.A.

*Also published in 1979 in hardbound edition by Reidel in
philosophical Studies Series in Philosophy, Volume 16,
edited by Wilfrid Sellars and Keith Lehrer*

Printed in The Netherlands

FOR ELLEN

TABLE OF CONTENTS

PREFACE   xi

ACKNOWLEDGEMENTS   xix

PART ONE: RIGHTS, JUSTICE, AND THE SOCIAL CONTRACT

The Killing of the Innocent   3
Rights and Borderline Cases   26
Violence and the Socratic Theory of Legal Fidelity   40
Hume and Kant on the Social Contract   58

PART TWO: PUNISHMENT AND RESPONSIBILITY

Three Mistakes About Retributivism   77
Kant's Theory of Criminal Punishment   82
Marxism and Retribution   93
Involuntary Acts and Criminal Liability   116
Moral Death: A Kantian Essay on Psychopathy   128

PART THREE: THERAPEUTIC INTERVENTION

Criminal Punishment and Psychiatric Fallacies   147
Preventive Detention and Psychiatry   159
Incompetence and Paternalism   165
Total Institutions and the Possibility of Consent to Organic Therapies   183

PART FOUR: DEATH AND THE SUPREME COURT

Rationality and the Fear of Death   205
Cruel and Unusual Punishments   223

LEGAL CASES CITED   250

NAME INDEX   251

SUBJECT INDEX   254

PREFACE

One might legitimately ask what reasons other than vanity could prompt an author to issue a collection of his previously published essays. The best reason, I think, is the belief that the essays hang together in such a way that, as a book, they produce a whole which is in a sense greater than the sum of its parts. When this happens, as I hope it does in the present case, it is because the essays pursue related themes in such a way that, together, they at least form a start toward the development of a systematic theory on the common foundations supporting the particular claims in the particular articles. With respect to this collection, the essays can all be read as particular ways of pursuing the following general pattern of thought: that a commitment to justice and a respect for rights (and *not* social utility) must be the foundation of any morally acceptable legal order; that a social contractarian model is the best way to illuminate this foundation; that a retributive theory of punishment is the only theory of punishment resting on such a foundation and thus is the only morally acceptable theory of punishment; that the twentieth century's faddish movement toward a "scientific" or therapeutic response to crime runs grave risks of undermining the foundations of justice and rights on which the legal order ought to rest; and, finally, that the legitimate worry about the tendency of the behavioral sciences to undermine the values of justice and rights must not cause us to miss the important insights and opportunities that these sciences might have to offer in understanding and dealing with crime or antisocial behavior. In other words, I hope that I have managed to remain properly skeptical of the pretensions of behavioral science without becoming a part of some ignorant and naively romantic antiscientific movement.

Three other reasons can justify the issue of a collection of previously published essays, and they too are present here. First, it is useful to publish a collection of essays which have previously appeared in journals not normally read by all the scholars who might have an interest in the essays. This problem is particularly acute in the philosophy of law. If one publishes in a law review, one knows that the article is likely to be missed by many philosophers who might find it of interest. If one publishes in a philosophy journal, the same problems arise with respect to potentially interested lawyers. Publication of the essays in one common source is thus of great assistance in reaching a larger number of scholars in one's desired audience.

Second, it is valuable to have the opportunity (frequently used here) of being able to correct mistakes in the essays, to improve clarity of expression at crucial points, and to re-write parts of them with a view toward making sure that they do indeed hang together successfully as a whole.

Third, and finally, such a collection gives the author the opportunity of publishing at least one *new* essay which seems more persuasive and valuable in the context provided by the other essays than it perhaps would if published alone. The previously unpublished essay 'Cruel and Unusual Punishments' fills this role in the present collection. It is in part a response to recent Supreme Court cases on capital punishment and is much more concerned with constitutional interpretation than any other essay I have published. It is my belief that it benefits from being in a context of other articles which flesh out the moral background presupposed by the constitutional interpretation presented.

In Part One, *Rights, Justice and the Social Contract*, four essays are presented which develop the general moral background upon which I draw in my later discussions of punishment. 'The Killing of the Innocent' attempts to develop the thesis that certain absolute moral prohibitions (e.g. never kill the innocent) are not necessarily bits of intuitive dogma or moral fanaticism (as utilitarian critics often charge) but can be rendered reasonable when seen as imbedded in a moral context of justice and respect for rights. The influence of Kant's moral philosophy on this essay is obvious and enormous. I began my career in philosophy as a scholar in the philosophy of Kant, and his powerful moral theory (particularly as I saw it developed by my teacher Lewis White Beck) still strikes me as the most impressive achievement in the history of moral philosophy – a resource not yet adequately mined for the philosophy of law. In 'Rights and Borderline Cases' I attempt to develop a conception of justice and rights by examining the status of such moral concepts in borderline or non-standard cases – e.g. children and the mentally retarded. I distinguish two concepts of rights and argue that a correct theory of justice and rights would have to keep them separate, since different kinds of arguments and considerations are relevant in the case of each. Here, as in other essays in the collecton, I employ a contractarian model for my discussions of justice; and the influence of some of John Rawls' writings on my use of the model is apparent. Finally, I present two historical pieces. 'Violence and the Socratic Theory of Legal Fidelity' is an exploration of the social contract theory as it was first developed in antiquity. In 'Hume and Kant on the

Social Contract,' I examine the historical development of the idea that the social contract may be used as a model for rational and moral social choice. I outline Hume's powerful arguments against the use of the social contract by such writers as John Locke and then consider the extent to which, if at all, later contract theorists (especially Kant and Rawls) are able to avoid these objections. From the four essays in Part I the reader will get a fairly clear picture of what I take the related claims of justice and respect for rights to amount to and why I believe that they are morally basic. This general vision of the moral foundation of the legal order will be appealed to in almost all of the essays to follow.

In Part Two, *Punishment and Responsibility*, essays are presented which explore the problem of the justification of punishment, defend a largely retributive conception of that justification, and develop an account of criminal responsibility founded on this conception. In 'Three Mistakes About Retributivism,' I attempt to clear up three common misunderstandings of retributivism — misunderstandings which pose obstacles to its acceptance and which account for a substantial amount of the "bad press" it has received. In 'Kant's Theory of Criminal Punishment,' the historical foundations of the retributive theory are explored through an examination of the writings of its most illustrious defender. In 'Marxism and Retribution,' I elaborate in detail the retributive theory of punishment sketched in the two previous essays. I argue that the retributive theory can best be defended in terms of a theory of justice which is contractarian in nature. Kant's belief that his theory of punishment is solidly grounded in his theory of justice is defended. Rawls, who shares with Kant a contractarian theory of justice, has not developed in print a theory of punishment as a part of his general theory of justice.[1] The only theory of punishment which he could consistently hold, I argue, should have to be retributive in nature.

General theories on the justifying aim of punishment require supplementation with an account of responsibility — i.e. with an answer to the question "who may legitimately be held accountable given the demands of the theory?" The retributivist argues that it is just to punish only those who *deserve* punishment and would oppose punishing those who act without fault (e.g. would oppose strict or absolute criminal liability) even if the social consequences of such punishment would be desirable. It is thus important that the concepts of desert and fault be given careful analysis and consideration. In the last three essays in this section, these issues are explored. In the last half of 'Marxism and Retribution,' I argue — in the spirit of Marx — that the basic demands of justice may not be satisfied in a class-divided society, that the only morally

acceptable theory of punishment (retributivism) will not be uniformly applicable in that society, and therefore it is by no means clear that the economically disadvantaged members of that society can truly be said to deserve
punishment for their crimes or that the society has a right to punish them. In
'Involuntary Acts and Criminal Liability' and 'Moral Death: A Kantian Essay
on Psychopathy,' I explore the question of the extent to which those suffering from certain mental or behavioral pathologies exhibit the kind of fault
which makes them deserving of punishment. These issues are commonly
looked at from a utilitarian perspective (e.g. is there any social good produced
by punishing such people?); but, as the reader should now expect, I evaluate
them from the perspective of justice and a respect for rights. I argue that
failure to be a responsible person is, in justice, an excusing factor; but it is
also a factor which diminishes one's moral personhood, loses one membership
in the moral community, and prevents one from justifiably claiming the moral
rights appropriate to that status. Adequate moral evaluation, of course, presupposes careful analysis of the concepts used to describe the objects of
evaluation. Thus these essays also contain analytical work on the concepts of
psychopathy and involuntary act.

In Part Three, *Therapeutic Intervention*, I attempt to come to terms with
the suggestion — often made by psychiatrists and other behavioral scientists —
that the crime problem should be viewed as mainly a scientific or medical
problem. The standard argument goes as follows: Our goal is the elimination
of crime. Punishment does not work very well as a technique for eliminating
crime. Thus we should replace punishment (and its outdated notions of
justice, desert, responsibility, and fault) with a technique that will work —
e.g. psychotherapy, behavior modification therapy, or even brain surgery.

The essays in this part are all attempts to come to terms with the above
line of argument — to expose its substantial weaknesses while still preserving
the insights which motivate it. In 'Criminal Punishment and Psychiatric Fallacies' and 'Preventive Detention and Psychiatry,' I examine the psychiatrist
Karl Menninger's well-known suggestion that criminality is a symptom of mental disease or disorder and should be dealt with accordingly — i.e. preventively
and therapeutically. I argue that Menninger's position is totally insensitive to
those due process considerations which are essential for the preservation of
rights in a just rule of law. In "Incompetence and Paternalism," I examine the
frequently made claim that, even in a free society, mentally incompetent
persons may legitimately have their liberty curtailed for their own good.
Coercing people for our notion of their good is, of course, a terrible danger in
a free society and should be done only if supported by an argument involving

careful analysis and solid empirical foundation. In this essay I attempt a careful analysis of the concept of incompetence and develop a contractarian justification for extremely limited paternalistic interference with incompetent persons. Finally, in 'Total Institutions and the Possibility of Consent to Organic Therapies,' I attempt to come to terms with some of the issues involved in the ongoing debate on behavior-corrective brain surgery (psychosurgery) on prison inmates and inmates of mental hospitals (so-called "total institutions"). While suspicious of the foundation of the claims made that psychosurgery is a valuable technique for dealing with some criminal violence, I still argue — much to the dismay of many of my liberal friends — that inmates of total institutions *can* give informed, voluntary, and competent consent to such surgery, In developing this position, I attempt to refute in detail the reasoning of the court in the important Michigan psychosurgery case, *Kaimowitz v. Department of Mental Health*. The judgment of the court that inmates of total institutions cannot give legally proper consent to psychosurgery is, in my judgment, supported by little more than knee-jerk liberal slogans. Though the ideological thrust of most of my essays can no doubt properly be characterized as "liberal," I hope that it is not liberalism of the sentimental variety which is prepared to use any argument, no matter how lame, to oppose anything which intuitively seems "anti-humanistic" in some unspecified sense. Reflective liberalism motivates the legitimate suspicion of the behavioral sciences, but it is sentimental knee-jerk liberalism which enlists vague slogans to attack everything of value which we might derive from those sciences. Even when defending the correct conclusion, such liberalism often does so by covering what are simply desirable fictions or useful policies with confusing abstract principles. In this essay, I attempt to reason carefully and thus leave open the possibility of our deriving future good from developments in such sciences as brain physiology by not using arguments of emotional overkill which will close off consideration of them entirely.

In the closing section, Part Four, *Death and the Supreme Court*, I have included two essays. The first, 'Rationality and the Fear of Death,' cannot honestly be said to stand in a very close logical relation to the other essays in the collection. The essay is primarily concerned to give an analysis of the concept of death and to consider the extent to which, if at all, the fear of death is rational. These issues should be of concern to philosophers of law interested in the death penalty and in the rational status of human emotions (a topic clearly relevant to questions of mental competence), but my primary reason for including the essay is much more direct: I happen to like it a great deal. The second essay, 'Cruel and Unusual Punishments,' has not been previously published. In this essay, I consider the decisions and opinions in the recent Supreme Court cases on the death penalty – particularly the claim that, under typical circumstances, the penalty constitutes constitutionally forbidden cruel and unusual punishment. I argue that a retributive theory of punishment provides the best argument in favor of capital punishment and also the framework for the best analysis of the constitutional concepts of cruel and unusual punishment. This suggests that the death penalty is most reasonably discussed, both pro and con, in terms of retributive considerations. This is not because such considerations are good in themselves but rather, as has been argued in many of the previous essays, because they rest on the morally vital basis of justice and respect for rights.

In putting together a collection such as this, an author is faced with some difficult decisions. Had I decided to issue all of my previously published essays, the collection would have been too long and would have failed to hang together as a coherent unit. Also, some of my previous essays I now judge to be so dreadful that I would not think of calling anyone's attention to them. Hopefully, if they are not included or even mentioned in this collection, they will be utterly forgotten or, if noticed, attributed to another person who happens to write under my name. Not all of the essays I omitted, however, fall into this camp. Some of them I genuinely like and was forced to leave them out solely for considerations of space or theme. Let me then at least mention them here so that they can be brought to the attention of potentially interested readers:

'Kant's Concept of a Right Action', *The Monist* **51**, No. 4 (1967) 574–98.

'Allegiance and Lawful Government', *Ethics* **79**, No. 1 (1968) 56–69.

'Kant's Second Analogy as an Answer to Hume', *Ratio* **XI**, No. 1 (1969) 75–78.

'A Paradox in Locke's Theory of Natural Rights', *Dialogue* **VIII**, No. 2, (1969) 256–271.

'In Defense of Obligation', *Nomos XII: Political and Legal Obligation*, ed. J. Roland Pennock and John W. Chapman (New York: Atherton Press, 1970, pp. 36–45).

One final note of thanks: Most of these essays were written after I joined the faculty of the Department of Philosophy at the University of Arizona. I want to take this opportunity to express my gratitude to the administrative officers of this university (and especially to President John Schaefer, Executive Vice President Albert Weaver, and Liberal Arts Deans Herman Bleibtreu and Paul Rosenblatt) for the tremendous support which they have given to our department and for their efforts in creating a genuine intellectual community

on this campus; to the College of Law (and especially to Professor David
Wexler) for encouragement and valuable discussion of my efforts in inter-
disciplinary work; to my colleagues in philosophy (and especially to Professor
Ronald Milo) for constructive discussion and criticism of my ideas; and to my
students — both undergraduate and graduate — for putting up with it all when
it was in a rough stage and for forcing me to rethink and clarify substantial
portions of it. All of these persons share in the credit for whatever is good in
my work and therefore must, of course, shoulder a portion of the burden of
responsibility and blame for whatever errors may still remain. Of course, I
sometimes *ignored* criticisms — including some very cogent ones made by
Professors Wexler and Milo. Even this does not free them from responsibility,
however, since they could have taken further steps — e.g. they could have
destroyed my manuscripts, had me arrested or subjected to civil commitment,
or even killed me. That they did none of these things clearly indicates that
they are not totally committed to the pursuit of truth.

J.G.M.

NOTE

[1] Rawls did discuss punishment in his early essay 'Two Concepts of Rules', *Philosophical
Review* 64, (1955) 3–32. However, his mature *A Theory of Justice* (Cambridge, Mass.:
Harvard University Press, 1971) does not contain a discussion of punishment and would
not, in my judgment, support the generally utilitarian views put forth in the early essay.

ACKNOWLEDGEMENTS

'The Killing of the Innocent' appeared originally in *The Monist* **57**, Number 4, (October 1973) 527–550. It is reprinted here with the permission of the publisher.

'Rights and Borderline Cases' appeared originally in *Arizona Law Review* **19**, Number 1 (1977) 228–241. Copyright © 1978 by the Arizona Board of Regents. Reprinted by permission.

'Violence and the Socratic Theory of Legal Fidelity' was presented as a lecture at the International Conference on Violence and Aggression in the History of Ideas, Temple University, 1972. This conference was conducted by the International Society for the History of Ideas, the organ of which is the *Journal of the History of Ideas.* This essay originally appeared in the volume *Violence and Aggression in the History of Ideas*, edited by Philip P. Wiener and John Fisher, Rutgers University Press, New Brunswick, 1974, pp. 15–33. It is reprinted here with the permission of the publisher and the editors.

'Hume and Kant on the Social Contract' was presented as a lecture at the David Hume Bicentennial Symposium, University of Arizona, 1976. It originally appeared in *Philosophical Studies* **33**, Number 1 (January 1978) 65–79. Copyright © 1978, D. Reidel Publishing Co., Dordrecht, Holland, and reprinted by permission of the publisher.

'Three Mistakes About Retributivism' appeared originally in *Analysis*, (April 1971) 166–169. It is reprinted here with the permission of the editor.

'Kant's Theory of Criminal Punishment' was presented as a lecture at the Third International Kant Congress, University of Rochester, 1970. It originally appeared in the volume *Proceedings of the Third International Kant Congress*, edited by Lewis White Beck, Copyright © 1972, D. Reidel Publishing Company, Dordrecht, Holland, pp. 434–441. It is reprinted here by permission of the publisher.

'Marxism and Retribution' originally appeared in *Philosophy and Public Affairs* **2**, Number 3 (Spring 1973) 217–243. Copyright © 1973 by Princeton University Press, Reprinted by permission.

'Involuntary Acts and Criminal Liability' originally appeared in *Ethics* **81**, Number 4 (July 1971) 332–342. Copyright © 1971 by the University of Chicago Press and reprinted with permission.

'Moral Death: A Kantian Essay on Psychopathy' originally appeared in *Ethics* **82**, Number 4 (July 1972) 284–298. Copyright © 1972 by the University of Chicago Press and reprinted with permission.

'Criminal Punishment and Psychiatric Fallacies' originally appeared in *Law and Society Review* **4**, Number 1 (August 1969) 111–122. Copyright © 1969 by the Law and Society Association and reprinted by permission.

'Preventive Detention and Psychiatry' originally appeared in *Dissent*, (Sept./ Oct. 1970) 448–450 and 460. It is reprinted here by permission of the publisher.

'Incompetence and Paternalism' originally appeared in *Archiv für Rechts-und Sozialphilosophie*, Volume 1974 LX/4, pp. 465–486. It is reprinted here by permission of the editor.

'Total Institutions and the Possibility of Consent to Organic Therapies' was presented as a lead symposium paper at the meetings of the American Philosophical Association, Pacific Division, 1975. It originally appeared in *Human Rights* **5**, Number 1 (Fall 1975) 25–45. It is reprinted here by permission of Southern Methodist University School of Law and the Section of Individual Rights and Responsibilities, American Bar Association.

'Rationality and the Fear of Death' originally appeared in *The Monist* **59**, Number 2 (April 1976) 187–203. It is reprinted here with the permission of the publisher.

'Cruel and Unusual Punishments' appears here for the first time. It was prepared for presentation as the opening paper in a symposium with M. D. A. Freeman at the Royal Institute of Philosophy Conference on Law, Morality and Rights in September, 1979. Copyright © 1979 by the Royal Institute of Philosophy and printed here, by permission of the Institute, in approximately the form for presentation to the conference. A revised text of the full symposium will be published in the conference proceedings by the Harvester Press.

A somewhat different version of 'Cruel and Unusual Punishments' was presented as a lecture in April, 1979, at a conference to honor Professor Lewis White Beck on the occasion of his retirement from the University of Rochester. I dedicate the essay to him with esteem and affection.

PART ONE

RIGHTS, JUSTICE, AND THE SOCIAL CONTRACT

There is nothing in the world so
sacred as the rights of others.

Immanuel Kant
Lectures on Ethics

PART ONE

RIGHT ... OF THE ... OF 1850

THE KILLING OF THE INNOCENT*

> After war has been begun, and during the whole period thereof up to the attainment of victory, it is just to visit upon the enemy all losses which may seem necessary for obtaining satisfaction or for securing victory, provided that these losses do not involve intrinsic injury to innocent persons, which would be in itself an evil.
>
> Suárez, *The Three Theological Virtues*

> Fight on land and on sea
> All men want to be free
> If they don't, never mind
> We'll abolish all mankind
>
> Peter Weiss, *Marat/Sade*

INTRODUCTION

Murder, some may suggest, is to be defined as the intentional and uncoerced killing of the innocent; and it is true by definition that murder is wrong. Yet wars, particularly modern wars, seem to require the killing of the innocent, e.g. through antimorale terror bombing. Therefore war (at least modern war) must be wrong.

The above line of argument has a certain plausibility and seems to lie behind much philosophical and theological discussion of such problems as the Just War and the nature of war crimes.[1] If accepted in full, it seems to entail the immorality of war (i.e. the position of pacifism) and the moral blameworthiness of those who participate in war (i.e. warmakers and uncoerced soldiers are all murderers). To avoid these consequences, some writers will challenge some part of the argument by maintaining (a) that there are no innocents in war or (b) that modern war does not in fact require the killing of the innocent or (c) that war involves the suspension of moral considerations

3

and thus stands outside the domain of moral criticism entirely or (d) that contributing to the death of innocents is morally blameless so long as it is only foreseen but not intended by those involved in bringing it about (the Catholic principle of the Double Effect) or (e) that the prohibition against killing the innocent is only *prima facie*[2] and can be overridden by even more important moral requirements, e.g. the defense of freedom.

In this paper I want to come to terms with at least some of the important issues raised by the killing of innocents in time of war. The issues I shall focus on are the following:

(1) What does it mean, in a context of war, to describe an individual as *innocent*?

(2) Why is it morally wrong to kill individuals so described?

(3) Is the moral wrongness merely *prima facie* (i.e. subject to being overridden by other, more weighty, moral considerations) or is it absolute?

I shall avoid making any final judgments on the morality of war (modern wars or otherwise) since such judgments would involve not just philosophical claims but also empirical claims, e.g. the claim that in fact modern wars cannot be waged so as to avoid the killing of the innocent. However, certain answers to the questions I shall explore will, when coupled with empirical premises, clearly have moral consequences. For example: *If* the killing of innocents is absolutely and not just *prima facie* immoral (a philosophical claim), and *if* modern wars necessarily involve the killing of innocents (an empirical claim), *then* war for modern times must be absolutely condemned, i.e. pacifism is the required moral posture for the twentieth century. I shall leave it to sociologists and military historians, however, to supply the correct factual premises.

I shall, then, mainly be concerned to seek answers to the above three questions. However, before launching into my discussion, I want to make one thing clear. Just because I am focusing upon the killing of innocents, it should not be thought that I am confident that it is right to kill the guilty and thus that it is *only* the killing of the innocent that stands in need of analysis and justification. I have no such confidence. I am starting with what any man who is not a moral imbecile must admit to be, at the very least, an obvious *prima facie* objection to indiscriminate war. In so doing, I do not mean to suggest that there may not be strong nonobvious objections to be made against discriminate war.

THE CONCEPT OF INNOCENCE

The notions of innocence and guilt seem most at home in a legal context and, somewhat less comfortably, in a moral context. Legally, a man is innocent if he is not guilty, i.e. if he has not engaged in conduct explicitly prohibited by rules of the criminal law. A man may be regarded as morally innocent if his actions do not result from a mental state (e.g. malice) or a character defect (e.g. negligence) which we regard as morally blameworthy. In any civilized system of criminal law, of course, there will be a close connection between legal guilt and innocence and moral guilt and innocence, e.g. murder in the criminal law has as one of its material or defining elements the blameworthy mental state (*mens rea*) of "malice aforethought." But this close connection does not show that the legal and moral concepts are not different. The existence of strict liability criminal statutes is sufficient to show that they are different. Under a strict liability statute, a man can be guilty of a criminal offense without having, at the time of his action, any blameworthy mental state or character defect, not even negligence.[3] However, the notion of strict *moral* responsibility makes little sense; for an inquiry into moral responsibility for the most part just is an inquiry into such matters as the agent's motives, intentions, beliefs, etc.[4] Also, the issue of legal responsibility is much more easily determinable than that of moral responsibility. For example: It is noncontroversial that negligence can make one legally responsible. Anyone who doubts this may simply be given a reading assignment in any number of penal codes.[5] But whether or not negligence is a mental state or a character defect for which one is *morally* responsible is a matter about which reasonable men can disagree. No reading assignment or simple inquiry into "the facts" will lay this worry to rest.[6]

Now our reasonably comfortable ability to operate with these concepts of guilt and innocence leaves us when we attempt to apply them to the context of war. Of course, the legal notions will have application in a limited number of cases, i.e. with respect to those who are legally war criminals under international law. But this will by no means illuminate the majority of cases. For example: Those who have written on the topic of protecting innocents in war would not want to regard the killing of an enemy soldier engaged in an attack against a fortified position as a case of killing the innocent. He is surely, in the right sense (whatever that is), among the guilty (or, at least, among the noninnocent) and is thus a fitting object for violent death. But he is in no sense *legally* guilty. There are no rules of international law prohibiting what he is doing; and, even if such rules were created, they would surely not involve the setting up of a random collection of soldiers from the other side to act as judges and executioners of this law. Thus the legal notions of guilt and innocence do not serve us well here.

What, then, about moral guilt or innocence? Even to make this suggestion plausible in the context of war, we surely have to attempt to narrow it down to moral innocence or guilt *of* the war or *of* something within the war — not just moral innocence or guilt *simpliciter*. That is, we surely do not want to say that if a bomb falls (say) on a man with a self-deceiving morally impure heart who is a civilian behind the lines that this is not, in the relevant sense, a case of killing an innocent. Similarly, I think it would be odd for us to want to say that if a soldier with a morally admirable character is killed in action that this is a case of killing an innocent and is to be condemned on those grounds. If we take this line, it would seem that national leaders should attempt to make some investigation of the motives and characters of both soldiers and civilians and kill the unjust among both classes and spare the just. (Only babes in arms would be clearly protected.) Now this sort of judgment, typically thought to be reserved for God if for anyone, is surely a very disquieting thing if advocated for generals and other war leaders. Thus the notions of moral innocence and guilt *simpliciter* must be dropped in this context.

Suppose, then, we try to make use of the notions of moral innocence *of the war* or moral guilt *of the war* (or of something within the war). Even here we find serious problems. Consider the octogenarian civilian in Dresden who is an avid supporter of Hitler's war effort (pays taxes gladly, supports warmongering political rallies, etc.) and contrast his case with that of the poor, frightened, pacifist frontline soldier who is only where he is because of duress and who intends always to fire over the heads of the enemy. It seems reasonable to say that the former is much more morally guilty of the war than the latter; and yet most writers on the topic would regard killing the former, but not the latter, as a case of killing an innocent.

What all this suggests is that the classical worry about protecting the innocent is really a worry about protecting *noncombatants*. And thus the distinction between combatants and noncombatants is what needs to be illucidated. Frontline soldiers are clearly combatants; babes in arms clearly are not. And we know this without judging their respective moral and legal guilt or innocence. And thus the worry, then, is the following: Under what circumstances is an individual truly a combatant? Wars may be viewed as games (terrible ones of course) between enemies or opponents. Who, then, is an enemy or opponent?

One suggestion for defining a combatant might be the following: Only soldiers engaged in fighting are combatants. But this does not seem adequate. For if killing an enemy soldier is right, then it would also seem to be right to kill the man who *orders* him to the frontline. If anything, the case for killing (say) a general seems better, since the soldier is presumably simply acting in some sense as his agent, i.e. the general kills *through* him. Perhaps the way to put the point, then, is as follows: The enemy is represented by those who are *engaged in an attempt* to destroy you.[7] And thus all frontline combat soldiers (though not prisoners, or soldiers on leave, or wounded soldiers, or chaplains, or medics) are enemies and all who issue orders for destruction are enemies. Thus we might try the following: Combatants are those anywhere within the *chain of command or responsibility* — from bottom to top. If this is correct, then a carefully planned attack on the seat of government, intended to destroy those civilians (and only those) directing the war effort, would not be a case of killing noncombatants or, in the relevant sense, innocents.

But what is a chain of command or responsibility? It would be wrong to regard it solely as a causal chain, though it is *at least* that. That is, the notion of responsibility has to be stronger than that expressed in the sentence "The slippery pavement was *responsible* for the accident." For to regard the chain here as solely causal in character would lead to the following consequence: If a combatant is understood solely as one who performs an action which is a causally necessary condition for the waging of war, then the following are going to be combatants: farmers, employees at a city water works, and anyone who pays taxes. Obviously a country cannot wage war if there is no food, no management of the basic affairs of its cities, and no money to pay for it. And of course the list of persons "responsible" for the war in this sense could be greatly extended. But if all these persons are in the class of combatants, then the rule "protect noncombatants" is going to amount to little more than "protect babies and the senile." But one would, I think, have more ambition for it than that, e.g. one would hope that such a rule would protect housewives even if it is true that they "help" the war effort by writing consoling letters to their soldier husbands and by feeding them and providing them with emotional and sexual relief when they are home on leave. Thus I think that it is wrong to regard the notion of chain here as merely causal in character.

What kind of chain, then, is it? Let us call it a *chain of agency*. What I mean by this is that the links of the chain (like the links between motives and actions) are held together logically and not merely causally, i.e. are held together, in this case, under the notion of who it is that is *engaged in an attempt* to destroy you. Perhaps the point can better be put in this way: The farmer's role bears a contingent connection to the war effort whereas the general's role bears a necessary connection to the war effort, i.e. his function, unlike the farmer's, is not logically separable from the waging of war. Or, following Thomas Nagel,[8] the point can perhaps be put in yet another way: The farmer is aiding the soldier *qua* human being whereas the general is aiding the soldier *qua* soldier or fighting man. And since your enemy is the soldier *qua* soldier, and not *qua* human being, we have grounds for letting the farmer off. If we think of a justified war as one of self-defense,[9] then we must ask the question "Who can be said to be *attacking* us such that we need to defend ourselves against him?" Viewed in this way, the farmer seems an unlikely candidate for combat status.

This analysis does, of course, leave us with borderline cases. But, since there *are* borderline cases, this is a virtue of the analysis so long as it captures just the right ones. Consider workers in a munitions factory. Are they or are they not combatants? At least with certain munitions factories (making only bombs, say) it is certainly going to be odd to claim that their activities bear only a contingent connection to the war effort. What they make, unlike food, certainly supports the fighting man *qua* fighting man and not *qua* human being. Thus I should be inclined to say that they are properly to be regarded as combatants and thus properly subject to attack. But what about workers in munitions factories that only in part supply the war effort, e.g. they make rifles both for soldiers and for hunters? Or workers in nonmunitions factories that do make some war products, e.g. workers in companies, such as Dow Chemical, which make both Saran Wrap and Napalm? Or workers in ball-bearing factories or oilrefineries, some of their product going to war machines and some not? Here, I submit, we do have genuine borderline cases. And with respect to these, what should we do? I should hope that reasonable men would accept that the burden of proof lies on those claiming that a particular group of persons are combatants and properly vulnerable. I should hope that men would accept, along with the famous principle in the criminal law, the principle "noncombatant until proven otherwise" and would attempt to look at the particular facts of each case as carefully and disinterestedly as possible. I say that I hope this, not that I expect it.

Who, then, is a combatant? I shall answer this question from the point of view of one who believes that the only legitimate defense for war is self-defense.[10] It is, in this context, important to remember that one may legitimately plead self-defense even if one's belief that one's life is being threatened is false. The only requirement is that the belief be *reasonable* given the evidence that is available. If a man comes to my door with a toy pistol and says, pointing the pistol at me, "Prepare to meet your Maker for your time has come," I act in my self-defense if I kill him even if he was joking so long as my belief was reasonable, i.e. I had no way of knowing that the gun was a toy or that he was joking. Thus: combatants may be viewed as all those in the territory or allied territory of the enemy of whom it is reasonable to believe that they are engaged in an attempt to destroy you.

What about our Dresden octogenarian? Is he a combatant on this analysis? Since he does not act *on authority*, it is at least *prima facie* odd to regard him as part of a chain of command literally construed — the concept of command being most at home in a context of authority. He does not, of course, have much to do with the war effort; and so we might find his claim that he is "helping to defeat the Americans" quaint on purely factual grounds. And yet none of this prevents its being true that he can properly be said to be engaged in an *attempt* to destroy the enemy. For people can attempt even the impossible so long as they do not *know* it is impossible. Thus I am prepared to say of him that he is, in fact, engaged in an attempt to destroy the enemy. But I would still say that killing him would count as a case of killing a noncombatant for the following reason: that the concept of attempt here is to be applied, not from the attacker's point of view, but from the point of view of the defender who proposes to plead self-defense in defense of his acts of killing. Combatants are all those who may *reasonably* be regarded as engaged in an attempt to destroy you. This belief is reasonable (though false) in the case of the frontline soldier who plans always to shoot over the heads of the enemy and unreasonable (even if true) in the case of our octogenarian. It would be quite unreasonable to plan a bombing raid on a nonmilitary and nonindustrial city and say, in defense of the raid, that you are just protecting yourself or your country from all those warmongering civilians who are attempting to destroy you. For making such a judgment imposes upon you a burden of proof which, given the circumstances of war, you could not satisfy. You probably could not get *any* evidence for your claim. You certainly could not get what the law calls a "preponderance of the evidence" — much less "proof beyond a reasonable doubt."

Combatants, then, are all those of whom it is reasonable to believe that they are engaged in an attempt at your destruction. Noncombatants are all those of whom it is not reasonable to believe this. Having the distinction, we must now inquire into its moral importance.

WHY IS IT WRONG TO KILL THE INNOCENT?

From what I have said so far, it should be obvious that this question cannot adequately be answered unless one specifies the sense of innocence that one has in mind. First, with respect to moral innocence, we can take babes in arms as paradigms. Here I should argue that no reasons can be given for why it is wrong to kill babies; neither are any reasons needed. If anything can be taken as a brute datum for moral philosophy, surely the principle "Do not kill innocent babies" is a very good candidate — much more plausible for an ethical primitive than, say, "promote your self-interest" or "maximize the general utility" (other candidates that have been offered for ethical primitives). The person who cannot just *see* that there is something evil about killing babies could not, I suspect, be made to see anything else about morality and thus could not understand any reasons that one might attempt to give. And any " ethical" theory which entailed that there is nothing wrong at all with killing babies would surely deserve to be rejected on the basis of this counterexample alone. G. E. M. Anscombe puts the point in the following way:

If someone really thinks, *in advance*, that it is open to question whether such an action as procuring the judicial execution of the innocent should be quite excluded from consideration — I do not want to argue with him; he shows a corrupt mind.[11]

Consider an example from literature: If a reader of Melville's *Billy Budd* cannot see why Captain Vere is deeply troubled because he has a legal obligation to execute Billy, a morally innocent (though legally guilty) man, what would one say to him? What could one do except repeat, in a louder tone of voice perhaps, "But, don't you see, Billy is morally *innocent*"? What I am saying is that, though it is reasonable to expect ethical theories to correct some of our moral intuitions or pretheoretical convictions, we cannot reasonably expect these theories to correct *all* of them — since there is a class of such intuitions or convictions which makes ethical theory itself possible and testable.[12] Kant, I think, was perhaps one of the first to begin to see this when he argued that utilitarianism cannot be correct because it cannot account for the obvious wrongness of making slaves of people, punishing the innocent, etc.

Now with respect to legal innocence (when this does not, as it often does, overlap moral innocence) a set of reasons for not killing (or punishing) the innocent *can* be given. These reasons will be in terms of *utility* (it makes people insecure to live in a society which punishes them whether they obey the rules or not), *justice* (it is not fair to punish people who conform their conduct to the rules), and general observations about the *purposes* and *techniques* of the criminal law as a system of control through rules. As John Rawls has argued,[13] a system of criminal law can be viewed minimally as a price system for controlling conduct (i.e. the rules state a price that has to be paid for certain bits of behavior in the hope that most people will regard the price as too high to pay). And obviously this sort of system is going to work only if the price is generally charged when and only when the "commodity" (i.e. the behavior) is "purchased."

When we move to war, however, difficulties begin to present themselves. We have seen that what people have had in mind when they have argued for the protection of innocents in war was neither clearly moral innocence nor clearly legal innocence. Rather it was *noncombatant* protection. But when we put the principle as "Do not kill noncombatants" we lose the background of moral and legal thinking which makes the principle seem plausible when formulated in terms of innocence.

Why, then, should we worry about killing noncombatants and think it wrong to do so — especially when we realize that among the noncombatants there will be some, at any rate, who are morally and/or legally guilty of various things and that among the combatants there will be those who are morally and/or legally innocent?

What I suggest is the following: If one believes (as I do) that the only even remotely plausible justification for war is self-defense, then one must in waging war confine one's hostility to those against whom one is defending oneself, i.e. those in the (both causal and logical) chain of command or responsibility or agency, all those who can reasonably be regarded as engaged in an attempt to destroy you. If one does not do this, then one cannot be said merely to be defending onself. And insofar as one is not defending oneself, then one acts immorally in killing one's fellow human beings. The enemy can plausibly be expanded to include all those who are "criminal" accomplices — those who, in Judge Learned Hand's phrase, have a "stake in the venture."[14] But it cannot be expanded to include all those, such as farmers, who merely perform actions causally necessary for the attack — just as in domestic law I cannot plead self-defense if I kill the one (e.g. the wife or mother) who feeds the man who is engaged in an attempt to kill me.[15]

In passing, I should note why I described my position as weakly as I did — namely, that self-defense is the only *remotely plausible* defense of war. I do this because, with respect to nations, the whole idea of self-defense is strongly in need of analysis. What, for example, is it for a state to die or to be threatened with death? Can nations, like individuals, fear death and act compulsively on the basis of that fear? And, insofar as the death of a state is not identical with the deaths of individual human beings, why is the death of a state a morally bad thing? Answering these questions (left notably unanswered in the

Just War Theory)[16] would be an object for another paper. I mention them here to point up latent problems and to further explain my unwillingness, expressed earlier, to affirm that even the killing of the "guilty" (combatants) is morally justified. I am certainly inclined to suspect the Just War Theory's willingness to regard war as an activity giving rise to autonomous moral problems (i.e. problems solely about war and not reducible to ordinary moral problems) and thus to make moral capital out of suspect notions like "national honor" and "national interests" and "national self-defense." Though I am obviously inclined to regard the concept of self-defense as having an important application in the context of war, I am sceptical that the "self" to be legitimately defended must always be the nation or state. It is at least worth considering the possibility that the only moral problems arising in war are the oldest and most common and most important — namely, are human beings being hurt and killed, who are they, and why are they?

IS KILLING THE INNOCENT ABSOLUTELY IMMORAL?

Is killing the innocent a *prima facie* immorality that can be overridden by other, more weighty, moral requirements or is it absolutely immoral, i.e. incapable of being overridden by any other moral requirements? Anscombe[17] holds that the prohibition against killing the innocent is absolute in this sense. And one would suspect that she would echo Kant's sentiments that we should do no injustice though the heavens fall. Unfortunately, she tends simply to assert her position rather than argue for it and so fails to come to terms with the worry that might bother anti-Kantians — namely, does it not matter upon whom the heavens fall? I agree with Anscombe that no argument can be given to demonstrate that there is *something* wrong with killing babies, but it does not follow from this alone that this "something" is not capable of being overridden by another "something" — saving the lives of even more babies, perhaps.

Now in trying to come to grips with this issue, I propose to start with the case of killing babies as a clear example of killing creatures innocent in every possible sense. If a case can be made out that it is sometimes right to kill them, then I assume it will follow *a fortiori* that it is sometimes right to kill those who may be innocent in a less rich sense, e.g. merely noncombatant. Of course if it is *not* ever right to kill babies, this will not in itself show that it is not ever right to kill noncombatants; for it may be the special kind of innocence found in babies (but not necessarily in noncombatants) which protects them.

First of all, we need to ask ourselves the question "What is it deliberately to kill a baby?" I am certain that Anscombe does not mean the following: that one deliberately kills a baby whenever one pursues a policy that one knows will result in the deaths of some babies. If anyone meant this, then that person would have to regard the construction of highways as absolutely immoral. For it is a statistical fact that on every completed highway a certain number of babies meet their deaths in accidents. Yet normally we do not regard this as a moral case against highways or as a moral proof that highway engineers are murderers. What is done is to weigh the social value of a highway against the knowledge that some deaths will occur and judge that the former outweighs the latter. (If we did not make this judgment, and if this judgment was not reasonable, then we *would* be acting immorally. For example: Suppose we let people blast with dynamite whenever they felt like it — conduct with little or no social value — in spite of our knowledge that this would result in many children dying.) Of course, situations comparable to the highway example arise in war. For example, consider the pinpoint bombing of a military installation in a war reasonably believed to be necessary and just coupled with the knowledge that bombs will occasionally go off target and that occasionally a wife, with baby in arms, may be visiting her husband on the base.

The natural way to interpret Anscombe's view is as follows: One kills a baby deliberately either when one (a) brings about the death of a baby as one's final purpose or (b) brings about the death of a baby as a *means* to one's final purpose.[18] Since war is hardly to be regarded as motivated by fetishistic infanticide, it is (b) which is crucial. And (b) lets off the highway engineer. For the highway engineer, whom we do not want to regard as a murderer, will not be a murderer on (b). The deaths of babies in highway accidents are in no sense *means* to the socially useful goal of good transportation but are rather accidental byproducts. That is, highway transportation is not furthered by these deaths but is, if anything, hindered by them. And so it is unreasonable to suppose that highway engineers desire the deaths of these babies because they want to use their deaths as a means to their goal of transportation. Similarly with the accidental deaths of babies resulting from a pinpoint bombing raid on a military installation.

But consider the following kind of case: One knows that one is fighting a war in defense of civilization itself. (It was not unreasonable to regard the war against Hitler in such terms.)[19] Suppose also that one knows that the only way (causally) to bring a power like Hitler's to a collapse is to undercut his support among the German people by achieving their total demoralization.

Further suppose that one knows that the only way to do this is by the obliteration terror bombing of civilian centers (e.g. Dresden) so that, by killing many German babies among others, one can create a desire on the part of the German people to abandon the venture. I am not suggesting that we could ever in fact know these things (they might be false) or that we should ever even let ourselves believe such things.[20] But my worry here is one of principle — namely, assuming the factual situation is as described, would it be wrong *in principle* to initiate a campaign of anti-morale obliteration bombing? Here I take it that Anscombe will say that, even in such circumstances, those making a decision to initiate such a campaign are murderers. For they will be deliberately killing the innocent as a means to their goal and that (no matter how good the goal) is absolutely wrong.

But why? Anscombe fails to bring fully into the open a latent issue that is absolutely crucial here — namely, are we as morally responsible for our omissions (e.g. failing to save lives) as for our commissions (e.g. killing people)? Of course there are differences between the two expressions, but are they *morally relevant* differences? If our basic value here is the sanctity of life, or the sanctity of innocents, or the sanctity of babies, then — as Jonathan Bennett has pointed out[21] — it is hard to see their moral difference. For consider the following kind of case: Suppose we know that a victory by Hitler would mean the extermination of all or a great many non-Aryan babies. And further suppose that these babies far outnumber the German babies to be killed in an obliteration bombing campaign.[22] Now, given this knowledge, what would a man who really values the lives of babies do? Is the moral case to rest upon the different descriptions "killing babies" and "letting babies die"? If so, *why*? If the argument is that by not positively killing we will at least be preserving our own moral purity, then it is important to note that this argument, in addition to being rather selfish, is question-begging. For to assume that one remains morally pure if one does nothing is to beg the question of whether we are as responsible for omissive as for commissive conduct. If moral purity means never choosing anything which one will have to regard as in some sense wrong and regret for all one's days, then moral purity may be impossible in a complex world. Albert Camus based his theory of rebellion on this kind of claim — a theory which Howard Zinn summarizes as follows:

Camus spoke in *The Rebel* of the absurdities in which we are trapped, where the very acts with which we seek to do good cannot escape the imperfections of the world we are trying to change. And so the rebel's "only virtue will lie in never yielding to the impulse to be engulfed in the shadows that surround him, and in obstinately dragging the chains of evil, with which he is bound, toward the good."[23]

The issue here is not over whether we should ever allow ourselves to be persuaded by any argument that killing the innocent is *in fact* necessary; and I am certainly not suggesting that I find plausible such arguments as have actually been given in the past. For a practical maxim I am much in favor of the slogan "Never trade a certain evil for a possible good." However, this does not solve the issue of principle. If the good (e.g. saving the lives of scores of babies) *is certain* and not just possible, is it anything more than dogmatism to assert that it would never be right to bring about this good through evil means? The maxim "Never trade a certain evil for a certain good" is by no means self-evidently true and, indeed, does not even seem plausible to many people. Thus I do not think that it has yet been shown that it is always absolutely wrong, whatever the consequences, to kill innocent babies. And thus it has not yet been shown that it is absolutely wrong to kill those innocent in a less rich sense of the term, i.e. noncombatants. Of course we may *feel* differently about actually killing innocents and simply letting innocents die; but I do not think that this phenomenological evidence in itself *proves* anything. Bomber pilots no doubt feel differently about dropping bombs on babies from thirty thousand feet than they would about shooting a baby face to face, but surely this does not show that the acts differ in moral quality.

Feelings do not prove anything in morality; but they sometimes *point* to something. And it is at least possible that we have not yet captured the worry which motivates the responses of Kant, Miss Anscombe, and those who want to defend some version of the doctrine of the Double Effect. If what they really value is the lives of babies and other innocents *simpliciter*, then – as Bennett argues – it does not seem that the distinction between "killing babies" and "letting babies die" will help them to save their principle. But perhaps this is to conceive their position too teleologically. That is, we have so far (with Bennett) been assuming that the person who says "never kill babies" says this because he sees the maxim as instrumental to *something else* that he values – namely, the lives of babies. But it is at least possible that he does not hold this principle to be instrumentally right (in which case he would be subject to Bennett's refutation) but intrinsically right, i.e. right in itself or from its very description. The problem is to explicate this notion of intrinsic rightness in such a way that it does not involve either of the two following pitfalls noted by Bennett:

(a) *Authoritarianism*, e.g. "God commands not killing babies."

(b) *Dogmatism*, e.g. "It is just absolutely wrong to kill babies; and, if you do not see this, you are just too corrupt to talk to."

Now the reason why (a) is a bad move is obvious – namely, it is an appeal to authority rather than reason and thus has no place in a philosophical discussion of moral questions. But (b) is more problematical. For I have said that I am willing to accept such a move if made in the name of there being *something* wrong with killing babies. Why will I not accept such a move in favor of its being *absolutely* wrong to kill babies?

Roughly, I should argue as follows: That there is something wrong with killing babies (i.e. that "*A* is a case of killing a baby" *must* count as a moral reason against *A*) explicates, in part, what may be called "the moral point of view." To be worried about moral issues just is, among other things, to be worried about killing innocents. But the judgment "Never kill babies under any circumstances" does not explicate the moral point of view but is, rather, a controversial moral judgment — or, if you prefer, explicates *a* moral point of view rather than *the* moral point of view. And so, to build *it* into the moral point of view is to beg a controversial question of moral substance — something which presumably meta-ethics should not do. Someone who said "I see nothing at all wrong with killing babies so let's bomb Dresden" would be an *a*moral monster — one with whom it would be senseless to conduct a moral argument. But one who sincerely said "Of course it is terrible to kill babies but I believe, to save more lives, we must regretfully do it in this case" is not such a monster. He is one with whom, if we think him wrong (*im*moral), we should hope to be able to argue.[24] Since, among war supporters, there are (one would hope) few of the former sort but many of the latter sort, being able to argue with and persuade the latter has some practical importance. It will hardly do simply to say to them "But I can just see the absolute wrongness of what you contemplate and, if you do not, I refuse to discuss the matter with you." We know, alas, what will then happen.

Now I am not going to pretend that I can given anything resembling a *proof* that it is absolutely wrong to kill the innocent (though not to allow them to die), but I hope at least to be able to elaborate a way of thinking which (a) does give some sense to such a prohibition and (b) cannot be condemned as simple dogmatism or authoritarianism, i.e. is a way of *thinking*.[25]

The way of thinking I want to elaborate is one in which the notion of people's having *rights* plays a predominate role. (Kant's ethical theory, in broad outline, is one such way of thinking.) And an ethical outlook in which the notion of rights looms large will want to draw a distinction between the following two claims:

(1) Doing *A* to Jones would be to violate one of his rights.
(2) It would be bad to do *A* to Jones.

To use Kant's own examples: If I have made a promise to Jones, he has a *right* to expect me to keep it, can properly regard me as having *wronged* him if I do not keep it, and could properly expect that others (the state) should *coerce* me into keeping it. Kant's opaque way of putting this is to say that keeping a promise is a *perfect* duty. A quite different situation is the following: If Jones is in distress (assuming I have not put him there) and I could help him out without extraordinary sacrifice, he would certainly want me to help him and I would be doing something bad if I did not help him. But he does not have a *right* to expect my help, is not *wronged* if I fail to help him, and it would be unreasonable to expect the state or anyone else to *coerce* me into helping him. Helping him is beneficence and (unlike justice) is a comparatively weak moral demand. Kant's opaque way of putting this is to say that the duty to help others in distress is *imperfect.*[26]

When a man has a right, he has a claim against interference.[27] Simply to refuse to be beneficent to him is not an invasion of his rights because it is not to interfere with him at all. When a person uses his freedom to invade the rights of others, he forfeits certain of his own rights and renders interference by others legitimate. (Kant calls this a moral title or authorization — *Befugnis* — to place "obstacles to obstacles to freedom.")[28] Thus if I have an imperfect duty to help others, I may interfere with those trying to harm those others because, by such an attempt, they have forfeited their right against interference. Here I have the imperfect duty; and, since those attacking have by the attack forfeited certain of their rights, I violate no perfect duty in interfering with them. Thus there is no conflict here. However, if the only way I could save someone from harm would be by interfering with an innocent person (i.e. one who has not forfeited his rights by initiating attack against others) then I must not save the person, for this would be to violate a perfect duty. And, in cases of conflict, perfect duties override imperfect duties.

Suppose that Jones is being attacked by Smith. In such a case it is certainly true to say that Jones's *rights* to liberty, security, etc. are being threatened and that Smith, therefore, is acting wrongly and thereby forfeits his right to be left free from interference. Thus I would not be acting wrongly (i.e. against Smith's rights) if I attacked him to prevent his attack on Jones. Similarly, Jones would not be acting wrongly if he defended himself. However, it does not follow from any of this that I have a *duty* to help Jones or even that Jones has a *duty* to defend himself. Defense, though permissible, is not obligatory. This being so, it does not follow that Jones has a *right to be saved* by me. Thus, since it is far from obvious that Jones has a right to be saved even from an attack by the guilty, it is even more implausible to assert that he has a right to be saved if so doing would involve killing the innocent. (Consider the following: We are all, at this very moment, sitting and talking philosophy and are thus omitting to save the lives of countless people we might save throughout the world. Are we acting wrongly in so doing? If we are, is this because all these people have a *right* to be saved by us?)

Now what sort of a moral view could one hold that would make one accept the principle that perfect duties, resting on rights, override imperfect duties, not resting on rights? I think it is this: a view which makes primary the status of persons as free or choosing beings who, out of respect for that status, are to be regarded as having the right to be left alone to work out their own lives — for better or worse. This is a basic right that one has just because one is a person. Respecting it is what Kant calls respecting the dignity of humanity by not treating people as *means* only. Part of respecting them in this sense is not to use them as a means in one's calculations of what would be good for others. It is fine (indeed admirable) for a person to sacrifice himself for others by his own choice; but it is presumptuous (because lacking in respect for his choices) if *I* choose to sacrifice him. This is his business and not mine. I may only interfere with the person who, by his own evil actions, has forfeited his right against interference. Innocent persons by definition have not done this. And therefore it is absolutely wrong to sacrifice the innocent, though not to kill aggressors. On this view there is something terribly perverse in arguing, as many do, that a defense of freedom requires a sacrifice of those who in no way give their free consent to the sacrifice.[29]

Of course babies are not yet, in the full sense, free or choosing beings who clearly have rights. They are, perhaps, only potential or dispositional persons and enjoyers of rights. But if one accepts the maxim "Innocent until proven otherwise" they may be regarded as equally protected in the above way of thinking. For they certainly cannot be described in the only way which, on this view, makes harmful interference permissible — namely, described as having, through their own deliberate acts of aggression, forfeited their right to be left in peace.

Now this view that what is central in morality involves notions like rights, dignity, freedom, and choice (rather than notions like maximizing the general utility) cannot be proven. But it is a plausible view which may lie behind the maxim "Never kill the innocent" and is a view which would be sacrificied (at least greatly compromised) by the maxim "Kill the innocent to save the innocent." I am myself deeply sympathetic to this way of thinking and would make neither the compromise nor the sacrifice. But I cannot *prove* that one ought not make it. Neither, of course, can my teleological opponent prove his case either. For we lie here at the boundaries of moral discourse where candidates for ultimate principles conflict; and it is part of the logical character of an ultimate principle that it cannot be assessed by some yet higher ("more ultimate"?) principle.[30] You pays your money and you takes your choice. It is simply my hope that many people, if they could see clearly what price they have to pay (i.e. the kind of moral outlook they have to give up and what they have to put in its place) would make the choice against killing the innocent.

Consider the following example: Suppose that thousands of babies could be saved from a fatal infant disease if some few babies were taken by the state and given over to a team of medical researchers for a series of experiments which, though killing the babies, would yield a cure for the disease. In what way except degree (i.e. numbers of babies killed) does this situation differ from the rationale behind antimorale obliteration bombing raids, i.e. is there not a disturbing parallel between Allied raids on Dresden and Tokyo and Nazi "medicine"? With respect to either suggestion, when we really think about it, do we not want to say with the poet James Dickey

Holding onto another man's walls
My hat should crawl on my head
In streetcars, thinking of it,
The fat on my body should pale.[31]

How can any such thing be in the interest of humanity when its practice would change the very meaning of "humanity" and prevent us from unpacking from it, as we now do, notions like rights, dignity, and respect? No matter how good the consequences, is there not some point in saying that we simply do not have the *right* to do it? For there is, I think, an insight of secular value in the religious observation that men are the *"children of God."* For this means, among other things, that other people do not *belong* to me. They are not *mine* to be manipulated as resources in my projects. It is hard to imagine all that we might lose if we abandoned this way of thinking about ourselves and others.

My appeal here, of course, is in a sense emotive. But this in my judgment is not an objection. Emotive appeals may rightly be condemned if they are masquerading as proofs. But here I am attempting to prove nothing but only to say — "Here, look, see what you are doing and what way of thinking your doing it involves you in." If one sees all this and still goes forth to do it anyway, we have transcended the bounds of what can be *said* in the matter.

What about noncombatants? Though they are not necessarily innocent in all the senses in which babies are, they clearly are innocent in the sense I have elaborated above — namely, they have not performed actions which forfeit their right to be free from execution (or, better: it is not *reasonable* for the enemy to believe this of them). Thus, in a very tentative conclusion, I suggest the following: I have not been able to prove that we should never kill non-combatants or innocents (I do not think this could be proven in any ordinary sense of proof); but I do think that I have elaborated a way of thinking which gives sense to the acceptance of such an absolute prohibition. Thus, against Bennett, I have at least shown that one can accept the principle "Never kill the innocent" without thereby necessarily being an authoritarian or a dogmatic moral fanatic.[32]

NOTES

*
Many people were kind enough to comment on this manuscript in various stages of its preparation, and I should like to take this opportunity to express my sincere appreciation for the help that they provided. In particular, I should like to thank the following: Lewis White Beck, Robert L. Holmes, Gareth Matthews, Ronald Milo, Richard Wasserstrom, Donald Wells, Peter Winch, and Anthony D. Woozley. I should also like to thank the members of my graduate seminar on war at the University of Arizona for stimulating discussion. Since I have perversely gone my own way on several points in spite of advice to the contrary, I alone am to be held responsible for any errors that remain. In setting a philosophical framework for a discussion of the problem of killing the innocent in war, I have been greatly influenced by Richard Wasserstrom's 'On the Morality of War: A Preliminary Inquiry' in his useful collection of essays *War and Morality* (Belmont, Calif.: Wadsworth Publishing Co., 1970). I am presupposing that the reader is familiar with G. E. M. Anscombe's two articles 'Modern Moral Philosophy', *Philosophy* 33, No. 124 (January, 1958), and 'War and Murder' (in the Wasserstrom collection). I am also presupposing a familiarity with Jonathan Bennett's 'Whatever the Consequences', *Analysis* 26, No. 3 (January, 1966).
[1] "Murder," writes Anscombe, "is the deliberate killing of the innocent, whether for its own sake or as a means to some further end" ('War and Murder', p. 45). Deliberate killing of the innocent (or noncombatants) is prohibited by the Just War Theory and is a crime in international law. A traditional account of the Catholic Just War Theory may be found in Chapter 35 of Austin Fagothey's *Right and Reason: Ethics in Theory and Practice* (St. Louis: C. V. Mosby Co., 1963). A useful sourcebook for inquiry into the nature of war crimes is the anthology *Crimes of War*, ed. by Richard A. Falk, Gabriel Kolko, and Robert Jay Lifton (New York: Random House, 1971).
[2] By "*prima facie* wrong" I mean "can be overridden by other moral requirements" — *not*, as a literal translation might suggest, "only apparently wrong."
[3] For example: In the criminal offense of statutory rape, the defendant is strictly liable with respect to his knowledge of the age of a girl with whom he has had sexual relations, i.e. no matter how carefully he inquired into her age, no matter how reasonable (i.e. non-negligent) his belief that she was of legal age of consent, he is liable if his belief is in fact mistaken. For a general discussion of such offenses, see Richard Wasserstrom's 'Strict

Liability in the Criminal Law', *Stanford Law Review* 12, (July, 1960).
[4] In discussion, Richard Wasserstrom has expressed scepticism concerning my claim that there is something unintelligible about the concept of strict moral responsibility. One could regard the *Old Testament* and *Oedipus Rex* as containing a strict liability conception of morality. Now I should be inclined to argue that the primitiveness of the *Old Testament* and of *Oedipus Rex* consists in these peoples' not yet being able to draw a distinction between legality and morality. However, I am prepared to admit that it might be better to weaken my claim by maintaining simply that no *civilized* or *enlightened* morality would involve strict liability.
[5] In California criminal law, for example, vehicular manslaughter is defined as vehicular homicide "in the commission of an unlawful act, not amounting to felony, with gross negligence; or in the commission of a lawful act which might produce death, in an unlawful manner, and with gross negligence . . . " (*California Penal Code* 192, 3, a).
[6] For an excellent discussion of moral and legal responsibility for negligence, see H. L. A. Hart's 'Negligence, *Mens Rea* and Criminal Responsibility,' in his *Punishment and Responsibility: Essays in the Philosophy of Law* (Oxford: Oxford University Press, 1963).
[7] I say "engaged in an attempt" rather than "attempting" for the following reason: A mortar attack on an encampment of combat soldiers who happen to be sleeping is surely not a case of killing noncombatants even though persons who are asleep cannot be attempting anything. Sleeping persons can, however, be engaged in an attempt – just as sleeping persons can be accomplices in crime and parties to a criminal conspiracy. Being engaged in an attempt, unlike attempting, is not necessarily a full time job. I am grateful to Anthony Woozley for pointing this out to me.
[8] Thomas Nagel, 'War and Massacre', *Philosophy and Public Affairs* 2, (Winter, 1972). In the same issue, Richard Brandt replies to Nagel in his 'Utilitarianism and the Rules of War.' I am grateful to Professors Nagel and Brandt for allowing me to read their articles prior to publication.
[9] For reasons of simplicity in later drawing upon important and instructive principles from the criminal law, I shall use the phrase "self-defense." (I shall later want to draw on the notion of *reasonable belief* in the law of self-defense.) However, what I really want to focus on is the concept of "defense" and not the concept of "self." For it seems to me that war can be justified, not just to defend oneself or one's nation, but also to defend others from threats that transcend nationality, e.g. genocide. If one wants to speak of self-defense even here, then it must be regarded as self-defense for the *human*, not just national, community. The phrase "self-defense" as it occurs in what follows should always be understood as carrying this qualification. And, of course, even clear cases of self-defense are not always necessarily justified. Given the morally debased character of Nazi Germany, it is by no means obvious that it acted rightly in trying to defend itself near the end of World War II (i.e. after it had ceased to be an aggressor).
[10] Remember that this carries the qualification stated in note 9. For a survey of the law of self-defense, the reader may consult any reliable treatise on the criminal law, e.g. pp. 883 ff. of Rollin M. Perkins's *Criminal Law* (Brooklyn, N. Y.: Foundation Press, 1957). The criminal law is a highly moralized institution, and it is useful (though by no means always definitive) for the moral philosopher in that it provides an accumulated and systematized body of reflection on vital moral matters of our culture. For my purposes, I shall in what follows focus upon the *reasonable belief* condition in the law of self-

defense. Other aspects of the law of self-defense (e.g. the so-called "retreat requirement") have, I think, interesting implications for war that I cannot pursue here.

[11] 'Modern Moral Philosophy', p. 17. For reasons I shall note later, Anscombe weakens her point by adding the word "judicial."

[12] See William H. Gass, 'The Case of the Obliging Stranger', *Philosophical Review* 66, (April, 1957).

[13] John Rawls, 'Two Concepts of Rules', *Philosophical Review* 64, (January, 1955).

[14] See, for example, *United States v. Falcone*, United States Court of Appeals, Second Circuit, 1940, 109 F.2d 579.

[15] Consider the case of the homicidal diabetic: He is chasing you through the woods of an enclosed game preserve, attempting to kill you for sport with a pistol. However, because of his medical condition, he must return to a cabin in the middle of the preserve every hour in order that his aged mother can give him an insulin shot. Without it, he will take ill or die and will thus be forced to abandon his attempt to kill you. Even if blocking that insulin shot seems your only hope, killing the mother in order to do it would be a very doubtful case of self-defense.

[16] Austin Fagothey, in his well-known statement of the Just War Theory cited previously, allows injury to national honor to count as a ground for a war of self-defense. I cite Fagothey's book because of its influence. It was, for example, appealed to by Justice Douglas in the 1971 *Gillette* case, a case where the defendant refused induction on the grounds of his belief that the Vietnam War is unjust (*Gillette v. United States*, 401 U.S. 437).

[17] "Modern Moral Philosophy."

[18] Another factor, relevant both of war and to the highway example, is the following: acting with the knowledge that deaths could be prevented by taking reasonable precautions and yet not taking those precautions. Such grossly negligent or reckless behavior, while perhaps not "deliberate" in the strict sense, is surely immoral in either context.

[19] See Michael Walzer, 'World War II: Why Was This War Different?', *Philosophy and Public Affairs* 1, No. 1 (Fall, 1971).

[20] As the citizens of London and Hanoi have illustrated, for example, terror bombing has a tendency to backfire. Rather than demoralizing the enemy, it sometimes strengthens their courage and will to resist.

[21] Jonathan Bennett, 'Whatever the Consequences', *Analysis* 26, No. 3 (January, 1966).

[22] I take it that, from a moral point of view, their being *German* babies is irrelevant. As Howard Zinn has argued, we should accept the principle that "all victims are created equal" (*Disobedience and Democracy: Nine Fallacies on Law and Order* [New York: Random House, 1968], p. 50).

[23] *Ibid.*, p. 40.

[24] One important metaethical inquiry that has been conducted in recent years concerns the nature of moral judgments and the moral point of view of "language game." The task here is to distinguish the moral from the *non*moral or *a*moral. Normative ethics, on the other hand, is concerned to distinguish the moral from the *im*moral. This is too large a dispute to enter here, but I can at least make my own commitments clear. Unlike the so-called "formalists" (e.g. R. M. Hare, *The Language of Morals* [Oxford: Oxford University Press, 1952]), I am inclined to believe that the moral point of view must be defined, in part, in terms of the *content* of the judgments it contains. Here I am siding, if I understand them correctly, with such writers as H. L. A. Hart (*The Concept of Law*

[Oxford: Oxford University Press, 1961]) and G. J. Warnock (*The Object of Morality* [London: Methuen, 1971]). Someone who does not see that "*A* is a case of killing an innocent" is a relevant reason against doing *A*, does not understand what moral discourse is all about, what it is *necessarily* concerned with. And this is so no matter how much he is prepared to universalize and regard as overriding his own idiosyncratic imperatives. If this is true, then the gulf between metaethics and normative ethics is not quite as wide as many have supposed, since the relevance of certain substantive judgments is now going to be regarded as part of the *meaning* of morality as a point of view, language game, or form of life. There still is some gulf between metaethics and normative ethics, however, since I should argue that only the *relevance* , and not the *decisiveness*, of certain substantive judgments (e.g. do not kill the innocent) can be regarded as a defining feature of the moral point of view. Normative ethics, however, is primarily interested in which of the relevant moral considerations are, in certain circumstances, decisive. (I am grateful to Ronald Milo for discussing these matters with me. He is totally responsible for whatever clarity is to be found in my views.)

25   Though I shall not explore it here, I think that the religious acceptance of the principle could be elaborated as a way of thinking and so distinguished from the authoritarianism and dogmatism that Bennett so rightly condemns. The view I shall develop also has implications (though I shall not draw them out here) for the abortion issue. For more on this, see Philippa Foot's 'Abortion and the Doctrine of the Double Effect', *Oxford Review* (1967). This has been reprinted in *Moral Problems: A Collection of Philosophical Essays*, ed. by James Rachels (New York: Harper & Row, 1971), and in my *An Introduction to Moral and Social Philosophy: Basic Readings in Theory and Practice* (Belmont, Calif.: Wadsworth Publishing Co., 1973). She sees the doctrine of the Double Effect as groping in a confused way toward an insight of moral importance: "There is worked into our moral system a distinction between what we owe people in the form of aid and what we owe them in the way of non-interference."

26   These well-known examples are drawn from Kant's *Foundations of the Metaphysics of Morals*, trans. by Lewis White Beck (Indianapolis: Bobbs-Merrill Co., 1959), pp. 39ff.; pp. 421 ff. of the Academy edition of Kant's works. Kant distinguished perfect duties (duties of respect) from imperfect duties (duties of love) in many places. See, for example, *The Doctrine of Virtue*, trans. by Mary J. Gregor (New York: Harper and Row, 1964), pp. 134–35; p. 463 of the Academy edition. The rights that grow out of the practice of promising are perhaps ultimately not the best ones persuasively to illustrate the moral force of those duties Kant calls perfect. To promise you to do *X* is indeed to give you a right to the performance of *X*; but if the content of the promise is trivial (e.g. to meet you for a drink after work), then many persons would intuitively be inclined to think that the right is also trivial – i.e. capable of being overridden by demands of utility. If such a person would consider the rights which he regards as morally basic (perhaps the right of maximum liberty compatible with like liberty for others), then the duties resting on these rights might seem to have the kind of force Kant attempted to capture in the concept of a perfect duty. The point here is not to draw up a list of moral rights or to determine which rights are morally basic, but is rather simply to suggest this: that whatever rights a person takes to be morally basic will, if he takes rights seriously, determine for him the most stringent set of moral duties.

27   Can the right created by a promise be regarded as a claim against interference? Not really; for the right is typically a right that someone positively do something – namely,

whatever he promised to do. I am inclined to think, however, that the right created by a promise has its *moral* force from being grounded in the same value that is respected and protected in more straight-forward cases of non-interference – namely, the basic human right to control one's destiny by one's own choices, the right not to be interfered with in the enactment of one's life plans. We might think of this as the right of autonomy – perhaps the most basic and important moral right of all. Normally, in making choices or life plans, I count on others only at my own risk or peril. If they do not help me, I cannot say that they have thereby shown a lack of respect for my autonomy. When someone has made a promise to me, however, I have been given a legitimate expection upon which to base my choices or life plans. In such cases I am invited to count upon another, am invited to expose a certain vulnerability to him, and am in a sense invited to entrust him with a portion of my autonomy. If he breaks the promise I can thus sensibly charge him with showing a lack of respect for my autonomy or status as a person; and, if my life plans fall through, I can legitimately blame him for the failure. Neither charge would make sense if directed against a stranger who simply ignored my need. Thus promise breaking is a kind of moral equivalent to interference in that, as with direct interference, it is a way of not recognizing the moral seriousness of meddling in the life of another.

28 Kant, *Metaphysical Elements of Justice*, trans. by John Ladd (Indianapolis: Bobbs-Merrill Co., 1965), pp. 35 ff.; pp. 230 ff. of the Academy edition. See also pp. 94 ff. and 107–9 of my *Kant: The Philosophy of Right* (New York: St. Martin's Press, 1970).

29 Someone (e.g. Jan Narveson in his 'Pacifism: A Philosophical Analysis', *Ethics* 75 [1965]) might say the following: If what you value are the *rights* of people, does this not entail (as a part of what it means to say that one values something) that you would recognize an obligation to take steps to secure those rights against interference? Perhaps. But "take steps" does not have to mean "do whatever is causally necessary." Such an obligation will presumably be limited by (a) what I can reasonably be expected to do or sacrifice and (b) my moral judgment about the permissibility of the *means* employed. It does seem perverse for a person to say "I value the rights of people above all else but I do not propose to do anything to secure those rights." However, it by no means seems to me equally perverse to say the following: "I deplore interferences with human rights above all else and I will do everything in my power to prevent such interferences – everything, of course, short of being guilty of such interferences myself."

30 See Brian Barry, 'Justice and the Common Good', *Analysis*, 21–22 (1960–61). Though the existentialists tend to overdo this sort of claim, there is truth in their claim that there are certain moral problems that are in principle *undecidable* by any rational decision procedure. Such cases are not perhaps as numerous as the existentialists would have us believe, but they do arise, e.g. when candidates for ultimate moral principles conflict. In such cases, we find it impossible to nail down with solid arguments those principles which matter to us the most. Perhaps this even deserves to be called "absurd." In his article "The Absurd" (*Journal of Philosophy*, 68, No. 20 [October 21, 1971]), Thomas Nagel suggests that absurdity in human life is found in "the collision between the seriousness with which we take our lives and the perpetual possibility of regarding everything about which we are serious as arbitrary, or open to doubt." It is here that talk about faith or commitment seems to have some life.

31 James Dickey, 'The Firebombing', in *Poems 1957–1967* (Middletown, Conn.: Wesleyan University Press, 1967), p. 185. Reprinted with the permission of the publisher.

[32] My claim in this paper that the superiority of a right-justice conception of morality over a teleological conception cannot be proven was (in my present judgment) a bit hasty. Though it no doubt cannot be proven in a strict logical sense, there are devices for rendering it more rationally credible which would be worth exploring. Two such devices are present in John Rawls's *A Theory of Justice* (Cambridge, Mass.: Harvard University Press 1971). One such device, which I actually use in the paper but mistakenly label "emotive," is the one which Rawls calls "reflective equilibrium" — i.e. we shall choose the moral conception which does the best job of ordering, systematizing, and accounting for the largest set of our considered moral judgments. The other device employs the idea of the social contract: moral principles will be justified if they would be unanimously chosen by a group of rational persons as the principles to goven their relations with each other. There is no reason in principle why principles relating to the rights of innocents in war might not be chosen in such a setting and thus, to that degree, rendered rationally credible. Any discussion of these issues should now, of course, make use of Michael Walzer's recent book *Just and Unjust Wars* (New York: Basic Books, 1977).

Another matter about which I now have some considerable hesitation is my use in this paper of babies or infants as paradigm examples of creatures enjoying the moral right protected in a prohibition against killing the innocent. I now see children as border-line cases of rights enjoyers — a theme I explore in my 'Rights and Borderline Cases', *Arizona Law Review*, 19, No. 1, 1977, pp. 228–241. (Reprinted in the present collection.)

One final note: Robert Nozick's characterization of rights as "side-constraints" nicely captures what I was trying to express in my claim to give a non-teleological account of rights. See *Anarchy, State and Utopia* (New York: Basic Books, 1974, pp. 28 ff.).

RIGHTS AND BORDERLINE CASES[*]

INTRODUCTION

Two competing theories of justice are currently dominating discussion within contemporary Anglo-American moral, social, political, and legal philosophy. The Welfare-State Liberal theory of John Rawls, developed most fully in his book *A Theory of Justice*,[1] contains a sustained defense of the partial redistribution of wealth within society in order to improve the position of the most unfortunate members of society. The Libertarian theory of Robert Nozick, presented in his book *Anarchy, State, and Utopia*,[2] is based on the claims that justice is the respecting of people's *rights*, that people's rights are respected when they are allowed to keep and control that to which they are *entitled*, and that people are entitled to any holding which they have legitimately acquired — that is, without using force, theft, or fraud (activities which would violate the rights of others). Since the kind of redistribution called for by Rawls' theory of justice would necessarily involve taking from some people (primarily through taxation) holdings to which they have a right, Nozick argues that an application of Rawls' theory will have unjust consequences: it will fail to show the proper respect for people's rights upon which any correct theory of justice must be based.

The present essay is an exploration of the concept of *a right* — a concept which is, as Nozick claims, central to the concept of justice. The essay is based on the assumption that one way to develop an understanding of this important moral concept is to examine cases — called "borderline" here — where the ascription of rights seems doubtful or problematic. If we can understand what goes wrong in the doubtful cases, then perhaps we can develop a more satisfactory account of the clear cases. Although not written with such a purpose in mind, the essay may also be viewed as a tentative start toward showing that a generally Rawlsian theory of justice or rights can make an important place for those moral claims which Nozick calls entitlements.

THE PROBLEM

The nature and importance of the problem to be discussed in this essay has been well stated by Joel Feinberg:

26

In the familiar cases of rights, the claimant is a competent adult human being, and the claimee is an officeholder in an institution or else a private individual, in either case, another competent adult human being. Normal adult human beings, then, are obviously the sorts of beings of whom rights can meaningfully be predicated. Everyone would agree to that ... On the other hand, it is absurd to say that rocks can have rights, not because rocks are morally inferior things unworthy of rights (that statement makes no sense either), but because rocks belong to a category of entities of whom rights cannot be meaningfully predicated. That is not to say that there are no circumstances in which we ought to treat rocks carefully, but only that the rocks themselves cannot validly claim good treatment from us. In between the clear cases of rocks and normal human beings, however, is a spectrum of less obvious cases, including some bewildering borderline ones. Is it meaningful or conceptually possible to ascribe rights to our dead ancestors? to individual animals? to whom species of animals? to plants? to idiots and madmen? to fetuses? to generations yet unborn? Until we know how to settle these puzzling cases, we cannot claim fully to grasp the concept of a right, or to know the shape of its logical boundaries.[3]

Feinberg's point can be summarized in this manner: We all recognize clear cases of individuals (competent adult human beings) to whom the ascription of rights, both moral and legal, is nonproblematic — indeed, it is obviously justified. We also recognize clear cases (such as rocks) of entities which not only do not have rights but *could not* have rights, such ascription being conceptually ludicrous. In addition to these clear cases, we also are confronted with a large class of borderline cases — individuals who have *some* of the features normally found in individuals who are clearly rights-bearers, but who do not seem to have *quite enough* of such features to make us confident in ascribing rights to them. They are of such a nature (for example, severely retarded) that they lack certain features (such as the power of rational choice) normally found in rights-bearers. Indeed they may even be of such a nature (for instance, irreversibly comatose) that they seem disturbingly similar in relevant respects to those entities (such as rocks) which clearly cannot be rights-bearers. All these considerations tempt us to say that they are *not* rights-bearers at all.

But there are temptations in the other direction as well. We are inclined to say that even the severely retarded, for example, may not be treated just *any* way we feel like — that a certain kind of decent treatment is *owed* to them, just as a certain kind of decent treatment is *owed* to animals and the insane. I use the term "owed" at this point merely to indicate that we feel that the decent treatment is done at least in part *for the sake of these creatures* and not simply for our own sakes — to protect our sensitive feelings with respect to the hardships of other creatures — and that the decent treatment is *obligatory* on us and is not optional or supererogatory in the way that certain acts of kindness or beneficence are. For example, the feeling that we owe the severely retarded something and that any decent treatment we give them is not just a matter of charity is behind the temptation to say that even creatures such as these borderline ones *do* have rights. Perhaps they do not have as many rights as properly ascribable to competent adult humans, but they have some rights nevertheless. It is my hope in what follows to make a start toward sorting out our conflicting temptations here and to suggest a way, both conceptually clear and morally adequate, in which both sides can be satisfied – at least partially.

THE NATURE AND IMPORTANCE OF RIGHTS

I shall argue that we use the language of rights to do at least *two different* (though related) moral jobs, and that a failure to keep clear the distinction between these two jobs is behind a substantial amount of the fruitless philosophical controversy surrounding the question of whether borderline cases do or do not have rights.

One important function of the language of rights, stressed by such philosophers as John Locke and especially Immanuel Kant, has been to mark out the special kind of treatment (called "respect" by Kant) which is particularly fitting or appropriate to *autonomous, rational persons*.[4] There does seem to be something special about such persons (Kant calls it their "dignity") in that their destinies, at least in large measure, can be rationally controlled by their own choices or decisions. They are, to use another Kantian phrase, self-legislating members of a kingdom of ends (a community of other self-legislators).

In the spirit of Kant, Robert Nozick uses the phrase "rational creature" as "short for beings having those properties in virtue of which a being has those full rights that human beings now have".[5] This special feature of persons seems to provide a ground for a special set of moral claims (natural or human rights) which are appropriate only for such creatures and not for any other animals. These basic natural or human rights are articulated by Locke as follows: "No one ought to harm another in his life, health, liberty or possessions".[6] This list is *negative* (it prohibits certain kinds of *interferences*) because only in this way can the special status of persons be protected and respected – their status as creatures who must be left their own "moral space" to work out their own destinies according to their own choices and decisions. Positive interference with them, even if benevolently or paternalistically motivated, would be an affront to their dignity or status as persons. Persons, Kant argued, are ends and not means only; they are not to be sacrificed or used as instruments or resources for the achieving of others' ends without their consent. They are inviolable. Stressing this inviolable nature of persons has been the central focus of many who have written on rights, and — for what I hope are obvious reasons — I shall label their accounts of rights as accounts of *Autonomy Rights*.

Those like Kant who have stressed Autonomy Rights have not regarded such rights claims as being the only important part of morality, but they have certainly regarded them as the *most important* part. Kant argues that those duties resting on rights are absolute and decisive (he calls them "perfect") when in conflict with any other moral considerations — for example, when in conflict with such "imperfect" duties as beneficence (helping others in need). These imperfect duties do not rest on rights (I do not violate another's rights simply by refusing to help him), admit of "latitude in time and manner of their fulfillment" (I must simply do *something* for *some* people *some* of the time) and never take precedence over claims of genuine rights. *Rights claims are morally basic because the value of autonomy which they capture is evaluatively basic.* This, in very general and oversimplified terms, is the view of such writers as Kant and Nozick.

Another quite different tradition in moral and social philosophy, best represented by John Stuart Mill and our contemporary John Rawls, involves the view that rights claims are *not* morally basic. Rather, they are *derivative* from more general moral principles. "To have a right," Mill suggests, "is to have something which society ought to defend me in the possession of ".[7] The central idea here is that rights claims function, not to mark some specially fine feature of persons, but rather to mark out which of all moral claims *ought to be enforced by the state*; in other words, which ones *ought to be law*. On this view, a creature may be said to have a right to *x* if and only if it is morally reasonable, all things considered, to *guarantee x* to that creature as a matter of law.

Mill's own version of rights theory meets shipwreck in the answer he gives to the question: "How do we decide what is morally reasonable?" Mill, alas, is a utilitarian — one who claims that the basic or most important moral requirement is to maximize human happiness. This theory is so obviously morally bankrupt[8] that very few contemporary moral philosophers take it at all seriously. I will not take time here to reiterate all the things wrong with the theory. Suffice it to say, as a summary objection, that utilitarianism fails to pay attention to those important *autonomy* values discussed above and thus fails to articulate a satisfactory conception of *justice* or *respect for persons*. It does not, as any correct theory of justice would, rule out the sacrifice of persons for the general good.[9]

Just because Mill's ultimate moral theory is defective, however, it does not follow that his analysis of rights as claims that society ought to enforce is defective. Though John Rawls (a contemporary anti-utilitarian) says very little about rights, his analysis appears similar to that of Mill.[10] However, he does not give a utilitarian answer to the question of what is morally reasonable for society to enforce. Rather, he says we should ask ourselves this question: "If a group of ideally rational beings came together in order to pick rules to govern their mutual relations, which rules would they be compelled (by the power of their rationality) to pick?" This decision-theoretical interpretation of classical social contract theory is basic in Rawls' outlook.

Since I believe that, in spite of certain very serious problems,[11] Rawls' theory is very helpful in illuminating certain moral issues, I should like to discuss it in a bit more detail. As already indicated, Rawls suggests that we use the idea of a social contract as a model of rational decision in morality. That is, we shall regard as rationally justified any moral principle (or any social practice) if that principle (or practice) would be unanimously agreed to, adopted, or contracted for by a group of rational agents coming together, in what Rawls calls the "original position," in order to pick principles and then practices to govern their relations with each other as members of a common community. The "original position" is simply a hypothetical situation of priority to moral rules and social practices. Unanimous consent is required because it captures our intuitive notion of what is *fair* as an agreement (because this precludes anyone's being coerced), and this intuitive notion of fairness is prior to developed moral rules or principles. Indeed, according to the theory, such rules or principles will grow out of this intuitively acceptable setting. This is why Rawls speaks of justice *as* fairness. In an attempt to avoid begging any moral questions (for example, by smuggling certain controversial moral values into the very conception of rationality), Rawls stipulates that rational agents in the original position are primarily *self-interested* – primarily concerned to promote their own welfare (which includes promoting the welfare of those about whom they care deeply, such as members of their families). An important and controversial restriction on Rawls' model of a rational being is that such a being is said to operate under a "veil of ignorance"[12] – he is said to know what in general can happen to persons in various positions in society but not to know what *his* own actual position is likely to be. According to Rawls, this prevents the rational contractors from making choices on the basis of *morally irrelevant* considerations such as skin color. For example, in trying to decide whether or not to adopt a practice of slavery, each agent would know in general what it is like to be a slave, but none of the agents would know the probability of *his* being a slave.[13] Finally, Rawls suggests that each rational agent will value a set of primary goods (liberty, security, self-respect) and will always choose to minimize, as far as possible, threats to these goods. Rawls defines primary goods as "things that every rational man is presumed to want. These goods normally have a use whatever a person's rational plan of life".[14]

Given this brief sketch of an elaborate intellectual machinery, we are now in a position to see how Rawls attempts to show that rational persons would *not* choose utilitarianism as a basic moral principle. Since utilitarianism allows for the sacrifice of the few if this results in substantial benefit to the majority, it would never be unanimously agreed to in the original position. Rational agents, caring most about protecting such primary goods as liberty ("mini-maxing," in the economists' language), and having no guarantee (because of the veil of ignorance) that they will not be members of the sacrificed class, will choose a principle which does not allow such sacrifice. To return to the slavery example: Since no rational agent would be willing to run the risk of being a slave, rational agents would not unanimously agree to a principle which allowed slavery. As one can easily see, Rawls views rational people as *cautious* people — people who plan their lives on the least favorable set of assumptions about how things will turn out. Though they perhaps miss out on the bliss and exaltation of the gambler, they also (and this matters much more to them) miss out on the irrevocable disasters to which gamblers are prone.

What does all this have to do with rights? I will suggest the following as a Rawlsian-inspired analysis: An individual should be understood as having a right to *x* if and only if a law guaranteeing *x* to the individual would be chosen by rational agents in the original position. This concept of a right I shall call a *Social Contract Right*.

We have, then, *Autonomy Rights*, concerned to respect the choices and decisions of persons, and *Social Contract Rights*, concerned to provide morally justified legal guarantees. These are related, but a few moments of reflection should persuade us that they are not identical. If you promise that you will meet me for dinner and then simply stand me up without good reason, you have shown insufficient respect for my humanity, treated me with contempt, and violated an autonomy right of mine. For surely it is part of the meaning of "I promise," sincerely uttered in the proper circumstances, that it gives a right to the person to whom the promise is made. But should all such rights be enforced by law? Surely not. Any state which sets for itself the goal of enforcing every promise, no matter how trivial, would be financially bankrupt and morally intrusive. This is why only certain promises (regarded as important enough to be made into *contracts*) are enforced by the state.

Consider another example: Suppose I am poor, unable to afford decent food and medical care. Does this mean that any of my autonomy rights have been violated? Not necessarily. Others may simply have exercised their right to leave me alone. They have neglected me but not interfered with me, and autonomy rights require only noninterference. And yet, many would want to say, the poor have a *right* to a decent standard of living, education, and health care. But why, if no considerations of autonomy are involved?[15] A Rawlsian answer here strikes me as plausible: Rational persons, in the original position, would want to protect themselves against certain major losses and harms. Thus they would probably agree to a *minimum floor* of security below which no member of society would be allowed to fall. Even selfish people, caring about their own welfare, would want to guard against the kind of destruction of primary goods that would result if they became severly disadvantaged, as people often do, through no fault of their own, but simply through their "bad luck on the social and natural lottery".[16]

In summary, most Autonomy Rights are going to be adopted as Social Contract Rights (though not all, as my promise example shows), because rational agents in the original position will surely want to protect themselves against interferences with their ability to determine their own future by their own choices. Social Contract Rights are going to be broader in scope than Autonomy Rights, however, because rational agents in the original position — in addition to caring about the protection of their autonomy against interference — are going to want to protect themselves against certain major hardships and sufferings. They know that they are sentient as well as sapient. They are thus likely to adopt minimum floors of security (income, health care, and the like) and speak of these as *rights*. There will be neither confusion nor immorality here so long as they remain clear about the status of these rights — that they are Social Contract Rights and not Autonomy Rights. The main point in calling them rights is to emphasize that they are *guaranteed* — nonoptional.

What if autonomy as a value seems to compete with minimum floors as a value? Which will take precedence? In the original position, decisions will be made — not just about what rights to recognize — but about the priority of these rights claims. This is a difficult problem, but not, in my judgment, obviously insoluble.[17] At this point, I shall resist the strong temptation to consider in even greater detail the fascinating abstract issues raised by the Rawlsian outlook on rights, and return to the more practical issues with which I began.

BORDERLINE CASES AGAIN

I shall not attempt to consider all of the borderline cases noted by Feinberg, but shall confine myself to a discussion of the extent to which, if at all, *children* have rights, and the extent to which, if at all, *retarded individuals* have rights. I shall further confine my discussion to *very young* children and individuals who are *more than minimally* retarded. If we consider 17 year-old "children," or "retarded persons" with IQs of 85, it would seem unduly severe to treat them as any less than autonomous persons with the rights appropriate to that status. The actual location of the dividing line between, for example, child and adult, is bound to be somewhat arbitrary and the cases barely on either side somewhat arbitrarily classified. Thus, it is useful, at least at the start of a discussion of these issues, to consider individuals noncontroversially within the class in question.[18]

Children

Young children certainly are not fully rational and autonomous (to the degree of normal competent adults) and thus clearly cannot be held to enjoy the basic Autonomy Right of having their destinies determined by their own choices and decisions. However, there is one very good reason for often *treating* them *as if* they had such a right. Treating children as though they are autonomous aids them in *developing* into genuinely autonomous persons; treating them as responsible persons aids them in *becoming* responsible persons. Such "fictions" have a way of becoming self-fulfilling prophecies. We shall, of course, want to place limits on such treatment in the interest of the child and pick our instances of fictional autonomy ascription wisely. For example, if a small child decides that he does not want to take the penicillin prescribed for a streptococcus infection in his throat, this would be a bad case in which to let his decision prevail in the interest of developing future autonomy.

Of course, as a normal child grows older, he will acquire greater and greater autonomy. Rights to self-determination can be correspondingly extended, paternalism being phased out gradually. But do not children sometimes, particularly when very young, have a *right* to paternalism – action in their interest either to prevent certain kinds of harms (such as child abuse, subjection to parental superstition with respect to proper medical care) or to provide them with certain benefits (such as a proper education) necessary for having or developing a satisfying life? Here I would answer *yes* – children do have such rights to paternalistic intervention on their behalf. However, the younger and less autonomous they are, the greater the need for intervention – it is *paternalism* after all. What this shows is that the rights here cannot be Autonomy Rights but must be understood as Social Contract Rights. Rational agents in the original position, knowing that they could be born into the class of children and knowing that — even as adults — they will care deeply about any children they may have, will surely want to establish certain minimum floors for children — certain levels of security and education below which no child will be allowed to fall. Thus, paradoxical as it may initially seem, I should argue that there are rights to be treated paternalistically. The paradox disappears, of course, if we remember that we are speaking of rights — not as ways of respecting autonomy — but as legal guarantees society should provide, perhaps as ways of allowing autonomy to develop in those cases where it is not yet present.

Retarded Persons

Autonomy considerations are even less relevant here than they were with respect to children. Retarded persons normally have little chance of ever becoming autonomous, and so the "fictional" argument given for sometimes treating nonautonomous children as if they were autonomous will not apply here — at least not nearly to the same extent. Here we are dealing with a class of persons who will never be in a position where it could reasonably be claimed that their destinies ought to be determined by their own choices and decisions; so, if there are rights here, they will for the most part be rights to a certain kind of paternalistic protection.

Are there such rights? Again I should be inclined to answer *yes*, and again the answer is based on social contract grounds. Anyone could become mentally defective or have a mentally defective child (about whom one might care very deeply), and thus rational persons presumably would want to provide a certain minimum floor below which such people would not be allowed to fall. Here what will be relevant is to guarantee a certain level of security and a certain level, not of education, but of training. At the very least (if we have any sense of the good)[19] we shall want to protect them against suffering, including any kind of mental suffering of which they may be capable. The right to be protected against such suffering is like the right to security and training in that it is clearly a Social Contract Right and not an Autonomy Right. In other words, it is simply that which any decent society would guarantee by law to its disadvantaged members.[20]

CONCLUSION

At this point, it would be useful to have a tidy *list* of exactly those rights which will be possessed by children and the retarded. I will plead my philosophical vocation as an excuse for not providing such a list, however, since it could be compiled only if we leave the world of abstract thought and begin to gather actual empirical information (which I do not possess) on the exact characteristics of children and retarded persons — what they are in fact capable of at various stages. I have been concerned simply to provide a moral framework in which discussions of their rights can be clarified; and I hope that others, if they accept the framework, will be able to fill in the practical and factual information necessary for its actual employment. At this point the philosopher must give way to the lawyer, the behavioral scientist, and the physician.[21]

I would, however, close with one caution to those who may be inclined to draw up lists of rights for children, the retarded, or any other disadvantaged people. The caution is simply this: Do not give into the romantic and knee-jerk liberal temptation to multiply rights beyond necessity. Autonomy Rights may seem restrictive, but Social Contract Rights are restrictive also — they are, remember, concerned with *minimum floors*. The more one attempts to go above the minimum to assert something more substantial as a matter of right, the more one runs the risk of developing a list of "rights" which are either so economically expensive to support or so morally intrusive to enforce that no sane society will in fact support or enforce them.[22] They will be paid at most a kind of lip service in manifestos — something which cheapens the concept of a right, makes people cynical about rights, and deprives them of their moral force. Social Contract Rights require, not simply noninterference, but *positive* steps to aid. The positive step taken in most complex modern societies, of course, is taxation. If, for example, we are going to have programs to benefit the retarded, someone is going to have to *pay* for such programs. If they are minimum floor programs resting on Social Contract Rights, then taxation may be the appropriate mechanism for funding. If they go beyond this, however, private funding seems in order. When we are under the spell of some good cause, and when we see that the chances of private funding of such a cause are unlikely, we are tempted to manufacture even more "rights" so that we can make our cause eligible for public funding through taxation. But the money available in society is not manna from heaven, to use Robert Nozick's metaphor, failing on the ground to be used for whatever good purpose we see fit. It is *earned* by people and is something over which they may plausibly claim to have a right.[23] Rational persons in the original position would want to protect themselves and their families against certain disasters, and this is why they would agree to minimum floors. Such persons also, however, would surely want to control at least a substantial portion of their earnings to spend as they see fit, and this is why they would be reluctant to agree to anything above minimum floors. Thus, crusades to go above minimum floors as a mater of *right* tend to themselves run the risk of inviting violations of other important rights. If such violations are also economically expensive, they will be opposed on both practical and moral grounds. The final victim of this sort of tension will simply be the important concept of a right itself.

NOTES

* An earlier version of this essay was originally delivered as a lecture at the 'Conference on the Rights of the Unborn, Children and Retarded Persons,' University of Rochester Medical Center, Nov. 19, 1976. It was also presented at the Mountain-Plains Philosophy Conference on 'Human Rights', University of Wyoming, Apr. 1, 1977. I am very grateful for the valuable discussions the essay received at both of these conferences, for these discussions forced me to see important changes that had to be made in the essay.

[1]   J. Rawls, *A Theory of Justice* (Cambridge, Mass.: Harvard University Press, 1971).

[2]   R. Nozick, *Anarchy, State, and Utopia* (New York: Basic Books, 1974).

[3]   Feinberg, 'The Rights of Animals and Unborn Generations,' in *Philosophy and Environmental Crisis*, edited by William T. Blackstone (Athens, Georgia: University of Georgia Press, 1974), pp. 44.

[4]   See generally I. Kant, *Foundations of the Metaphysics of Morals* (1785); I. Kant, *Metaphysical Elements of Justice* (1797); J. Locke, *Second Treatise of Government* (1690).

[5]   R. Nozick, *supra* note 2, at 299.

[6]   J. Locke, *supra* note 4, section 6.

[7]   J. Mill, *Utilitarianism* (1863), Chapter 5. According to Mill, society's mechanisms of defense are the *law* and the social pressure of *opinion*. In order to simplify matters, I shall concern myself only with the former.

[8]   As John Rawls has shown, this theory could be used to justify such morally heinous practices as slavery. See J. Rawls, *supra* note 2, at 158–59.

[9]   Even if a utilitarian does rule out such sacrifice, he will do so for the *wrong reason*. As Rawls has noted, slavery cannot be wrong because the benefits derived by the slaveholder can never outweigh the burdens imposed on the slaves. See *id*. This kind of argument fails to appreciate that any benefits derived by the slaveholder are *immoral to count* because they are benefits which are unjustly acquired by the exploitation of human beings and to which he thus has no *right*. Analogously, we do not wait before morally condemning a rape in order to make sure that the pleasure derived by the rapist did not outweigh the pain experienced by the victim.

[10]   What follows is not an attempt to give an accurate depiction of the exact details and structure of Rawls' argument in *A Theory of Justice*. As any student of Rawls will immediately realize, I am collapsing together certain elements in his theory (for instance, the distinction between the stage of the "original position" and the stage of the

"constitutional convention") and am skimming over details (such as the distinction between "self-interested" and "mutually disinterested" motivation) which Rawls regards as theoretically important. I am also ignoring some serious problems faced by the theory. While such matters are of theoretical interest, a careful exploration of them is, in my judgment, simply not necessary for present purposes. It would be, indeed, merely a distraction in the present context. Thus the reader should perhaps view the following simply as a set of variations on a Rawlsian theme. The notion of a *minimum floor* which I shall employ is drawn from R. M. Hare's discussion of "insurance strategies" in Part II of his review of *A Theory of Justice*. Hare, Book Review (pt. II), *Philosophical Quarterly* **23**, (1973) 241–52.

One important point of detail, however, should perhaps be stressed. In suggesting that Rawls' theory can be used to provide a derivative analysis of at least certain rights as guarantees that society should enforce, no suggestion is being made that autonomy is unimportant in this theory. On the contrary, the contractors in Rawls' social contract theory are thought of as autonomous in something like Kant's sense; and what these contractors agree to protect or legally guarantee first is a set of certain basic liberties.

[11] See *Reading Rawls*, edited by Norman Daniels (New York: Basic Books, 1976). This is an anthology of critical essays on *A Theory of Justice* and contains a bibliography of other critical essays on Rawls' theory. Two book length attacks on Rawls' theory are Brian Barry, *The Liberal Theory of Justice* (Oxford: Oxford University Press, 1973), and Robert Paul Wolff, *Understanding Rawls* (Princeton: Princeton University Press, 1977). Though serious and fundamental problems have been located in Rawls' theory, no one has yet, in my judgment, done to Rawls' theory what Rawls has done to the theory of utilitarianism – Rawls has not simply shown its weak points, but also *replaced it* with a theory that is clearly superior. Rawls' theory is certainly not the only game in town, but is still seems to me the best.

[12] See J. Rawls, *supra* note 1, at 12, 19.

[13] For Rawls, basic social choice is choice under nearly total uncertainty.

[14] J. Rawls, *supra* note 1, at 62.

[15] In real, as opposed to hypothetical cases, it is going to be difficult to claim that autonomy is not involved at all. One's status as a rational agent, a maker of free choices and decisions, is going to be impaired by severe hardships.

[16] J. Rawls, *supra* note 1, at 74.

[17] Whatever the rational solution will be, it will *not* be the highly counter-intuitive one sometimes suggested by Kant – namely, that all autonomy rights (grounding perfect duties) will, no matter how trivial, take precedence over any other moral consideration (perhaps grounding an imperfect duty), no matter how serious. To borrow an example from Joshua Rabinowitz: No morally decent society is going to forbid that I simply take Jones' rope to throw to a drowning person if Jones, who (let us grant) has a Nozickian entitlement to the rope, refuses to let me have it or says I may have it only if I pay him several thousand dollars for it. It is a Kantian perfect duty that I do not take Jones' rope and "only" an imperfect duty that I attempt to save the drowning person. What response can we make to this point except "so what?"

There is insight in Kant's attempted ordering, however, and I think it is this: That the *most important* of the perfect duty requirements resting on the *most important* rights (those which protect autonomy in a serious sense) can be said to take precedence over even the most important of the imperfect duty requirements. Killing Jones, spoiling his health, or taking his liberty away for a substantial amount of time, for example, do not seem acceptable steps to take even to save a drowning person. Taking his rope, however, does not seem to be in the same ballpark with these intrusions. Unless Jones is really weird, the temporary loss of his rope will not interfere with his autonomy in any serious way – it will not keep him from leading one of those meaningful lives which are, according to Nozick, bound up with the concept of rights. (See R. Nozick, *supra* note 2, at 50–51.) Some of these Kantian insights are captured in Rawls' notion of the priority of liberty, and his claim that his principle of "most extensive liberty compatible with like liberty for others" is lexically ordered prior to all other moral principles. In saying all this, I am admittedly making some assumptions I cannot presently defend: (1) that autonomy rights claims can be ordered on a scale of moral importance and; (2) that interferences with life, health, and liberty are typically more serious rebukes to autonomy than are threats to money and possessions. I think this ordering will have something to do with what I want to call the "internal" relation that one's very self (the person that one is, the meaning in one's life) stands in to one's life, liberty, and bodily integrity, as contrasted with the "external" relation that one stands in with respect to money and tangible things. These are themes I hope to be able to develop at some length in a future paper: to try to make sense of the "internal-external" metaphor (now admittedly just a vague intuition), establish its moral significance, and put it to use. For example, I will attempt to show where philosophers like Nozick go wrong in identifying taxation with forced labor.

[18] A full treatment of these issues would obviously require finer distinctions – with rights graded accordingly – than can be captured by the vague terms "very young" and "more than minimally retarded." Here I am simply concerned to give a general idea of how, in my judgment, discussion of these issues should proceed. For a more detailed treatment, see Murphy, 'Incompetence and Paternalism,' *Archiv für Rechts-und Sozialphilosophie* 60 (1964) 465–86. (Included in the present collection.)

[19] I believe that rational agents, as parties in the original position, can have a less selfish conception of the good than that which seems to be stipulated by Rawls. The primary good which Rawls allows them to value is good *to themselves* or *their immediate families* – it is *their* liberty, security, and self-respect which they value and want to secure. The motive for this restriction seems to be the laudable one of wanting to avoid begging any substantive questions in the theory by smuggling controversial moral claims into the model of rational choice. But are there not noncontroversial moral views, views which constitute the "facts" on which morality is based or which are the presuppositions for its very intelligibility? Surely, for example, it is noncontroversial that *suffering is bad* and, within moral limits, is to be opposed. Another way of stating this is that the *interests* of any creature have a *prima facie* claim to satisfaction – something which rational agents, who understand what morality is, can surely accept. (See Feinberg, *supra* note 3, at 49.) This expanded notion of primary good will have two interesting results. With respect to borderline cases it will, unlike a theory totally grounded in self-interest, make it possible to see the social contract rights extended in these cases as at least in part extended for *their* sakes, and not merely our own. The alternative, as Feinberg notes, is highly counterintuitive. Second, even animals may gain entry into the world of rights given an expanded conception of the good. Rawls himself might want to agree with much of this, for his conception of the good might not be as selfish or individualistic as I have suggested, though it is extremely common for his critics to interpret him in

this way. See Rawls, 'Fairness to Goodness', *Philosophical Review* 84 (1975) 536.

[20] Parties in the original position may know that people frequently value objects, such as works of art, and thus may want legal protections for these objects. Does this mean that a stone (if made into a sculpture) may have rights after all? In answering this question *no*, I should want to make three points: First, the Rawlsian apparatus requires our imagining certain misfortunes that might befall us and attempting to protect ourselves against them. It could befall me that I might become mentally disabled, but it seems to make no sense at all to suggest that it might befall me that I could become a stone. I cannot imagine myself as an occupant of *that* position. Animals pose interesting problems in this regard. See Thomas Nagel, 'What is it Like to be a Bat?', *Philosophical Review* 83 (1974) 435. Second, given the expanded conception of the good noted above, (see discussion note 19 *supra*), parties in the original position will sometimes act for the sake of sentient creatures in order to protect the interests of those creatures. But a stone (even if a great work of art) does not have either a sake nor does it have any interests. Third, my entire discussion is to be understood as accepting Feinberg's conceptual restrictions on the meaningful use of the concept of a right, and I agree with him that ascription of rights to stones is unintelligible. This is why I used phrases such as "creatures have a right to *x* if and only if" and "individuals have a right to *x* if and only if" and *never* the phrase "objects have a right to *x*." The upshot of this is the following: Laws protecting works of art or any other objects do not confer rights on these objects. If any rights are recognized here, it is simply *our* rights as human beings (or the rights of future generations) to enjoy these objects. Here we are acting for our own sakes. See D. Clayton Hubin, 'Justice and Future Generations', *Philosophy and Public Affairs* 6 (1976) 70–83.

[21] After reading the present essay, Professor David Wexler of the University of Arizona College of Law called my attention to the monograph, A. Stone, *Mental Health and the Law: A System in Transition* (National Institute of Mental Health, 1975). Its author, Alan A. Stone, is a Professor of Law and Psychiatry at Harvard University. His discussion, see especially *id*. at 15–19, overlaps mine to a certain extent and explores some of the interesting constitutional issues arising in this area.

[22] A reasonable minimum floor will, of course, be in part a function of what any particular society, or the entire world, is economically and technologically capable of at a given time in history.

[23] Granted the insight of this Nozickian claim, a qualification (perhaps overly cynical) must be added: Many people with substantial wealth in society have done nothing remotely resembling *working for* or *earning* that wealth as we normally understand these terms. Nozick sometimes seems to attempt to marshal our Puritan sympathies for the work ethic (and even our Marxist sympathies for the labor theory of value) on behalf of people who, though very wealthy, neither work nor "mix their labor" with anything: "Consider . . . how they grow; they toil not, neither do they spin."

VIOLENCE AND THE SOCRATIC THEORY OF
LEGAL FIDELITY*

I

We are inclined to think of Socrates as a rebel against the society of his day. We also think of him as a man whose intellectual rebellion took a negative form — i.e., instead of propounding philosophical theories of his own, he revealed his wisdom in destroying through rational criticism the theoretical pretensions of his fellow citizens. Given these expectations, the dialogue *Crito* contains substantial surprises. For, though containing negative criticisms of Crito's arguments, it is in the main an elaborate theoretical defense of obedience to the political powers that be. A part of this theoretical defense consists of a statement of a political theory, the social contract theory, which — at least until the time of Hegel and Marx — was the most influential theory in political thinking about such matters as obedience to law and political violence. For it is primarily a theory of legal fidelity — i.e., a theory which attempts to establish a *moral* obligation to obey the law, a moral obligation to honor one's legal obligations. This theory has strongly affected philosophical thinking about violence because, according to most social contract theory, the greatest criticism to be made against violence is that it is illegal. Indeed, some of these theorists (e.g., Hobbes and Kant) are inclined to *define* violence as the illegal use of force or coercion. This assimilation of the problem of violence to the problem of disobedience, and the related tendency to regard *law* as the central concept of politics, are both present in the *Crito*.[1] For Socrates in that dialogue sometimes seems to regard any disobedience to law (even the passive refusal to to accept the state's punishment) as the use of destructive violence against the state and condemns it on those grounds. And it is obvious that his relation to Athenian law is the only political aspect of his situation that strongly engages his interest.[2]

Because of its historical influence, and because it is philosophically interesting in its own right, I propose in this essay to subject the Socratic theory of legal fidelity to critical examination. In the spirit of Socrates himself, I propose to push the theory at its weak points to see if I can thereby generate its collapse. At the end of the paper, I shall make a few general remarks about social contract theory and political violence.

40

Now in examining the Socratic theory, I propose in the main to explore the ideas presented in the *Crito* rather than those presented in the *Apology*. This is not because, like some commentators, I view the arguments of the two dialogues as inconsistent. Rather I believe that the consistency between them is bought at the price of a theoretical poverty in the *Apology*. Let me explore this point briefly. In the *Apology*, Socrates claims that he would disobey the state under one set of circumstances — namely, if the state released him subject to the condition that he give up his practice of philosophy. Here, it is sometimes suggested, Socrates is proposing an act of civil disobedience (disobeying a law because it is believed unjust) of the very kind he rejects in the *Crito*. But this seems to me to be the wrong way to read Socrates' claim in the *Apology*, for I do not see him there to be clearly proposing civil disobedience at all. First of all, if the court order or "law"[3] reads "Socrates is at liberty unless Socrates practices philosophy," it is by no means clear that, by practicing philosophy, Socrates would be violating that order at all — so long as he openly accepts loss of liberty as a consequence. For the law gives him a choice; and, so long as he confines his choices to those contained in order, it is not clear that he would be strictly violating anything. If it would be a violation of any kind, it is (as A. D. Woozley has argued)[4] more like violating conditions of probation or parole than violating a law. A man who violates conditions of his people is simply sent back to serve the remainder of his sentence; and a man who violates conditions of probation is simply required to begin serving his sentence. In neither case is such a person regarded as having violated yet some other law carrying additional punishment over and above that prescribed for the offense of which he was originally convicted. Second, even if one would regard Socrates' practicing philosophy after the order to be a violation of law, the situation still differs markedly from the situation in *Crito*. For Socrates, in claiming that he would violate the condition of not practicing philosophy, justifies his refusal, not by claiming that the order would be unjust, but rather by claiming that God (his "divine inner voice") has commanded him to pursue philosophy as his vocation and that he will "obey God rather than men" (*Apology*, 29). In the *Crito* and end of *Apology*, however, he is inclined to believe (since no inner voice has tried to restrain him) that God approves of his dying as a martyr and that such a death will indeed be a benefit rather than a harm to him. Thus Socrates' position in the *Apology* is "Obey the law unless God commands otherwise." And thus, since in the *Crito* God has not commanded otherwise, his acceptance of punishment there is quite consistent with the argument of *Apology*. However, as I suggested before, this consistency is bought at the price of theoretical poverty. For no general political theory, at least not one of any intellectual respectability, can be built on such a subjective and private notion as an inner divine voice. This "voice" may by psychologically interesting in understanding the character of Socrates, but it can hardly be of use in constructing a universal theoretical position for the giving of reasons or justifications (not merely causal explanations) of obedience and disobedience to law.[5] Thus, since such non-rational appeals are pleasantly absent in the *Crito*, I propose to limit my examination in the main to its teachings.

The *Crito* divides into two main parts. In the first part, Crito gives reasons why Socrates should flee his legal punishment and Socrates counters these reasons. Having silenced Crito (who henceforth says little more than "That is correct, Socrates"), the second part contains Socrates' own attempt to construct a positive theoretical defense of obeying the law and accepting his punishment. I propose to examine both parts, but I shall give special emphasis to the second, where I shall attempt to do the job Crito fails to do — namely, subject Socrates' arguments to criticism.

II

Crito gives three main arguments in favor of Socrates' escaping. And Socrates, in responding to them, shows really what an advanced thinker he was for his era. Earlier Greek rebels, even Sophocles' Antigone, were primarily caught between the demands of competing social conventions (in Antigone's case between political conventions and religious conventions). Socrates, however, proposes to stand outside conventional expectations entirely and to concern himself not with what anyone else thinks, or what he himself *feels*, but solely with what, according to reason, it is just or right to do.[6] He is so rebellious on this point that he offers what have to be called *persuasive definitions* for the concepts "harm," "injury," and "evil" — definitions which would surely have struck his fellow Athenians as bordering on linguistic absurdity. For, according to Socrates, what really harms or injures a man, or what is really evil for him, is not bodily pain or death or loss of reputation but simply the loss of moral integrity that comes from being unjust (not from being thought unjust).[7] Only in this radical spirit can his responses to Crito be understood and appreciated.

Crito's arguments, quite plausible on their face, are the following:

(1) If you do not escape, your friends will be ridiculed and suffer loss of reputation because it will be said that they lacked the courage to save you;

(2) If you do not escape, you will not be able to provide for your children;

(3) If you do not escape, you will have to give up the practice of philosophy and your enemies, who wanted this, will thereby have won and you will have abandoned that which, as you said at your trial, was your God-given vocation.

Many commentators suggest that Socrates' dismissal of these arguments is superficial. For Socrates claims that these arguments are just irrelevant appeals to his feelings (e.g. his desire to continue doing philosophy) and to common conventional expectations (e.g., the belief that reputation is important) and that he will only be moved by what is right or just. But, so some commentators argue, Socrates is simply wrong on this point. For what happens to one's friends, one's family, and one's vocation in life are *not* just matters of feeling or convention but are of substantial importance. It may be all right for Socrates to be indifferent to his own reputation, for example, but it is hardly right to be indifferent to the harm that will come to his friends if they lose theirs. A. D. Woozley, arguing that Socrates' response to Crito is totally unsatisfactory, puts the criticism in the following way:

Although it has not always been appreciated, the reasons which Crito advances are moral ones, reasons why Socrates *ought* to agree to escape; appeals to Socrates' sense of prudence or personal advantage would, no doubt, have been useless, and Crito sensibly makes none.[8]

Though I shall admit that Socrates' attack on Crito is disorganized and enthymematic, I think that Woozley's criticism does not really give it a fair interpretation. For Woozley seems to be suggesting that there are factors present in the situation which clearly are morally relevant and that Socrates has negligently overlooked them. I should argue, however, that Socrates (a) knows full well that these factors are present, (b) knows full well that these factors are regarded as morally relevant by most people, but (c) does not himself believe that they are morally relevant (not, at any rate, as Crito interprets them). Woozley's real disagreement with Socrates, then, is a *moral* disagreement — a disagreement about what is important in morality. And thus it is oversimplified to suggest that there is just something obvious here which Socrates has overlooked. I do not here want to defend Socrates' moral outlook, only to elaborate it. And this elaboration will show, I think, that Socrates could not accept Woozley's point without sacrificing a main tenet his own moral theory — i.e., the tenet often summarized in the Socratic slogan that "a good man cannot be harmed" (*Apology*, 41). Thus it can hardly be said that Socrates' disagreement with Woozley and his other critics is just a matter of negligence on his part. With this in mind, let me take up his response to Crito in more detail.

In responding to (1) I think that we may take it that Socrates is assuming (though he does not mention) his theory that one is harmed, or injured, or suffers evil only insofar as one is unjust. Thus Crito, if he does not act unjustly, cannot really be harmed by loss of reputation, by being called "coward" by other Athenians. If Crito thinks that this is harm, then Crito is simply ignorant. For he views harm or evil as the world views it and not as (in Socrates' judgment) a rational man should view it.

I wish that the multitude could do a man the greatest evil, Crito, for then they could also do the greatest good. And that would have been well. But the truth is they can do neither good nor evil: they cannot make a man wise or foolish; and whatever they do is the result of chance [*Crito*, 44].

Thus Socrates can, I think, be interpreted as agreeing with Woozley fully on the principle that one should not harm one's friends but disagreeing with him (and almost everyone else) on the meaning to be given "harm." What interests him is what might be called harm to the soul, not harm to the body; and it is the former sort of harm that he wants to avoid both for himself and for his friends.[9] (Surely his theory of harm is meant to be universal — i.e., he is not saying that for Socrates being unjust is harm but for everyone else other things, such as pain and loss of reputation, are harm.) Thus Crito's appeal (1) comes too early in the discussion. It must first be decided if escape would be unjust before it can be decided how to apply the principle, "Do not harm your friends." For if the escape is unjust, Crito will, in engineering it, be acting unjustly. And if he acts unjustly he will be truly harmed — regardless of how secure his public reputation as a man of courage.

The same ideas, I think, help us to come to terms with (2) and (3) above. As the final section of *Apology* shows, Socrates is not indifferent to the welfare of his sons. He seeks to provide for thier benefit. But again we must ask what counts, on his theory, as doing this? As I would interpret him, he believes that he will benefit his sons primarily by acting to insure that they will be just rather than unjust men — *not* that they will be well fed and well thought of.

When my sons grow up, punish them, my friends, and harass them in the same way that I have harassed you, if they seem to you to care for riches or for any other thing more than excellence; and if they think that they are something when really they are nothing, reproach them, as I have reproached you, for not caring for what they should, and for thinking they are something when really they are nothing. And if you will do this, I myself and my sons will have received justice from you [*Apology*, 41].

Thus I should suggest that Socrates may have had in mind, or at the very least could have made out, a fairly plausible case of the following sort against (2): Of course, it is important to care for my children, but the important kind of care is for their souls – i.e., the inculcation of justice. Now if, in escaping, I set for them an example of injustice in their father, I will have failed them in what really matters – regardless of how well I feed or clothe their bodies in the future. (Remember, by the way, that Socrates believes that his friends will do this anyway.) Thus, important though the question of caring for my children is, I must *first* determine the question of whether escaping would be just before I can be sure of the best way to care for them in the circumstances.

Similarly with point (3). Of course, Socrates is concerned to pursue his vocation and not let his enemies win. But what is it to pursue his vocation; and what counts as "winning" in such a context? Here too, I think, his primary concern is with being just. For being unjust would, as the Laws point out to him, render him unfit for the practice of philosophy.

If you go to [well-governed states]. you will come to them as an enemy, Socrates, and their governments will be against you, and all patriotic citizens will cast an evil eye upon you as a subverter of the laws, and you will confirm in the minds of the judges the justice of their own condemnation of you ... Will you then flee from well-ordered cities and virtuous men? And is existence worth having on these terms? Or will you go to them without shame, and talk to them, Socrates? And what will you say to them? What you say here about virtue and justice and institutions and laws being the best things among men? Would that be decent of you? Surely not [*Crito*, 53].

And as for the question of who is "winning," Socrates or his enemies, it is perfectly clear that Socrates believes that this too depends upon who is being just.

I think it is a much harder thing to escape from wickedness than from death, for wickedness is swifter than death. And now I, who am old and slow, have been overtaken by the slower pursuer; and my accusers, who are clever and swift, have been overtaken by the swifter pursuer – wickedness. And now I shall go away, sentenced by you to death; and they will go away sentenced by the truth to wickedness and injustice. And I abide by the award as well as they. Perhaps it was right for things to be so. I think that they are fairly balanced ... No evil can happen to a good man, either in this life or in death ... And so I am not angry with my accusers or with those who condemned me to die; they have done me no harm although they did not mean to do me any good; and for this I may gently blame them [*Apology*, 41].

Thus again Socrates seems to be expressing his conviction that, before he can decide the important issue of whether to continue practicing philosophy, he must first decide the *prior* question of whether he would be acting unjustly in escaping. Thus he is not necessarily holding that a consideration for his friends, or sons, or future is unimportant. Rather he seems to be holding that these issues, important as they are, *presuppose* an answer to a more basic question: What is the just thing to do here? Thus his initial inquiries must be directed to this basic question. For the answer to this question helps to determine what it is to consider or care for his friends, his children, and himself in this setting. If escape is unjust, he will in escaping (given his theory of harm) harm those who aid him, harm his children by example, and harm himself. By harming himself and forfeiting his right to practice philosophy, he will insure that his enemies — who sought his harm — will have won. One can morally disagree with Socrates here, but one can hardly charge him simply with overlooking things whose moral importance is obvious and unambiguous.

III

Having considered Socrates' reasons for rejecting Crito's appeals, I shall now turn to Socrates' positive theory of legal fidelity. In justifying his refusal to disobey the law and flee his punishment, he makes the following three claims:

(1) We should never return injury for injury, evil for evil, injustice for injustice. Thus, even though the state has unjustly injured Socrates, he should not return the injury (*Crito*, 49ff.).

(2) The state is like a parent. And just as we have a duty to obey our parents and not use violence against them, so too do we have (by analogy) a duty to obey the state and not use violence against it (*Crito*, 50ff.).

(3) We have, in some sense, contracted to obey the law; and we have a moral obligation to honor our contracts (*Crito*, 51ff.).

Point (3) is developed at the greatest length and is also the most interesting and persuasive; and thus I shall spend most of my time in commenting on it. However, I shall first attempt to demonstrate the weakness of points (1) and (2).

(1) *Never Return Injury for Injury.*[10] This principle is simply put forth by Socrates as a bit of unargued dogma, and yet surely it is controversial. Most people approve of institutions of criminal punishment, and there is no reason to suppose that Socrates would not share this approval. But such institutions, at least on a retributive model, involve the returning of injury for injury in some sense.[11] We can, of course, make the principle appear more plausible by equating injury here with injustice. Then we might agree that punishment, if just, is not really injury. But if by "injure the state" Socrates means "act unjustly with respect to the state," he is simply begging the question at issue

by assuming that his leaving would constitute injury to the state. For he is supposed to be arguing that it would be unjust to leave, and he defends this by claiming (a) that it would be unjust to injure the state and (b) that his leaving would injure the state. But if "injure" just means "be unjust to," then a premise of Socrates' argument here is that his leaving would be unjust. But this cannot be a premise, for it is supposed to be the conclusion.[12]

There are serious problems, therefore, with interpreting "injure the state" as "act injustly with respect to the state." Suppose, then, we try out a more plausible notion of injury. Drawing on Socrates' previously discussed theory of harm or injury, we can let "injure the state" mean, not "treat the state unjustly," but rather "make the state unjust." However, if the state can be injured in this sense ("deteriorated by injustice" as he says at *Crito*, 47), then it must be possible to draw some kind of distinction between a state's soul (its constitution, perhaps) and a state's body (its efficacious use of power, perhaps). Only interference with the former's justice would constitute true injury or harm. But, if this line is taken, it seems quite plausible to argue as follows: If really harming the state means increasing the likelihood of its being unjust (and therefore maimed or deteriorated in soul), then the question of whether or not to accept unjust punishment at its hands depends upon the answer to another question — namely, will acceptance of injustice be more likely than resistance to deter the state from future acts of injustice? This is in some sense an empirical question, and it is by no means obvious on these grounds that Socrates' decision to remain was the correct one. It is not implausible to argue, for example, that if the victims of injustice effectively resist their oppression, the government will be deterred from future acts of injustice, whereas passive acceptance may encourage the government to greater excesses of injustice and thereby fulfill Socrates' prophecy (at *Apology*, 28), that he will not be the "last victim." If this is so, then to remain and accept punishment would be to harm the state (in the relevant sense of harm) and to escape or resist in some other way would be to benefit the state (in the relevant sense of benefit) — i.e., by resisting one would be giving the state an incentive for acting more justly in the future (though not, it must be admitted, an incentive of morally the best sort).

In summary: By "injure the state" Socrates must mean either "act unjustly with respect to the state" or "make the state unjust or more unjust." If he means the former, his appeal to the "do not return injury for injury" principle is circular as a justification for his conviction that it would be unjust for him to escape. If he means the latter, then it is by no means clear that his resistance would make the state more unjust. It just might make it better. Thus argument (1) has to be rejected.[13]

(2) *The State as Parent*.[14] There are several problems with this appeal. First, the principle "honor your parents" seems to be drawn from conventional morality — the very source for moral guidance of which Socrates is supposed to be so suspicious. Socrates seems to put the principle forth as a bit of unargued dogma, and the skeptical reader might well wonder how this principle differs in kind from Crito's "protect the reputation of your friends" — a principle which Socrates regards as irrelevant. Second, the principle, even if accepted, surely gives rise only to a *prima facie* obligation — i.e., we have a duty to obey our parents *unless* there are good moral reasons to disobey them (e.g., suppose your father tells you to murder someone or to kill yourself). Thus the principle admits of exceptions. Since it does, Socrates must not appeal to the principle *simpliciter*, but must consider whether his predicament, given the analogy, might not constitute an exception. But he does not pursue this worry at all. Third, Socrates seems to shift (at *Crito*, 50–51) between a principle of the form (a) "obey your parents" and a principle of the form (b) "do not strike or do violence against or destroy your parents." But this linking of violence with disobedience is problematic. For example: we can surely accept (b) without thereby being logically or morally required to accept (a) — e.g., we think of ourselves as *outgrowing* (a) but not (b). And of course this shift muddies up the very point at issue in the *Crito*; for Socrates' escape would be a clear case of disobedience but a very doubtful case of violence or destruction. This close linking of disobedience with violence, which as I suggested earlier is common in social contract theory, will be explored later in more detail. At present it is sufficient to warn the reader to be on guard against such a simple identification. Fourth, and finally, if harming one's parents is what is at issue, and to harm means either to act unjustly to or to make unjust, then it is not established that to escape would be to harm the state (as parent) unless it is already established that escape is unjust or will cause injustice. But it is not already established, for it is the very point at issue.

Of course, one might argue that the appeal to the parent analogy is not an attempt to appeal to a conventional duty to honor parents *simpliciter*. Rather it is only *some* parents who are to be honored — namely, those who, like the state, have in some way conferred benefits on one (nurturing, educating, etc.) for which feelings such as gratitude are appropriate. This may be, but then the argument will not hang on the parental relation *simpliciter* but rather upon some obligation-creating property which is typically (but not necessarily) found in the parental relation. And this point, in my judgment, can best be discussed as one of the ideas making up the social contract theory to which I shall now pass.

(3) *The Social Contract*. Socrates' final argument states, or at least anticipates, the social contract theory of legal fidelity — a theory held (in different forms) by such later writers as Hobbes, Locke, Rousseau, Kant, and (in our own day) John Rawls. Though Socrates' elaboration of the theory is defective, and though his application of it misfires, it is still rather impressive as a first try. Its main points are the following:

(i) The state (like a parent) has conferred benefits on the citizen through its law.

(ii) By accepting the benefits voluntarily (i.e., when it was possible to leave) one can be said to have consented or contracted to obey the law as a kind of payment or act of gratitude for those benefits. (This clearly is an anticipation of Locke's famous — or notorious — notion of "tacit consent.")

(iii) Another reason why obedience is owed is that disobedience is destructive of law, and it is wrong to seek to destroy that from which you have voluntarily accepted benefits.

(iv) In agreeing to obey the law, you also agree to accept all court decisions as final.

This is interesting both for what it contains ((iv) is particularly puzzling) and for what it leaves out. Two important omissions are the following: First, since it is obviously false that one act of disobedience tends to destroy the law (only widespread disobedience could do that), this argument for obedience will not work unless it is supplemented by a principle of fairness: if it would be wrong for everyone to do A, then it is wrong for anyone to do A.[15] Second, in his principle (iii), Socrates seems to be overlooking the fact that his moral obligation to obey is not owed to the laws (though the laws are, in a sense, the object or beneficiary of this obligation) but is rather owed to his fellow citizens. This is because of the fact (noted by John Rawls[16]) that the benefits of law are possible (because law itself is possible) only because most citizens most of the time obey the law. Thus since the benefits I derive result from other people's sacrifices of obedience, it is only just or fair to them that I too be willing to make a comparable sacrifice, to insure their benefits, when my turn comes.

Without these two supplementations, Socrates' theory would not be a *social* contract theory at all. (And since it is not clear that Socrates would accept these supplementations, I am prepared to admit that it may be wrong to interpret him as doing anything more than anticipating some parts of social contract theory.) For without these supplementations, Socrates' appeal is either not really a contractual appeal at all (but rather an appeal to some principle like "show gratitude for benefits") or is simply an *individual* contract with the laws: "I agree not to destroy you who have benefited me. " But since, as Woozley notes, one act of disobedience will not harm (much less destroy) the law, even this individual contract, unsupplemented by a principle of fairness, will give Socrates no conclusive reason for obedience.

With the supplementation, however, one does get, I think, an extremely plausible argument for why there is a *prima facie* obligation to obey the law. But of course (and this is a point Socrates misses) it is, like the obligation to honor parents, only *prima facie*. And this can be explained on purely contractual grounds — namely, no rational man in his right mind would contract for a rule of the form " I shall obey the law *no matter what*." Even Hobbes (no flaming radical) realizes this and thus gives citizens the right to resist the government when their lives are threatened. So Socrates, except for the "divine voice" exception, seems even more absolutist than Hobbes, and one would hardly have thought this possible. This same point can be brought out by considering the principle of fairness: If it would be wrong for everyone to do *A*, then it is wrong for anyone to do *A*. [17] The application of the principle, of course, depends upon what *A* is. If *A* is "disobey the law whenever you jolly well feel like it," then of course it would be wrong (disastrous) for everyone to do this and so wrong for anyone to do it. But what if *A* is "disobey the law when it is reasonable to believe the law is grossly unjust" or "refuse to accept your punishment from a witchhunt tribunal?" It is by no means clear that the result would be bad if everyone acted on these maxims (I am inclined to think the result might be very good indeed) and thus it is by no means clearly wrong for an individual person to act on such a maxim.

But here Socrates has an extremely complex point to make — namely, that the rule of law in some sense precludes the individual's making and acting upon his *own judgment* about what is and what is not worthy of obedience in the legal system. And this, I take it, is part of the point of (iv) above — that in agreeing to obey the law, one also agrees to accept as final all court decisions.

Do you think that a state can exist and not be overthrown, in which the *decisions of law* are of no force, and are disregarded and undermined by private individuals? How shall we answer questions like that, Crito? Much might be said, especially by an orator, in defense of the law which makes judicial decisions supreme [*Crito*, 50]. [18]

Here Socrates seems to be making the point that legal systems are worthless unless they can be authoritatively applied by a court. And thus anyone who challenges a court decision is also challenging the law. Now why might Socrates (or anyone else) think this? There are, I think, three possible reasons:

(A) It may be the case that the legal system itself contains, as one of its laws, the law "judicial decisions are supreme." According to Socrates, the Athenian system contains such a law.

(B) One might hold a naïve form of legal realism – i.e., the theory that the law just is whatever a court says it is.[19]

(C) Even if the law and court decisions are different, and even if there is no law which says "judicial decisions are supreme," the only workable system of law (both in terms of justice and efficacy) is one where decisions are accepted as final.

Point (A) seems of little help. At most, it shows that in some legal systems there will be a legally specified limit to formal legal appeal. But this does not demonstrate, without an independent moral agrument for legal fidelity, that one is morally obligated to accept this limit in all cases. Indeed, unless the theory of legal realism (B) is true, it does not show that one could not disobey the court decision on *legal* grounds – i.e., by arguing that the court, even if it has the final say, has had the *wrong* say in that it has misinterpreted or ignored the law.[20]

Point (B) is useless because, as H. L. A. Hart has demonstrated, the naïve theory of legal realism is false.[21] It makes sense to disagree with court decisions (even Supreme Court decisions) on legal grounds (as dissenting judges do); courts are thought of as interpreting and not making law; courts reverse themselves; court judges are surely not, in making legal decisions, simply trying to predict what they will decide; and, finally, the very concept of a *court* is itself defined in terms of legal rules. Surely no rational man would contract for membership in a society whose master rule was "we will do whatever a group of men who happen to be called a 'court' tell us to do;" for that (like Hart's game of "scorer's choice"[22]) would be contracting for rule by men, not rule by *law*. For a rule of law requires that even government officials (including court judges) be subject to legal obligations.

Therefore (C) seems the only plausible appeal. But it is, again, only a principle establishing a *prima facie* obligation – i.e., one which might be overridden in particular circumstances. For it is important to distinguish the following cases:

(1) A man violates the law and is convicted by the court.

(2) A man does not violate the law but is honestly convicted by the court (i.e., the court acts in the belief that he is guilty).

(3) A man does not violate the law but is cynically and dishonestly convicted by the court (i.e., the court neither believes in nor cares about the actual guilt of the man but convicts him out of personal spite or on grounds of social utility).[23]

Now in a case like (1), a man who claims to respect and have allegiance to the law will have a strong *prima facie* obligation to accept his punishment. And it would not be implausible (though it would perhaps be heroic) for a man to reason similarly in Case (2), since he has no reason to doubt the integrity (only the knowledge) of the system. But what about Case (3)? Socrates clearly thinks that his case is of this sort, and there is every reason to accept his interpretation of the situation.

I have not committed the act of injustice for which Meletus is prosecuting me. What I have said is enough to prove that. But be assured it is certainly true, as I have already told you, that I have aroused much indignation. That is what will cause my condemnation if I am condemned; not Meletus nor Anytus either, but that prejudice and resentment of the multitude which have been the destruction of many good men before me, and I think will be so again. There is no prospect that I shall be the last victim. [*Apology*, 28.]

Even the Laws say that Socrates is a victim "not of the Laws, but of men" (*Crito*, 54).

Now in a case of this sort, one must raise the following question: If Socrates' punishment flows from these men and not from the law (i.e., his punishment is in some sense *illegal*), how in the world does his acceptance of this punishment necessarily demonstrate a loyalty to the *law*? One might think that by quietly accepting it he is showing his loyalty to these men (the very thing he presumably does not want to do) and that by fleeing he would show his loyalty to the law, since he has done nothing illegal! By staying, he seems to give a sanction to the proceedings and, if anything, increases the prospect that he will not be the last victim. He clearly rejects legal realism in some places (otherwise he could not say that he is a victim of men — the court — and not of the law); and yet his acceptance of punishment can be defended only on the assumption that he accepts legal realism (for otherwise how is accepting punishment at the hands of the court an act of fidelity to the law?) His confusion on this point is very deep and (if one will pardon the pun) fatal.

In summary, then, I suggest the following: Socrates gives very good arguments to establish a *prima facie* obligation to obey the law — even when (perhaps especially when) the law requires a consequence one does not relish. Thus if the law required his punishment, Socrates' fidelity to the law would

prima facie require his accepting it. But it is not the law requiring his punishment, but rather a group of unjust men — (Woozley very rightly calls them
Macarthyites) — men not even honestly attempting to apply the law. This
being so, I should argue that his obligation to the *law* is to flee and make it
perfectly clear that his prosecution and conviction were "legal" in name only.
For a contemporary parallel, consider the plight of the draft resister who
sincerely and reasonably believes (a) that the Vietnam War is illegal (unconstitutional) and (b) that the Supreme Court, in refusing to hear cases where
the charge of the illegality of the war has been made, reveals itself as nothing
more than a slave of the executive branch of government. Is it so clear that
such a person, if he flees to Canada rather than go to jail for draft refusal, is
revealing a lack of respect for the *law*? It is just as plausible to me to view him
as respecting the law but showing his contempt for a group of men who
happen to have power.

IV

I have strayed very far indeed from the symposium topics of force and
violence; and so perhaps in closing I should say a few words about these
matters and their relation to legal fidelity and civil disobedience. Civil disobedience, I should argue, is disobedience to particular laws coupled with
fidelity to the system as a whole. This is what distinguishes civil disobedience
from revolution — the revolutionary desiring the total overthrow of the
system. Now it seems to me that violence against persons is always incipiently
revolutionary. For whatever is controversial about government, one thing is
not — namely, that it must enjoy a monopoly on the force in a given society.
This is the main thing, on all social contract theories, we contract for: the institutional control of force, the transforming of violence into legal coercion.
Thus anyone who challenges the state's right to control force is challenging
the state at its basis and is thus revolutionary, not civilly disobedient.[24] Given
this, one can build up a deceptive and dangerous case for the status quo by
attempting to equate all disobedience with violence. It is not uncommon,
alas, to hear leading United States Government officials speak as though
draftcard burning, breaking windows at the Pentagon, and killing policemen
are all actions morally on a par. If one accepts this, it is then essay to see all
rebels as dangerous revolutionaries seeking and effecting the violent overthrow and destruction of the state. Socrates and other social contract theorists, insofar as they are tempted by this sort of equation (e.g., tempted to
regard "refusal to accept an illegal witchhunt verdict" as morally equivalent

to "striking a violent blow against one's parents"), are helping to establish a way of thinking about man and society and the law which encourages a slavish devotion to the state and which therefore threatens the spirit of rebellion so vital to a free and decent society — threatens indeed the idea that the proper allegiance is to law and justice and not to men. For the choice they hold out (and even Locke is guilty here) is one between total obedience and open violent revolution. But surely this is a false dichotomy.

NOTES

* In the following essay, I have for the most part death with *Apology* and *Crito* (relying on the translations by Benjamin Jowett and F. J. Church) as though they are philosophical works in English. I do not think this is totally unjustified because (a) the issues raised in the translations are of intrinsic philosophical interest and (b) it is primarily in translation that these works have had an impact in the recent history of ideas. Where some issue of translation did seem important, I was able to obtain assistance, for which I am very grateful, from my colleague Ronald Milo. I also found it useful to consult W. D. Adkins' *Merit and Responsibility, A Study in Greek Values* (Oxford: Oxford University Press, 1960).

1 This assimilation of the problem of violence to the problem of disobedience to law still crops up in some surprising places. See for example, Robert Paul Wolff's essay 'On Violence', *Journal of Philosophy* **LXVI** (Oct. 2, 1969) 601–16, where what starts to be a discussion of violence very quickly shifts into a discussion of civil disobedience. In my reply to Wolff ('Violence and the Rule of Law', *Ethics* 80 [July 1970], 319–21) I was guilty of the same assimilative tendency.

2 I should think that a Marxist, viewing legal institutions as a suspect part of an ideological superstructure, would find Socrates' focus in the *Crito* to be wrongheaded.

3 What we have here is really an order addressed specifically to Socrates; and, since it lacks generality, it should perhaps not strictly speaking be called a law at all.

4 'Socrates on Disobeying the Law', *The Philosophy of Socrates*, ed. Gregory Vlastos (Garden City: Anchor Books, 1971), pp. 299–318. I have had the opportunity of discussing this article, in conjunction with an early draft of my own present essay, with Professor Woozley. I have learned much from these discussions though not, I suspect, as much as I should have.

5 Private and subjective appeals on matters of this nature did not by any means end with Socrates but are still represented, for example, in attempts to justify civil disobedience by appeals to the "voice of conscience." The appeals made in Thoreau's famous 'On the Duty of Civil Disobedience' are roughly of this sort and are, in my judgment, to be rejected for lacking what Kant would call universalizability.

6 This decision of Socrates to stand above the authority of convention could almost be regarded historically as the creation of morality and is surely the greatest contribution made by Socrates to our civilization. In its most radical form, of course, it leads to the atomistic individualism characteristic of later social contract theory — i.e., the notion that man's nature and rationality can be understood in complete isolation from social

forces. In this radical form, the position may well be challenged by Hegelians and Marxists.

7 The Greek adjective generally translated as harmful, injurious, or evil is *kakon*, and the Greek verbs for harming or causing injury are *blapto* and *kakourgeo*. We must suppose that Socrates is persuasively defining these terms to make any sense at all of his famous claim (*Apology*, 41) that "no evil or harm can happen to a good man." For good men can surely be treated unjustly and made to suffer pain and death. What a good or just man cannot be, however, is bad or unjust. Thus only if being harmed is being unjust can it be true (though tautologically true, of course) that a good man cannot be harmed. This notion of harm runs throughout much of Plato's writings. See, for example, *Republic*, 335, where Socrates argues that to harm a man is to injure him and that to injure a man is to make him unjust. The term "persuasive definition" was coined by C. L. Stevenson in his article of that title in *Mind* (1938). One persuasively defines a term when, for evaluative purposes, one attempts to alter its normal usage (e.g. extend it to a new class of things) while preserving its emotive overtones. For the use of such definitions in Greek ethics, see W. D. Adkins, *Merit and Responsibility, A Study in Greek Values* (Oxford: Oxford University Press, 1960). On 265 he discusses the Socratic claim (at *Crito*, 47) that committing injustice is harmful, *kakon*, to the man who commits it.

8 *Op. cit.*, 308.

9 The notion that injustice deteriorates or maims the soul is explicitly expressed at *Crito*, 47.

10 The Greek word translated by Jowett as "injure" here is *antadikeo*. This is perhaps better translated as "unjustly retaliate." Unfortunately, as I shall argue in the following, this will render Socrates' argument from the principle question begging, since the very point at issue is whether Socrates' escape would be unjust.

11 There is no reason to suppose that Socrates, like Plato, rejected a retributive theory of punishment. Indeed, the issues raised by Socrates in the *Crito* (e.g., contractual obligation) are much more at home with a retributive conception of punishment than they would be with a utilitarian outlook.

12 No matter how the principle at issue is translated, confusion results. If we translate the principle as "never return injury for injury," we have the problems of (a) interpreting what Socrates here means by injury and (b) wondering why Socrates thinks the principle applies at all since he has already argued, at the end of *Apology*, that he had not been harmed or injured. Perhaps injury is here to be understood in its ordinary, and not in Socrates' technical, sense – e.g., *pain* will now count as injury. But on this interpretation, we have the problem, already noted, of squaring the principle with Socrates' apparent acceptance of criminal punishment – an institution which certainly does often return pain for pain. If, probably being more accurate to the Greek, we translate the principle as "never return injustice for injustice" or "never retaliate unjustly against injustice," we have Socrates merely begging the question at issue by assuming that the principle applies to his situation.

13 It is possible that Socrates does not intend the principle "never return injury or injustice for injury or injustice" to be an argument for his decision at all. It is perhaps just a reminder to Crito that only justice matters. Given this reminder, Crito will be in a position to appreciate the force of the arguments to follow.

14 It is interesting to note that a *family* model for understanding political obligation is

much more at home within an organic theory of the state than within a social contract theory. Thus Socrates' total outlook in the *Crito* is an interesting (and perhaps inconsistent) anticipation of a variety of different political views.

[15] This necessity for supplementing Socrates' argument with a principle of fairness is stressed in Woozley, *op. cit.*, 315 ff. The principle I have given above would obviously need refinement (e.g., specification of the act description *A*, elaboration of relevant circumstances, etc.) before it would be acceptable, but that would be an object for another paper.

[16] 'Legal Obligation and the Duty of Fair Play', *Law and Philosophy*, ed. S. Hook (New York: New York University Press, 1964), reprinted in my *Civil Disobedience and Violence* (Belmont, Calif.: Wadsworth Publishing Co., 1971). See, for a further elaboration of his social contract theory, his 'Justice as Fairness', *The Philosophical Review*, 67 (1958) 164–194. See also my 'In Defense of Obligation' in *Nomos XII: Political and Legal Obligation*, ed. J. Roland Pennock and John W. Chapman (New York: Atherton Press 1970), pp. 36–45.

[17] A more Kantian, and perhaps better, way of putting the principle might be as follows: It is unjust for anyone to claim for himself a liberty in action that could not be extended to all other persons in similar circumstances.

[18] I italicize the phrase "decisions of law" to note its importance and, in my judgment, its ambiguity. For suppose a court, applying a law *L* requiring *R*, decides not-*R*. Is it clear, even given the judicial supremacy law, that this decision is in every sense a decision of *law*?

[19] By a *naïve* (one might say "simpleminded") theory of legal realism, I mean one of the form summed up by Justice Holmes in the following slogan: "The prophecies of what the courts will do are what I mean by the law." There are more sophisticated versions of the theory that need not concern us here.

[20] See on this point Ronald Dworkin's 'On Not Prosecuting Civil Disobedience', in my *Civil Disobedience and Violence* (Belmont, Calif.: Wadsworth Publishing Co., 1971). See also my 'The Vietnam War and the Right of Resistance' in the same volume.

[21] Chapter VII, *The Concept of Law* (Oxford: Oxford University Press, 1961).

[22] As Hart points out on p. 140 of his *The Concept of Law*, there is a great difference between the following two games: (a) a game with a scoring rule *R* and an official scorer with final say, within the game, concerning the application of *R* and (b) a game where the scoring rule just is "the score is whatever the scorer says it is." Game (b) can be called the game of the "scorer's choice," and it is this kind of game which the naïve legal realist would have us accept as a model for understanding legal systems. But surely game (a) is a better model. Judges may, within the system, have the last legal word. But this does not show, since the rules are independent of their wills, that the last word is necessarily the correct word. In baseball, for example, we know that umpires sometimes make mistaken calls (i.e., baseball is not a game of scorer's choice); but we also know there is nothing we can do about it.

[23] The very fact that we can distinguish these three cases is sufficient to demonstrate that no naïve form of legal realism can be correct.

[24] This is not, of course, to say that such challenges are always morally wrong. They certainly are sometimes required. For a government, if it fails to use its coercive power with justice, and itself be regarded as violent and may require strenuous opposition. I take it that Nazi Germany would be a noncontroversial example here, an example of

what might be called *institutionalized or structural violence*. It is, in my judgment, a grave detriment of some forms of social contract theory (e.g., the theories of Hobbes and Kant) that, defining violence as the *illegal* use of force or coercion, they render it extremely difficult to speak of violence as being institutionalized. Thus they deprive us of what is, at the very least, a valuable rhetorical device.

HUME AND KANT ON THE SOCIAL CONTRACT*

Hume and Kant were both political philosophers of remarkable originality, subtlety and profundity; and yet their contributions in this area are largely unrecognized. Both are generally relegated to footnotes in comprehensive texts on political theory — e.g. Hume gets only eight of the 948 pages in Sabine and Kant gets even less (only a few references in passing). This is perhaps particularly unfair to Hume who claimed that the ultimate goal of *all* of his philosophy was to introduce into morals and politics the kind of scientific inquiry that Newton had brought to external nature; but it is also unfair to Kant, who wrote at great length on these matters as well. Probably the chief explanation for the relative obscurity in political philosophy of both men is the same — namely, that the overwhelming genius exhibited in their writings on epistemology and metaphysics simply eclipsed the importance of their writings in other, less 'primary' areas of philosophical inquiry (thereby illustrating the maxim that no good deed ever goes unpunished).[1] Whatever the total reasons for the neglect, however, I hope that I can present a convincing case — by a discussion of some central arguments in the political thought of both men — that the neglect is extremely unfortunate and ought not to be allowed to persist among serious teachers and scholars in the area of legal, social and political philosophy.

Now of course the time-honored device for discussing Hume and Kant in epistemology and metaphysics is to place them in fundamental conflict with each other. (I have in mind here the tradition, to which I have myself contributed, of essays in the 'Kant vs. Hume' or 'Kant answers Hume' *genre*.) At least for a *start* in this lecture, I shall use the same device for developing central themes in their social and political thought. And to do this I shall focus on the doctrine of the *social contract* or *original contract*. I think it is safe to say that this was the central or dominant intellectual model which provided the structure of social and political thought in the 18th century, and both Hume and Kant felt obliged to assess it carefully — Hume coming out a qualified opponent and Kant a qualified supporter of the model. This opposition is particularly interesting for the following reason: Hume's attack on social contract theory is directed primarily against Hobbes and Locke, and it is interesting to see if post-Humean social contract theories (especially

Kant's and that of our own contemporary John Rawls) succeed in avoiding his very powerful objections to this line of thought. Without further preliminary, then, let us turn to Hume.

HUME

With Hume, it is always useful to start with the *negative* aspects of his thought — Hume on the attack, refuting and debunking the dominant patterns of thought of his age. As Sheldon Wolin has suggested, Hume can initially be viewed as a man who "turned against the Enlightenment its own weapons, . . . whittling down the claims of reason by the use of rational analysis".[2] This is why, in studying Hume's epistemology, it is usually wise to start with his scepticism, his attack on the pretensions of reason in giving us knowledge. (It is, of course, a great mistake to *end* here — as many commentators do — for we shall thereby miss his equally important *positive* doctrine of natural belief.) Similarly, in social and political philosophy, it is a good starting (but not ending) point to consider his attack on the pretensions of reason in moral, social, and political matters — his attack on what he calls "the *speculative* systems of politics." His contempt for such systems, and even the *motives* which prompt them, is boundless — as the opening passage of his important essay 'Of the Original Contract' indicates:

As no party, in the present age, can well support itself without a philosophical or speculative system of principles annexed to its political or practical one, we accordingly find that each of the factions into which this nation is divided has reared up a fabric of the former kind, in order to protect and cover that scheme of actions which it pursues. The people being commonly rude builders, especially in this speculative way, and more especially still when actuated by party zeal, it is natural to imagine that their workmanship must be a little unshapely, and discover evident marks of the violence and hurry in which it was raised.

There are, according to Hume, two speculative systems competing in political philosophy in his day — appeals to the *Deity* and appeals to the *Original contract*. Apparently believing that the former doctrine very nearly carries its absurdity on its face, Hume spends only a brief paragraph on its refutation. The rest of his attention is focused on the theory of the original contract, and that is where my attention will rest also.

What is the theory of the original contract, and how and why does Hume seek to refute it? Here it is important to stress that Hume understands the contract theory to be primarily a theory of *allegiance* — i.e. an answer to the question "Why do we have a moral obligation to obey the law?" It is the theory in this role which Hume so abhors. He is prepared to admit that the theory may be accepted if it is nothing more than a statement, admittedly a confused one, of the ideal that government should in some sense be based upon the consent of the governed, in so far as this is possible. He writes in the essay:

My intention here is not to exclude the consent of the people from being one just foundation of government where it has place. It is surely the best and most sacred of any. I only pretend that it has very seldom had place in any degree, and never almost in its full extent. And that therefore some other foundation of government must also be admitted.

Hume also is prepared to agree that primitive people must have come to co-operative terms with each other at some time in order to survive; and that, if this is all the doctrine of the original contract amounts to, he can accept it. What he opposes is any attempt to draw a theory of present legitimacy of government and thus citizen allegiance from such fragile axioms.

What, then, is the original contract as a theory of allegiance? Very roughly put, it is the following: All obligation is based upon consent. If citizens have a moral obligation to government or the state (to obey the law), this is either because they presently consent (at least tacitly) to the government and its laws or because this government and its laws grow out of an original consent, or contract, or promise by their ancestors. In sum, the obligation to obey the law is based upon either *tacit* consent (e.g. remaining in a country when I have a chance to leave) or *explicit* consent (e.g. a promise or contract); and this consent can be either *present* or *inherited*.

Hume makes much sport with the theory thus formulated, and can I think be said to deal it – in *this form* – a death blow. (Whether this form is a fair representation of the views of such writers as Locke is another matter.) Hume's case against the theory can be divided into five main lines of attack: (1) the original contract is an historical and anthropological fantasy; (2) even if the original contract were accepted as a fact this could not explain how it morally binds the *present* generation; (3) certain basic concepts in the theory – e.g. that of tacit consent – are used in absurd ways; (4) the theory employs a false account of moral obligation – i.e. it is incorrect in maintaining that all obligations are based upon consent; and (5) allegiance to government cannot be founded upon fidelity to promises since they both have exactly the *same* foundation and, if problematic at all, are problematic to the same degree. Let us examine each of these in somewhat more detail.

(1) *The Original Contract as Historical and Anthropological Fantasy*. Here

Hume's *negative* case is quite simple to state: Of all the actual states, both past and present, we know of, only a few can be said even to approximate an original contract-consent origin; *no* actual states fully accord with the theory. And yet these are clearly viable states in which citizens believe they owe allegiance to those who rule. "Obedience or subjection," Hume writes, "become so familiar that most men never make any enquiry about its origin or cause, more than about the principle of gravity, resistance, or the msot universal laws of nature" ('Of the Original Contract').

But, we may be inclined to object, this is simply a statement of what *is* the case — namely, that people even in such states *believe* that they owe a duty of allegiance. But surely the point of social contract theory is to provide the framework in which beliefs in allegiance are not merely held in fact but are also *correct* or *morally justified*. Only in a government of consent, founded on an original contract, is it *rational* to believe that citizens morally owe allegiance.

Hume's full response to such an objection must await the discussion of his own account of moral obligation; but at this point it will be useful partially to respond to the objection by bringing in Hume's own *positive* social and political theory. For Hume would say that this way of objecting, noble as it sounds, grows out of a fundamentally wrongheaded way of thinking about social institutions — namely, that they are or could be a product of rational or intellectual design. This is the way it is made to appear in philosophy books and in the rhetoric of revolutionaries, but it is not the way the social and political world really is. A few aspects may be changed here and there (and often should be), but the social and political fabric itself in which such changes take place (and even the *language* at our disposal to talk about the suggested changes) are the products of a process of undesigned social evolution over the inheritance of which we have no control. Christian Bay has called Hume a precursor of Darwin in the field of ethics and social philosophy, and this claim strikes me as fundamentally correct.[3] As we know from Part VIII of the *Dialogues Concerning Natural Religion*, Hume clearly anticipated the doctrine of natural selection as an explanatory mechanism for biological evolution (thus dispensing with the need for teleological explanations), and I believe that these same patterns of thought are to be found in his moral and social writings. As Friedrich von Hayek has put it: "Hume undertakes to show that certain characteristics of modern society which we prize are dependent on conditions which were not created in order to bring about these results, yet are nevertheless their indispensable presuppositions".[4] In Hume, this line of thought is most clearly developed in the section of the

Treatise 'Of the Origin of Justice and Property'. There Hume argues that individual men are naturally vulnerable (and thus with doubtful potential for survival) and can therefore survive only if ways are evolved to allow them to live together (and thus gain collective strength) in communities. Obstacles to such social unions are individual selfishness, the narrow bounds of human understanding (i.e. limited knowledge), and scarcity of the objects of desire. Ways to overcome these obstacles *had* to develop (otherwise humanity would not have survived) and the primary mechanism that evolved was the *largely unquestioned obedience to certain rules of conduct*. Which rules? — those with utility or survival value. These rules (because of the very limitations of men noted above) must evolve by a natural selection process and cannot be the result of rational human design.

To balance a large state of society, whether monarchial or republican, on general laws, is a work of so great difficulty, that no human genius, however comprehensive, is able by the mere dint of reason and reflection, to effect it. The judgments of many must unite in this work: Experience must guide their labour: Time must bring it to perfection: And the feeling of inconveniences must correct the mistakes, which they inevitably fall into, in their first trials and experiments ('Of the Rise and Progress of the Arts and Sciences').

The point with respect to allegaince is obvious: If we acknowledge moral allegiance only to those states which, both in origin and present structure, fit some conception we have of ideal rationality and reserve the right to resist them whenever, in our judgment, they deviate from this ideal, we shall sacrifice the tangible and accumulated benefits of civilization in the pursuit of illusion. This does not mean that states are never rightfully to be changed or even resisted. Hume's point is simply that in doing either we should not seek our justification in a comprehensive theory having such pernicious consequences. What J. L. Austin said in our own century about words, Hume would echo for social institutions and practices as well — namely, that they embody

all the distinctions men have found worth drawing, and the connexions they have found worth marking, in the lifetimes of many generations: these surely are likely to be more numerous, more sound, since they have stood up to the long test of the survival of the fittest, and more subtle, at least in all ordinary and reasonably practical matters, than any that you or I are likely to think up in our armchairs of an afternoon — the most favoured alternative method.[5]

So much for the theory of social evolution. Let me now turn to the next two lines of attack which Hume mounts against social contract theory. These can be treated briefly because I could not possibly improve on Hume's own words and shall thus for the most part merely quote him.

(2) *The Present Generation Could Not be Bound by an Original Contract.*
According to the original contract theory, moral obligation is founded on
consent. But surely the only even remotely plausible version of such a theory
is one which bases *my* obligation on *my* consent — not on someone else's. As
Hume writes:

The original contract cannot now be supposed to retain any authority. If we would say
anything to the purpose, we must assert that every particular government, which is
lawful, and which imposes any duty of allegiance on the subject, was, at first, founded
on consent and a voluntary compact. But besides that this supposed the consent of the
fathers to bind the children even to the most remote generations (which republican
writers will never allow), besides this, I say, it is not justified by history or experience
in any age or country of the world ('Of the Original Contract').

(3) *The Absurd Use of the Concept of Tacit Consent.* Suppose it is argued
that the present generation does consent but consents *tacitly* — merely, as
Locke says, by walking on the highways of the state rather than leaving.
Hume's withering attack on this claim occurs in what is probably the most
famous passage in his political writings — one which cannot be quoted too
many times.

Can we seriously say that a poor peasant or artisan has a free choice to leave his country,
when he knows no foreign language or manners, and lives from day to day, by the small
wages which he acquires? We may as well assert that a man, by remaining in a vessel,
freely consents to the dominion of the master, though he was carried on board while
asleep, and must leap into the ocean, and perish, the moment he leaves her ('Of the
Original Contract').

(4) *Original Contract Theory Rests on a Mistaken Analysis of Obligation.*
According to contract theory, as Hume interprets it, all moral obligation rests
upon voluntary consent. This is why contract theorists are able to argue that,
in the absense of such consent, there is no obligation to government or law.
But, Hume retorts, such a theory would rule out a substantial amount of
what we all agree constitutes our moral obligations, and is thus absurd as an
analysis of the essential nature of such obligations. Seeing the importance of
counter-examples in moral theory, Hume says "nothing is clearer proof that a
theory of this kind is erroneous than to find that it leads to paradoxes repugnant to the common sentiments of mankind and to the practice and
opinion of all nations and ages" ('Of the Original Contract').

What, then, are our moral duties or obligations? Hume says that they are
of two kinds — those toward which immediate instinct impels normal persons
(love of children, gratitude to benefactors, pity to the unfortunate) and those
we perform, not because they appeal to us in themselves, but because we

"consider the necessities of human society, and the impossibility of supporting it if these duties were neglected." These duties, then, rest on *general social utility*. And Hume's basic point is this: All persons would agree that these are our primary categories of moral obligation, and *voluntary consent clearly has nothing to do with either.*[6]

(5) *Allegiance to Government and Fidelity to Promises Have the Same Foundation.* In response to Hume's demonstration that at least not all moral duties are based on consent, the defender of the contract doctrine might argue that at least *some* moral obligations (e.g. the obligation to keep a promise or honor a contract) *are* founded on consent and that allegiance to government is in turn founded upon such a promise or consent obligation.

In response to this, Hume considers the following three moral obligations or duties:

(i) the obligation to do what one consents to do;

(ii) the obligation to keep a promise; and

(iii) the obligation of allegiance to government or law.

Now it is no doubt true that obligations (i) and (ii) arise at a time historically prior to obligation (iii) because institutions of government and law are rather late developers in the evolution of mechanisms of social cohesion. But the *moral status* of each obligation, argues Hume, is exactly on a par; for all three have exactly the same *moral foundation* — namely, *time tested general social utility*. Given this, no one of them can be used for the moral legitimization or authorization of the others. No one of the three is any more morally basic than the other two. Hume writes as follows:

Allegiance and fidelity to promises stand precisely on the same foundation, and are both submitted to by mankind on account of the apparent interests and necessities of human society. We are bound to obey our sovereign, it is said, because we have given a tacit promise to that purpose. But why are we bound to observe our promise? It must here be asserted that the commerce and intercourse of mankind, which are of such mighty advantage, can have no security where men pay no regard to their engagements. In like manner it may be said that men could not live at all in society, at least in civilized society, without laws and magistrates and judges to prevent encroachments of the strong upon the weak, of the violent upon the just. The obligation to allegiance being of like force and authority with the obligation to fidelity, we gain nothing by resolving the one into the other. The general interests and necessities of society are sufficient to establish both ('Of the Original Contract').

Having surveyed Hume's attack on social contract theory, we may now turn to Kant's later version of that theory to determine the extent to which — if at all — it escapes the Humean attack.

KANT

Let me begin the discussion of Kant by quoting at some length from three different discussions which he provides of the original contract. (I have not apologized for lengthy quotation; but perhaps I should at least apologize for not apologizing. I feel obliged to provide lengthy quotations because, as I noted at the outset, the social and political writings of Hume and especially Kant are not nearly as well known as they deserve to be; thus I do not think it is reasonable for me to presuppose a familiarity with them in a public lecture.)[7]

From *Rechtslehre*:

The act by which the people constitute themselves a state is the original contract. More properly, it is the Idea of that act that alone enables us to conceive of the legitimacy of the state. According to the original contract, all the people give up their external freedom in order to take it back again immediately as members of a commonwealth, that is, the people regarded as the state. Accordingly, we cannot say that a man has sacrificed in the state a part of his inborn external freedom for some particular purpose; rather, we must say that he has completely abandoned his wild, lawless freedom in order to find his whole freedom again undiminished in a lawful depency, that is, in a juridical state of society, since this dependency comes from his own legislative Will.

From the essay *Theory and Practice:*

The contract, which is called *contractus originarius*, or *pactum sociale* . . . need not be assumed to be a fact, indeed it is not [even possible as such. To suppose that would be like insisting] that before anyone would be bound to respect such a civic constitution, it be proved first of all from history that a people, whose rights and obligations we have entered into as their descendants, had *once upon a time* excuted such an act and had left a reliable document or instrument, either orally or in writing, concerning this contract. Instead, this contract is a *mere idea* of reason which has undoubted practical reality; namely, to oblige every legislator to give us laws in such a manner that the laws *could* have originated from the united will of the entire people and to regard every subject in so far as he is a citizen as though he had consented to such [an expression of the general] will. This is the testing stone of the rightness of every publicly-known law, for if a law were such that it was impossible for an entire people to give consent to it (as for example a law that a certain class of subjects, by inheritance, should have the privilege of the *status of lords*), then such a law is unjust, On the other hand, if there is a mere *possibility* that a people might consent to a (certain) law, then it is a duty to consider that the law is just, even though at the moment the people might be in such a position or have a point of view that would result in their refusing to give their consent to it if asked.

And from the *Nachlass*:

The original contract is not a principle explaining the origin of civil society; rather it is a principle explaining how it ought to be . . . . It is not the principle establishing the state; rather it is the principle of political government and contains the ideal of legislation, administration, and public legal justice.

To understand the theory thus presented in these passages, let us examine it against the background of Hume's five basic challenges.

(1) *The Historical Status of the Original Contract*. Here Kant is quite explicit that the original contract is *not* to be regarded as an historical fact. Indeed Kant suggests (for largely Humean reasons) that it would be absurd to regard it as such because, even so regarded, it could not perform any useful moral function. Thus one Humean objection is avoided at the outset.

But if the original contract is not historical, what is it and what role does it serve in Kant's social and political philosophy? Here it is extremely important to see that the doctrine of the original contract is not for Kant a theory of *allegiance*, is not an answer to the question 'Why do I have a moral obligation to obey the law?' (Another Humean worry is thereby sidestepped.) Rather for Kant the original contract or social contract theory provides a way for answering the question 'When is a law just?' What we find in Kant (and here lies a large part of his influence on John Rawls) is the use of the social contract as the basis for a *theory of justice*. (This is not a theory of allegiance because Kant is well-known — perhaps notorious — for his belief that the injustice of a law does *not* free us from a moral obligation to obey that law.)

How does the original contract provide the basis for a theory of justice? It does this, according to Kant, as an *Ideal of Reason* — as a model of rational choice. Kant's original contract theory is thus a start (admittedly a primitive start) toward the development of those theories which play such a large role in contemporary economic theory and in the social philosophy of John Rawls — those theories we now call game theories, decision theories, or social choice theories. According to Kant, the only coercive social rules that are morally (because rationally) justified are those which a group of ideal rational beings could agree to adopt in the hypothetical position of having to pick social rules and practices to govern their relations with each other. In attempting to determine the justice of any rule or practice, then, we are to ask ourselves the following question: *Could* a group of rational beings have unanimously agreed to the rule or practice in an antecedent position of choice — in what Rawls calls 'the original position'? If the answer is yes, the rule is just; if no, then unjust.

Would Hume be happy with this? I am afraid not. Though this formulation of original contract theory does not commit the simpleminded mistakes Hume thinks he finds in Hobbes and Locke, it is still an instance of the *constructive rationalism* Hume wants to oppose in morals and politics. For it presupposes (what to Hume is absurd) that we can at any time simply step outside of history, put aside the accumulated and evolved patterns of moral and political thought and feeling, and become 'ideally rational'. According to Hume, theories of this sort are defective for two main reasons. First, since it is desire or passion − not reason − which motivates men to act, such ideal models could have no behavioral efficacy. Second, it is Hume's belief that such ideal rational models cannot be developed 'without any circuit' − i.e. without question-begging circularity. Inevitably, we shall build into our model of raionality a substantial number of our current beliefs and feelings about what is morally and socially correct. This is a point I shall expand on a bit later.

Now since *inheritance of obligation, tacit consent,* and a *theory of allegiance based upon a promising model* are simply not present in Kant's version of the social contract theory, we can simply ignore objections (2), (3) and (5) on my list of Hume's lines of attack. I shall therefore close with a discussion of what I listed as Hume's objection (4) − that social contract theory rests upon a mistaken theory of moral obligation. And this is the point where we would expect Hume and Kant to meet headon. For it would be hard to imagine moral theories or theories of moral psychology more fundamentally opposed than those found in Hume and Kant.

(4) *The Moral Basis of Social Contract Theory.* The moral theories of Hume and Kant are, of course, both incredibly complex; and all I can hope to give here is a very superficial overview of the aspects of those theories which have a direct bearing upon the contract theory and the basic issues of social and political philosophy.

Hume's conception of morality is that it is primarily an enterprise concerned to maximize the objects of human *desire.* Desire or passion is what moves us to act, sets our ends for us; and reason is properly only its instrument or 'slave'. The main business of ethics, then, is (a) to discover what people do in fact primarily desire or at least feel approval toward and (b) discover the best (i.e. most rational) *means* for the attainment of these approved or desired objects. This is not an egoistic theory, becuase Hume believes that many of our basic desires are sympathetic or benevolent. The importance of sympathy and benevolence are given by our *nature,* however; and, in the absence of such a nature, reason could never 'prove' their importance to us. In certain places (e.g. the essay 'Of the Standard of Taste') Hume qualifies this account of morality in the direction of what we now call an Ideal Observer theory of ethics − i.e. he argues that the proper objects of moral persuit are not just any desires or approved objects, but rather only desires that would be found in or objects that would be approved by a *competent* or *rational* or *disinterested* observer or judge.

Now we might charge that this final move is (like ideal social contract theory) bound to be *circular* or *question-begging* — i.e. that we will inevitably build the results we want to get into our conception of who constitutes a competent judge, persons not approving what we think ought to be approved losing their status of competence. Hume, interestingly enough, might not seek to avoid this charge. Rather he might openly accept it and use it to remind us of a fundamental claim of his entire philosophy — namely, that our capacity to provide rational justifications for our practices can never catch up with our capacity to raise sceptical doubts about those practices — that ultimately any such justifications we can give, whether for the practice of morality or the practice of induction, *will* be characterized by question-begging circularity. What works so well to distinguish justified from unjustified moves *within* a practice does not work at all when the objective justification of the practice itself is called into question. And Hume's view that our passionate nature forces us, for the most part, to *act* and *believe* as though we had such rational justifications is not, of course, an attempt to show that we do have them but is rather a theory about how we are able to get along *without* them. Ultimately what saves us (all rationalist philosophers including Kant to the contrary) is not reason, but our passionate nature and the personal and social habits it has evolved. If we ever lose a grip on our lives, reason will never give it back to us.[8]

Kant, of course, regards this whole conception of morality as fundamentally wrong — so grotesque, indeed, as not even to *be* a conception of *morality*. To view human beings in this way, simply as utility maximizers, is to see them as heteronomous — as fundamentally no different from the brutes, mere slaves or prisoners of irrational passions. Surely, Kant insists, it is just our status as *rational beings* which essentially distinguishes us from the brutes and founds that which is morally sacred and inviolate about our human nature. This value Kant calls *autonomy* — a kind of rational freedom which gives us dignity and makes us *deserve* a special kind of respect (captured in the value of *justice*) which is fitting to our nature as persons — i.e. ours by *right*. The morally basic and related concepts of *rights*, *justice*, and *desert* have no proper home in a Humean or any other utilitarian outlook; and thus such accounts of morality must be rejected.

What does this have to do with social contract theory? The following: Given that Kant's basic moral value is autonomy, he is forced to consider the possibility that state coercion (or any other kind of coercion) is evil and can *never* be justified. For coercion seems to be, by definition, forcing people to do that which they will not do of their own free will. And how can that involve a respect for autonomy? We are thus on the verge of being forced into *anarchism* as the only morally acceptable social philosophy.

How can this move toward anarchism be avoided? Only, as Robert Paul Wolff has suggested,[9] if we can develop a theory of state coercion which is *consistent* with individual moral autonomy – a theory which makes the state's coercion in some sense a product of *my own* will. What we need is a conceptual reconciliation of coercive political authority and individual autonomy; and, according to Kant, it is exactly this which his own version of original contract theory will provide. This theory, remember, is a model of rational decision. And, according to Kant's view, respecting a person's autonomy is not respecting whatever he now happens, however uncritically, to desire – coercion will, of course, always interfere with this. Respecting autonomy is respecting what the person desires (or would desire) *as a rational agent*. A person is genuinely free or autonomous only in so far as he is rational. Thus it is a person's rational will that is to be respected.[10]

How is the rational will to be determined? According to Kant's contract theory, a person may be said to rationally will X if, and only if, X is called for by a rule that the man would have adopted in the original hypothetical position of choice – i.e. in a position of coming together with others to pick rules for the regulation of their mutual affairs. Let us consider an example: I may not, in our actual society, desire to treat a certain person fairly – e.g. I may not desire to honor a contract I have made with him because so doing would adversely affect my own self-interest. However, if I am forced to honor the contract by the state, I cannot charge that my rights, dignity, or autonomy are being violated by my being coerced into doing it. Indeed, it can be said that I rationally will this very coercion since, in the original position, I would have chosen a rule of the form "contracts are to be honored'. This, I take it, is the point Kant is making in the passage I quoted earlier where he describes state coercion as a dependency coming from the citizen's 'own legislative Will'. For Kant contrasts the legislative will (autonomy of a rational being) with the elective will (simple empirical freedom of choice). Coercion and autonomy are hereby supposedly reconciled.

How might Hume respond to all of this? With scepticism and cynicism, of course. He would certainly make at least the following three charges: (1) the concept of rational will involved in the theory cannot, for reasons already noted, be developed in a non-circular, non-question-begging way. It will inevitably smuggle in the very judgments we would hope to be able to derive from it. Let me elaborate: A right or just action (or law) on this theory is going to be one which ideal rational agents would agree to. But would we ever accord the status of ideal rationality to any agent who chose or approved of actions or laws we already strongly *dis*approved of? Surely not. As Hume says, "in all questions with regard to morals, as well as criticism, there is really no other standard except an appeal to general opinion by which any controversy can ever be decided." In modern jargon, we might say that we will only accept a moral theory which is consistent with our pretheoretical intuitions or judgments — e.g. 'do not punish the innocent', 'do not inflict unnecessary suffering', etc. Agreement with these judgments will be *criterial* for rationality in morality, and thus the concept of rationality cannot be the *basic* concept in moral theory from which all else can be derived. (2) Kantian *autonomy* seems to involve a kind of contra-causal freedom, and as such has very doubtful metaphysical credentials. A reading of his chapter 'Of Liberty and Necessity' is persuasive evidence that Hume would have no sympathy with such a view. If reason is not part of the causal nexus of natural desires and passions, then it cannot motivate or move us to act and is thus morally useless. If it *is* part of this nexus, then why pretend that it has some exalted special status which other motives — e.g., sympathy — lack? Finally (3): Hume simply *denies* the possibility of reconciling, in any totally consistent way, human freedom with coercive authority. The impossibility of such reconciliation is, he thinks, simply one of the many unhappy features of our world with which we shall just have to live. The moral and political universe is just not as well-ordered as, given our rational pretensions, we would like to believe. Some conflicts are basic and lie beyond the scope of any rational resolution. We shall want to respect liberty, of course, but doing that — according to Hume — will consist in something much more modest than anything Kant had in mind. It will consist primarily in devising means to check, through public rules, the grosser potentials for abuse that are latent in any political authority. Hume writes as follows:

In all governments, there is a perpetual intestine struggle, open or secret, between *authority* and *liberty*; and neither of them can ever absolutely prevail in the contest. A great sacrifice of liberty can never, and perhaps ought never, in any constitution, to become quite entire and uncontrollable. . . . The government which, in common appellation, receives the appellation, of free, is that which admits of a partition of power among several members, whose united authority is no less, or is commonly greater than that of any monarch, but who, in the usual course of administration, must act by general and equal laws that are previously known to all the members and to all their subjects. In this sense, it must be owned that liberty is the perfection of civil society ('Of the Origin of Government').

CONCLUSION

In this lecture I have attempted to survey the main points of contention between Hume and Kant with respect to their treatment of social or original contract theory. I have tried to show that their conflicts, running as they do to the heart of each thinker's *moral* philosophy, are very deep indeed. If nothing else, they show the conceptual dependence of social and political philosophy upon moral philosophy and were worth exploring at least for that reason. I have not, of course, as yet said anything about the most important question of all: which, if either, of the two theories is *true*? Limitations of space and time (and perhaps even of talent) do not permit me to explore this question in detail; but I should like very briefly to suspend Bicentennial piety and sketch the reasons which incline me to think that Hume's position, powerful as it is, is inferior to that developed by Kant.

It seems desirable that we attempt to develop a coherent set of principles for ordering our evaluative judgments and discourse about law and politics. As Ronald Dworkin has argued, "men and women have a responsibility to fit the particular judgments on which they act into a coherent program of action or, at least, that officials who exercise power over other men have this sort of responsibility".[11] The basic question with respect to competing moral theories, then, is simply this: which theory will do the best job of fitting our judgments into a coherent system?

On the basis of this test for theoretical adequacy, Kantianism seems to fare much better than utilitarianism of the Humean variety. The values of justice, rights, respect for persons, and autonomy can (unlike the utilitarian value of the general good) form the basis for a coherent and intuitively satisfying ordering if they are made basic — e.g. "After first doing justice and respecting rights then promote the general good" has a plausibility lacking in "First promote the general good and then respect whatever rights it is still possible to respect." Thus Kantianism, which does make rights basic, seems a plausible basis for a public morality. This is not to say that it is not vulnerable to many serious objections (many of the kind Hume would make) but is rather to say that it is worth attempting to save against those objections, that it is worth working hard to patch up the weak spots so that the entire structure (being the best there currently is) can stay afloat. Attempting to patch up utilitarianism, however, is rather like rearranging the furniture on the decks of the Titanic. Thus it is not an accident, in my judgment, that the three most exciting and persuasive works recently published in moral and social philosophy start from the assumption that utilitarianism is theoretically hopeless and that the best alternative theory will, in some sense, have a Kantian base.[12] I mention this fact, not in the attempt to give an argument from authority, but merely to issue the following invitation to the reader: study these three works (and also the other essays in the present collection) and then ask yourself which theory, utilitarianism or some form of Kantianism, does a better job of introducing coherence and system into your moral judgments? This is a contest which, in my judgment, Kantianism is likely to win.

NOTES

[*] A lecture presented at the David Hume Bicentennial Symposium, University of Arizona, September 17, 1976. An earlier version of the lecture was presented to the Department of Philosophy, Loyola University (Chicago), in 1975. The lecture was also presented at the 1977 meeting of the Hume Society, University of Virginia, October 29, 1977.

[1] Hume also suffers under the additional handicap that his levity is often taken as evidence of superficiality. It is important to remember that Hume is perhaps unique among philosophers in that he succeeds in being profound without being solemn.

[2] Quoted in F. A. Hayek's 'The Legal and Political Philosophy of David Hume', *Hume*, ed. by V. C. Chappell (Garden City: Doubleday, 1966), p. 335. My interpretation of Hume has been greatly influenced by Hayek's work.

[3] Bay's discussion occurs in his *The Structure of Freedom* (Stanford: Stanford University Press, 1958), p. 33.

[4] *Op. cit.*, p. 344. Robert Nozick presents an interesting discussion of such 'invisible hand' explanations in his *Anarchy, State and Utopia* (New York: Basic Books, 1974), esp. pp. 18ff.

[5] J. L. Austin, 'A Plea for Excuses', *Philosophical Papers* (Oxford: Oxford University Press, 1961), p. 130.

[6] This account is drawn from 'Of the Original Contract'. Hume would surely have applauded the following remark by George Eliot: "Duty has a trick of behaving unexpectedly — something like a heavy friend whom we have amiably asked to visit us and who breaks his leg within our gates" (*Middlemarch*, Chapter 52).

[7] For a fuller discussion of Kant's views on the social contract (plus fuller and documented textual citation) see my *Kant: The Philosophy of Right* (London: Macmillan, 1970), esp. Chapter 4.

[8] See Thomas Nagel, 'The Absurd', *Journal of Philosophy* 68, (1971) 716–727.

[9] *In Defense of Anarchism* (New York: Harper, 1970). See also my "Marxism and Retribution", *Philosophy and Public Affairs* 2, (1973) 217–243. (Reprinted in the present collection.)

[10] Perhaps the following example will make a distinction between the *empirical* will (what one now happens to desire) and the *real* or *autonomous* will (what one rationally desires or would desire) less ludicrous than it might initially seem: Recall the story of Odysseus who wanted to hear the voices of the Sirens but who did not want to succumb to their fatal seductive power. He had himself lashed to the mast of his ship and instructed

his crew not to release him no matter how much he might beg for release when under the Sirens' spell. When he fell under the spell he made it clear through his gestures (the crew had stopped their ears) that he desired release so that he could go to the Sirens. His crew ignored this desire and left him lashed to the mast. Was not this truly to respect his real will, his autonomy?

11 'Justice and Rights', Chapter 6 of his *Taking Rights Seriously* (Cambridge: Harvard University Press, 1977), p. 160. Dworkin is here attempting to interpret John Rawls' notion of "reflective equilibrium" and to defend Rawls' Kantian contractarian theory of justice by arguing that it rests upon a "deep theory" of respect for natural rights.

12 I am referring to John Rawls' *A Theory of Justice* (Cambridge: Harvard University Press, 1971), Robert Nozick's *Anarchy, State and Utopia* (New York: Basic Books, 1974), and Ronald Dworkin's *Taking Rights Seriously* (Cambridge: Harvard University Press, 1977).

PART TWO

PUNISHMENT AND RESPONSIBILITY

Judicial punishment can never be used merely as a
means to promote some other good for the criminal
himself or for society, but instead it must in all cases
be imposed on a person solely on the ground that he
has committed a crime; for a human being can never
be confused with the objects of the law of things . . .
He must first be found to be deserving of punishment
before any consideration can be given to the utility of
this punishment for himself or his fellow citizens.

Immanuel Kant
The Metaphysical Elements of Justice

THREE MISTAKES ABOUT RETRIBUTIVISM

Retributive theories of punishment maintain that criminal guilt merits or deserves punishment, regardless of considerations of social utility. Such theories may be put forth for either of two reasons: (1) It could be argued (e.g. by a Moral Sense theorist) that the claim is a primitive and unanalysed proposition which is morally ultimate. Every ethical theory necessarily involves at least one such primitive (e.g. 'happiness is good', 'freedom is to be respected', etc.) and the retributivist may be offering this as his candidate. We can, he may argue, just *intuit* the "fittingness" of guilt and punishment. (2) It might be maintained (as it was, I believe, by both Kant and Hegel) that the retributivist claim is demanded by a general theory of political obligation which is more plausible than any alternative theory. Such a theory will typically provide a technical *analysis* of such notions as crime and punishment and will thus not regard the retributivist claim as an indisputable primitive. It will be argued for as a kind of theorem within the system.

The objection to the first sort of theory is obvious: the retributivist may be able to intuit the fittingness of guilt and punishment, but most of us cannot — not, at any rate, in a sense strong enough to make us want to appeal to the notion in justifying punishment. Thus the first theory is subject to all the classical objections to intuitionism, and these do not have to be repeated here. Let us, then, try to make sense of a theory of the second sort. What sort of theory of political obligation would render it plausible?

Consider a quasi-contractual model (found in Kant and John Rawls)[1] that seeks to analyse political obligation in terms of *reciprocity*. Such a model will proceed as follows: In order to enjoy the benefits that a legal system makes possible, each man must be prepared to make an important sacrifice — namely, the sacrifice of obeying the law even when he does not desire to do so. Each man calls on others to do this, and it is only just or fair that he bear a comparable burden when his turn comes. Now if the system is to remain just, it is important to guarantee that those who disobey will not thereby gain an unfair advantage over those who obey voluntarily. Criminal punishment thus attempts to maintain the proper balance between benefit and obedience by insuring that there is no profit in criminal wrongdoing. This is at least one point behind the *jus talionis* (return like for like) principle and was no doubt at least part of what Kant had in mind when he spoke, in a misleading idiom, of the criminal as owing a *debt* to the law-abiding members of his community. (The idiom of owing and paying a debt is misleading in that it tends to obscure the fact that (i) criminal "debts" differ from ordinary debts in that we have an antecedent moral obligation not to incur them and (ii) undergoing punishment for (say) murder, unlike paying the final installment on a loan, can hardly be said to make things all right again, to make the world morally the same as it was before.)

Now the above theory is one possible form retributivism might take and is, at least, not absurd on its face. What I want to do now is to show how retributivism, at least of this variety, does not fall to three stock objections which are frequently put forth to "demonstrate" that no reasonable man could be retributivist.

(1) *Retributivism as necessarily involving Utilitarianism and as being obviously unacceptable without it*. Rule utilitarians often maintain that retributivism, to be coherent, must involve a tacit appeal to utility – i.e. must tacitly presuppose that the principle 'Do not allow men to profit from their criminal wrongdoing' has more desirable social consequences than any alternative principle. But I should argue that Kant's theory, for example, is (i) perfectly coherent and (ii) quite independent of utilitarian considerations. His principle is that no man should profit from his own wrongdoing, and retribution attempts to keep this from happening. If a man does profit from his own wrongdoing, from his disobedience, this is *unfair* or *unjust*, not merely to his victim, but to all those who have been obedient. Now it may be, as the utilitarian might argue, that such unfairness – if widespread – would have socially undesirable consequences. But this is not Kant's argument. His argument is that the *injustice* or *unfairness itself*, regardless of consequences, demands retribution. As H. L. A. Hart has argued, 'a theory of punishment which disregarded these moral convictions [about justice] or viewed them simply as factors, frustration of which made for socially undesirable excitment is a different kind of theory from one which *out of deference to those convictions themselves* [justifies] punishment . . . ' [2] Kant's theory is clearly of the latter sort.

But if this line is taken, the utilitarian may argue, retributivism becomes obviously unreasonable – a bit of primitive, unenlightened and barbaric emotionalism. But why is retributivism so condemned? Typically the charge is that infliction of punishment, with no attention to utility, is pointless vengeance. But what is meant by the claim that the activity in question is pointless? If 'pointless' is to be analysed as 'disutilitarian', then the whole question is being begged. One cannot refute a retributive theory merely by noting that it is a retributive theory and not a utilitarian theory. This is to confuse refutation with redescription. That the maximization of social utility is important is no more *obviously* true than that a man should not unfairly profit from his own criminal wrongdoing; and, if the utilitarian proposes simply to dig in his heels on the former, it is important to note that the charge of emotionalism cuts both ways.[3]

(2) *The Inapplicability of Jus Talionis.* Perhaps the most common criticism of Kant's theory is the claim that the principle *jus talionis* (return like for like) cannot with sense be taken literally. As Hegel observes, 'it is easy enough . . . to exhibit the retributive character of punishment as an absurdity (theft for theft, robbery for robbery, an eye for an eye, a tooth for a tooth – and then you can go on to suppose that the criminal has only one eye or no teeth).'[4]

But this objection, as Hegel rightly sees, is superficial. Surely the principle *jus talionis*, though requiring likeness of punishment, does not require *exact* likeness in all respects. There is no reason *in principle* (though there are practical difficulties) against trying to specify in a general way what the costs in life and labour of certain kinds of crime might be, and how the costs of punishments might be calculated, so that retribution could be understood as preventing criminal profit. And it is certainly possible retributively to *rank* punishments so that the most serious punishments are matched with the most serious offenses.

(3) *The Gap between Theory and Practice.* Another common criticism against the Kantian theory may be regarded as Marxist in character. Kant's theory, it may be argued, involves an ideal Utopian model of society which is in fact so utterly different from the actual character of society as to render it useless in understanding or evaluating any existing practice of criminal punishment. Indeed, the theory is dangerous. For it allows us to hide from ourselves the vicious character of actual social arrangements and thereby perpetuate gross injustice.

Let me elaborate: Punishment as retribution (paying a kind of "debt" to one's fellow-citizens) makes good sense with respect to a community of responsible individuals, of approximate equality, bound together by freely adopted and commonly accepted rules which benefit everyone. This is an ideal community, approximating what Kant would call a kingdom of ends. In such a community, punishment would be justly retributive in that it would flow as an accepted consequence of accepted rules which benefited everyone (including, as citizen, the criminal). But surely existing human societies are not *in fact* like this at all. Many people neither benefit nor participate but rather operate at a built-in economic or racial disadvantage which is in fact, if not in theory, permanent. The majority of criminals who are in fact punished are drawn from these classes, and they utterly fail to correspond to the model which underlies the retributive theory. Surely we delude ourselves in appealing to the retributive theory to justify their punishment.

The moral doubts raised here are extremely important. However, they may be doubts which testify to *strengths* rather than weaknesses in a retributive theory of the Kantian variety. Decent men surely want to object to the wanton handing out of punishments to those who, in a socially uneven community, always get the short end of the stick. But does not Kant's theory explain (or at least give one good reason) *why* we do want to object? Just punishment rests upon reciprocity; and is not one of the most serious moral problems confronting most existing communities the absence of such reciprocity, the absence of a balance between benefit and burden? Punishment is unjust in such a setting because it involves pretending (contrary to fact) that the conditions of justified punishment are met. Thus could not Kant, given this theory, easily share the Marxist scepticism about punishing in certain actual states? I believe that he could.

Now Kant may have thought that in defending a retributive theory he was also defending all of our present punitive practices. If so, his mistake is simply about *facts* and not about the *principles* involved. In developing his theory, Kant is attempting to outline the characteristics that a society must have if punishment within it is to be justified. Being right on this question will not prevent one from mistakenly believing that a particular society has these characteristics when in fact it does not.

My purpose here has not been to claim that a retributive theory of the Kantian variety is obviously true. I have rather been concerned to show that it is not, as is so often supposed, obviously silly. It is a *theory*, not just a primitive bit of intuitive vindictiveness, and should be taken seriously and criticized as a theory. It is not to be refuted by stock arguments such as the above three; for these rest upon nothing but misunderstanding and question-begging.[5]

NOTES

[1] See, for example, Rawls' 'Legal Obligation and the Duty of Fair Play' in *Law and Philosophy*, edited by Sidney Hook, (New York: New York University Press, 1964). For Kant's views see his *Metaphysical Elements of Justice* (translated by John Ladd,

Indianapolis, 1965) and my *Kant: The Philosophy of Right* (London: Macmillan, 1970).
[2] 'Murder and the Principles of Punishment', in *Punishment and Responsibility* (Oxford: Oxford University Press, 1968), p. 79.
[3] It is commonly charged that retributivism is simply a way of giving vent to some of the most degrading and barbaric of human emotions — bloodlust, vindictiveness, the desire for vengeance, and the passion for revenge. Certainly these emotions are, at least under normal circumstances, rather unattractive; but they have no necessary connection at all to the kind of retributivism I am here outlining. The only emotion necessarily tied to this form of retributivism is the *desire to do justice.*
[4] *Philosophy of Right*, translated by T. M. Knox (Oxford: Oxford University Press, 1952) p. 72.
[5] I am grateful to Robert Gerstein, Gareth Matthews, Herbert Morris, and A. D. Woozley for helpful discussion of issues involved in this paper.

KANT'S THEORY OF CRIMINAL PUNISHMENT*

Kant maintains that guilt is a necessary condition for the legitimate infliction of punishment. Punishment of the innocent is a conceptual and moral pathology. It is largely to avoid such punishment that Kant inveighs against private revenge, vigilante activities, war, and any other activity which allows a disputant to judge his own case and punish according to his own biased decision. Criminal punishment is coercive social power in its most brutal domestic form, and thus it is absolutely essential (in order to preserve freedom) that it be administered only under those procedures of due process found in a just Rule of Law. Such procedures, by securing fairness to the individual, interfere with the utilitarian goals of crime control and criminal rehabilitation. But this, Kant argues, is the price we must pay for liberty and justice.

Judicial punishment can never be used *merely* as a means to promote some other good for the criminal himself or for civil society, but instead it must in all cases be imposed on him only on the ground that he has committed a crime; for a human being can never be manipulated *merely* as a means to the purposes of someone else ... He must first be found to be deserving of punishment before any consideration is given to the utility of this punishment for himself or for his fellow citizens.[1]

That guilt is a necessary condition for the legitimate infliction of punishment will be accepted by most people — even, I suppose, by all but the most simple-minded utilitarians. What will not to be so readily accepted, however, is Kant's belief that guilt is a *sufficient* condition for justifying punishment, regardless of utility. The famous and much scorned passage is worth quoting:

Even if a civil society were to dissolve itself by common agreement of all its members (for example, if the people inhabiting an island decided to separate and disperse themselves around the world), the last murderer remaining in prison must be executed, so that everyone will duly receive what his actions are worth and so that the bloodguilt thereof will not be fixed on the people because they failed to insist on carrying out the punishment; for if they fail to do so, they may be regarded as accomplices in this public violation of legal justice.[2]

This theory of punishment is clearly *retributive* in character, holding that criminal guilt merits or deserves punishment and that the non-criminal members of the community have a moral duty to inflict (through official authorities, of course) the punishment. This is the claim that is universally

82

condemned — particularly by utilitarians — as primitive, unenlightened, and barbaric.

But why is it so condemned? Typically the charge is that infliction of punishment in such circumstances is pointless vengeance. But what is meant by the claim that the activity in question is pointless? If 'pointless' is to be analyzed as 'disutilitarian', then the whole question is being begged. One cannot refute a retributive theory merely by noting that it is a retributive theory and not a utilitarian theory. This is to confuse refutation with redescription.

Why, then, might someone claim that guilt merits punishment? Such a claim might be made for either of two reasons: (1) It could be argued (e.g. by a Moral Sense theorist) that the claim is a primitive and unanalyzed proposition which is morally ultimate. Every ethical theory necessarily involves at least one such primitive (e.g. "happiness is good," "freedom is to be repected," etc.) and the retributivist may be offering this as his candidate. We can, he may argue, just *intuit* the 'fittingness' of guilt and punishment. (2) It might be maintained that the retributivist claim is demanded by a general theory of political obligation which is more plausible than any alternative theory. Such a theory will typically provide a technical *analysis* of such notions as crime and punishment and will thus not regard the retributivist claim as an indisputable primitive. It will be argued for as a kind of theorem within the system.

Kant's theory is of this latter sort. He offers a theory of punishment which is based on his general view that political obligation is to be analyzed, quasi-contractually, in terms of *reciprocity*. In order to enjoy the benefits that a legal system makes possible, each man must make certain sacrifices — e.g. the sacrifice of obeying the law even when he does not desire to do so. Each man calls on others to do this, and it is only just or fair that he bear a comparable burden when his turn comes. Now if the system is to remain just, it is important to guarantee that those who disobey will not gain an unfair advantage over those who obey voluntarily. Criminal punishment thus attempts to maintain the proper balance between benefit and obedience by insuring that there is no profit in wrongdoing. The criminal himself has no complaint, because he has rationally willed or consented to his own punishment. That is, those very rules which he has broken work, when they are obeyed by others, to his own advantage as *citizen*. He would have chosen such rules for himself in an antecedent position of choice — what John Rawls calls "the original position".[3] And since he derives benefit from them, he owes obedience as a *debt* to his fellow-citizens for their sacrifices in maintaining them. If he chooses not to sacrifice by exercising self-restraint and obedience, this is tantamount to his choosing to sacrifice in another way — namely, by paying the prescribed penalty:

A transgression of the public law that makes him who commits it unfit to be a citizen is called . . . a crime . . . What kind and what degree of punishment does public legal justice adopt as its principle and standard? None other than the principle of equality (illustrated by the pointer of the scales of justice), that is, the principle of not treating one side more favourably than the other. Accordingly, any undeserved evil that you inflict on someone else among the poeple is one you do to yourself. If you vilify him, you vilify yourself; if you steal from him, you steal from yourself; if you kill him, you kill yourself.

To say, 'I will to be punished if I murder someone', can mean nothing more than, 'I submit myself along with everyone else to those laws which, if there are any criminals among the people, will naturally include penal laws'.[4]

This is one point of the *jus talionis* principle. The criminal owes a *debt* to the law-abiding members of his community; and, once the debt has been paid, he may be re-enter the community of good citizens on equal status.

Now it is essential to see that Kant's theory is not a disguised form of utilitarianism. His principle is that no man should profit from his own wrongdoing, and retribution attempts to keep this from happening. If a man does profit from his own wrongdoing, from his disobedience, this is *unfair* or *unjust*, not just to his victim, but to all those who have been obedient. Now it may be, as the utilitarian might argue, that such unfairness — if widespread — would have undesirable consequences. But this is not Kant's argument. His argument is that *justice or fairness itself*, regardless of consequences, demands retribution. As H. L. A. Hart has argued, "A theory of punishment which disregarded these moral convictions [about justice] or viewed them simply as factors, frustration of which made for socially undesirable excitement is a different kind of theory from one which *out of deference to those convictions themselves* [justifies] punishment . . . "[5] Kant's theory is clearly of the latter sort.

Having outlined Kant's theory, I should now like to sketch five of the most interesting objections to it. Some of these are anticipated by Kant himself in his correspondence and other writings (e.g. the *Religion*). Some of them, I think, can be met. Others remain deeply troublesome.

(1) *The Inapplicability of Jus Talionis*. Perhaps the most common criticism of Kant's theory is the claim that the principle *jus talionis* (return like for like) cannot with sense be taken literally. As Hegel observes, "It is easy enough . . . to exhibit the retributive character of punishment as an absurdity (theft for theft, robbery for robbery, an eye for an eye, a tooth for a tooth — and

then you can go on to suppose that the criminal has only one eye or no teeth."[6]

But this objection, as Hegel rightly sees, is superficial. Surely the principle *jus talionis*, though requiring likeness of punishment, does not require *exact* likeness in all respects. There is no reason in *principle* (though there are practical difficulties) against trying to specify in a general way what the costs in life and labor of certain kinds of crime might be, and how the costs of punishments might be calculated, so that retribution could be understood as preventing criminal profit.

There are still more remaining difficulties here, however — the chief being that, once a literal reading of *jus talionis* is abandoned, its application "in spirit" seems to be merely a matter of intuition unguided by any systematic theory. Kant's favorite example of *jus talionis* is the penalty of death for the crime of murder — this in spite of the fact that the punishment for *almost everything else* is imprisonment, a punishment which can literally satisfy "like for like" only for the offenses of false imprisonment or kidnapping. And even he is prepared to admit that there are some things which we should not do to the criminal even if he has done them to others. The state should never, he argues, do anything to a criminal that humiliates and degrades his dignity as a man. (So Kant presumably should oppose punishing the torturer and mutilator with torture and mutilation.)[7]

The problem here seems to be the following: Though a conception of reciprocity explains why the guilty should be punished, it is not clear that this same principle will explain why like should be returned for like or even why the evil inflicted on the criminal should be of equal gravity with that which the criminal has inflicted on others. The criminal has acted unfairly and that is why he must be punished. But unfairness is unfairness, murder being no more *unfair* than robbery. Thus if murder is worse than robbery (and thus deserves a worse punishment), this cannot be shown on the basis of purely formal or conceptual considerations. Consider, for example, the punishment for rape if the "Like for like" position were taken literally. If it be argued that the position does not entail that we rape the rapist but only do to him something of *equal* evil, it can be replied that the question 'What evils are equal?' does not admit of a purely formal answer. Thus a retributivism grounded on fairness can at most demand a kind of *proportionality* between crime and punishment — i.e. demand that we rank acceptable punishments on a scale of seriousness, rank criminal offenses on a scale of seriousness, and then guarantee that the most serious punishments will be matched with the most serious crimes, the next most serious punishments with the next most serious crimes, and so on. The ranking must be reasonable, of course, but there is no reason to suppose that it will be determined solely or even primarily by considerations of fairness, i.e. no reason to suppose that seriousness can be analyzed in terms of fairness.[8]

(2) *The Gap between Theory and Practice.* Another common criticism of Kant's theory may be regarded as Marxist in character. Kant's theory, it may be argued, involves an ideal model of society which is in fact so utterly different from the actual character of society as to render it useless in understanding or evaluating any existing practice of criminal punishment. Indeed, the theory is dangerous. For it allows us to hide from ourselves the vicious character of actual social arrangements and thereby perpetuate gross injustice.

Let me elaborate: Punishment as retribution (paying a debt to one's fellow-citizens) makes good sense with respect to a community of responsible individuals, of approximate equality, bound together by freely adopted and commonly accepted rules which benefit everyone. This is an ideal community, approximating what Kant would call a kingdom of ends. In such a community, punishment would be justly retributive in that it would flow as an accepted consequence of accepted rules which benefited everyone (including, as citizen, the criminal). But surely existing human societies are not *in fact* like this at all. Many people neither benefit nor participate but rather operate at a built-in economic or racial disadvantage which is in fact, if not in theory, permanent. The majority of criminals who are in fact punished are drawn from these classes, and they utterly fail to correspond to the model which underlies the retributive theory. Surely we delude ourselves in appealing to the retributive theory to justify their punishment. In his letters, Kant himself considers this problem and reaches a position which appears to be diametrically opposed to that of the *Rechtslehre*:

In a world of moral principle governed by God, punishments would be categorically necessary (insofar as transgressions occur). But in a world governed by men, the necessity of punishments is only hypothetical, and that direct union of the concept of transgression with the idea of deserving punishment serves the ruler only as a prescription for what to do ... [Criminal punishment], even if its goal is merely medicinal for the criminal and setting of an example for others, in indeed a *symbol* of something deserving punishment.[9]

Here Kant seems to be admitting that human society is not the kind of society, and human criminals not the kind of individuals, corresponding to the ideals of community and personality needed to make punishment as retribution legitimate. To make a man suffer punishment as a *symbol* may have good consequences and may be very edifying, but it has nothing to do with the question of whether the man morally *deserves* his punishment and whether, in getting it, he is being treated as a person and not a mere thing.

The moral doubts raised here are extremely important. However, they may be doubts which testify to *strengths* rather than weaknesses in Kant's theory. Decent men surely want to object to the wanton handing out of punishments to those who, in a socially uneven community, always get the short end of the stick. But does not Kant's theory explain (or at least give one reason) *why* we do want to object? Just punishment rests upon reciprocity; and is not the most serious moral problem which confronts most existing communities the absence of such reciprocity, the absence of a balance between benefit and burden? Punishment is unjust in such a setting because it involves pretending (contrary to fact) that the conditions of justified punishment are met. Thus could not Kant, given his theory, easily share the Marxist scepticism about punishing in certain actual states? I believe that he could.

Now Kant may have thought that in defending a retributive theory he was also defending all of our present punitive practices. If so, his mistake is simply about *facts* and not about the principles involved. In developing his theory, Kant is attempting to outline the characteristics that a society must have in order for punishment within it to be justified. Being right on this question will not prevent one from mistakenly believing that a particular society has these characteristics when in fact it does not.

(3) *Good Reasons and Sufficient Reasons*. The utilitarian, I have argued, typically begs the question against Kant. But Kant, alas, does the same thing to the utilitarian. For Kant confuses or collapses the distinction between a *good* moral reason for doing x and a *sufficient* moral reason for doing x. Kant has established that at least one non-utilitarian consideration (reciprocity) is involved in the justification of punishment. It is a morally relevant factor and is not susceptible to a utilitarian analysis. Retribution (paying the debt) thus explains why there is a good reason, or a good *prima facie* case, for punishing the guilty. But this analysis cannot establish, in a non question-begging way, the sufficiency of the case. Why not? For the following reason: When considerations of justice or fairness *compete* with utilitarian considerations (presenting, let us suppose, a good case against punishment in a particular case) one cannot decide this conflict by an appeal to justice. One cannot evaluate some value system S by the very same values definitive of S. Now it may be that considerations of justice should always override considerations of utility; but if this claim is correct, its correctness will have to be established by some principle *independent* of either justice or utility.[10]

(4) *Let Him Who is Without Sin Cast the First Stone*. Let us grant that

Kant has established that the criminal deserves his punishment. A question that still must be considered is the following: Do the other members of the community (given their moral failings) have a *moral right* to administer the punishment through their representatives? If they have no right to do this, then they surely can have no duty to do it.

Kant believes that he can meet this worry in the following way: First, he draws a distinction between *juridical* duties or duties of justice and *ethical* duties or duties of virtue. No man is without ethical failings, without failings of virtue. But society typically does not punish for such failings, does not punish for such things as omissions or bad motives. Society only punishes for injustice, for the active violation of the rights of others, for the breach of juridical duty. Most of us are without these failings (failings of justice) and thus we can, without hypocrisy, demand punishment for these failings in others. Bad though our motives may be, most of us do not actively harm others. Regardless, then, of our failings of virtue, we are the moral superiors of the criminal in at least one sense: we are *just* and he is not.

But are we? Can motives be so easily disregarded? According to Kant's official theory, the unjust man is morally less than the rest of us because we have exercised restraint whereas he has not — regardless of his or our motives in the respective cases. But in the *Religion*, he begins to develop some doubts about this.

[Men] may even picture themselves as meritorious, feeling themselves guilty of no such offenses as they see others burdened with; nor do they even inquire whether good luck should not have the credit, or by reason of the cast of mind which they could discover, if they only would, in their own inmost nature, they would not have practiced similar vices, had not inability, temperament, training, and circumstance of time and place which serve to tempt one (matters which are not imputable), kept them out of the way of those vices. This dishonesty, by which we humbug ourselves and which thwarts the establishing of a true moral disposition in us, extends itself outwardly to falsehood and deception of others.[11]

The point here (for our purpose) is the following: The criminal has not restrained himself and thus appears to manifest a moral failing sufficient for excluding him from the community of the just, those who have restrained themselves. But the lurking question is the following: *Why* have the so-called just restrained themselves? Suppose they have not restrained themselves from any morally creditable motive (respect for duty, say) but only self-interest — e.g. fear of punishment. In what sense are they more *deserving* of citizenship than the criminal? Of course, the preservation of political liberty demands that we punish only those who commit overt acts. But if a man's failure to commit an overt criminal act rests on some *fortuity* rather than principled restraint, how can he claim (in conjunction with people like him) the moral right to demand punishment for others for their criminal acts? Consider the following two cases: (1) The man who intends a criminal act and carries out his intentions and (2) The man who intends a criminal act and loses his nerve to carry it out or fails through a fortuity. In whatever sense, if any, (2) is more just than (1), it is hardly a sense which will allow us to say that (2) is the *moral* superior of (1). (2) retains his citizenship in the kingdom of ends by *luck*, not by deserving it any more than (1). The criminal is, of course, *eligible* for his punishment in a way that most of us are not. But this does not show that he *deserves* punishment any more than the rest of us. Consider the following analogy: Jones, a superior athlete, has a cramp and loses his race to Smith, an inferior runner. Given the rules, Smith is eligible for the award and gets it. But surely Jones deserved it; Smith would surely have no right to regard himself as superior to Jones.[12]

The reason all this is relevant for Kant is that, given his views on radical evil in the *Religion*, it seems that we may *all* be in the position of (2) above — that is, in the position of one who can never be sure that he has, from a morally creditable motive, restrained himself. Though such a judgment is an intensely personal affair, the possibilities for bad faith and self-deception are enormous. Thus there is tension between the official theory presented in the *Rechtslehre* and the position of humility adopted, for example, in the *Religion*. The insights of the latter work do not sit well with the rather self-righteous tone of the official theory.[13]

(5) *Shared Guilt*, Suppose that Jones commits a criminal act. Our initial temptation is to regard his guilt as individual for this and to regard ourselves as acting rightly in demanding his punishment alone. But even in the law there are inroads against stopping here. Those who counsel Jones, aid him, and profit from his act may be criminally prosecuted. It would be unfair to make Jones bear the burden for what has been a collective endeavor.

Some writers have sought to extrapolate from the legal notion of complicity and argue that our collective responsibilities are wider than we might at first imagine. Though not many would follow Dostoevsky in believing that we are all responsible for everything, we have in recent times heard such charges as that most law-abiding Germans were responsible for Nazi crimes and that most white Americans are responsible for black violence. Though these claims go against the grain, they are by no means clearly silly. Consider the following sort of case: If preventing a crime (through befriending a homeless and alienated child, say) would have caused me less personal sacrifice than the sacrifice that was later required of the child (when adult) to refrain from crime, can I really judge myself his superior or claim that he is more guilty of the crime than I? Surely I and my fellow citizens have some share in the pathology.

In a rather obscure passage at *Rechtslehre*, 336–337, Kant worries about a similar problem. There he seems to argue that since society persists in fostering stupid prejudices (such as hatred of illegitimacy or love of military honor), it is hypocritical for society to punish those who act (bastard infanticide, duelling) on the basis of such prejudices.

Such a door, once opened, is hard to close. And once we begin to look at the moral world in this way, we will perhaps be hesitant in being too certain in our judgments as to just what punishment we can in justice demand for others. Once again, here is an insight which leads to moral humility and which is thus in tension with the smug tone of the official theory.

In conclusion, I should note (as I suppose has been obvious) that my reaction to Kant's theory of criminal punishment is one of deeply mixed feelings. On the one hand, it is a theory which respects human dignity, regards human beings as responsible agents and not merely as things or resources to be manipulated for the social good. On the other hand, it tends perhaps to encourage blindness to the way things really are and to give rise to smugness and self-righteousness. It is a theory built on tension — tension between justice and utility, tension between ideal states and actual states, tension between righteousness and humility. This, I suspect, accounts for its eternal fascination.

NOTES

* This essay was originally presented as a lecture at the Third International Kant Congress held at the University of Rochester in 1970 and was published in the proceedings of that Congress. It is an expansion of the discussion of Kant's theory of punishment in my book *Kant: The Philosophy of Right* (London: Macmillan, 1970) and has been extensively revised for inclusion in the present volume. It still overlaps other essays in this volume more than I would like, but this could not be avoided without destroying its integrity as an independent essay. Kant's theory of punishment is presented in his *Metaphysische Anfangsgründe der Rechtslehre* (1797). Pagination cited in the present essay is from Volume VI of the edition of Kant's works issued by the Royal Prussian Academy in Berlin. I have relied upon the English translation by John Ladd (*Metaphysical Elements of Justice*, Indianapolis: Bobbs-Merrill, 1965) which provides the Prussian Academy pagination in the margins.

[1] *Rechtslehre*, 331. I have italicised the word 'merely' to point out that Kant is not committed in principle to opposing such *additional* goals as deterrence and rehabilitation for a man being justly punished.

[2] *Rechtslehre*, 333.

[3]   See John Rawls, *A Theory of Justice* (Cambridge, Mass.: Harvard University Press, 1971).

[4]   *Rechtslehre*, 331, 332, 335.

[5]   'Murder and the Principles of Punishment', in *Punishment and Responsibility* (Oxford: Oxford University Press, 1968), p. 79.

[6]   *Philosophy of Right*, translated by T. M. Knox, (Oxford: Oxford University Press, 1952), p. 72.

[7]   At *Rechtslehre* 363, Kant clearly sees that there is a problem in applying *jus talionis* to "punishments that do not allow reciprocation because they are either impossible in themselves or would themselves be punishable crimes against humanity in general." With respect to rape, pederasty and bestiality, Kant believes that imprisonment is inadequate as a punishment and proposes castration for the former two offenses and expulsion from society for the latter. He admits, however, that this is not a literal application of *jus talionis* but only in some sense captures the intuitive "spirit" of the principle.
   Speaking of the death penalty at *Rechtslehre* 333, however, Kant argues that this punishment must be "kept entirely free from any maltreatment that would make an abomination of the humanity residing in the person suffering it." And he earlier suggests (*Rechtslehre* 331) that the "innate personality" of the criminal protects him against morally indecent treatment. Kant here seems to be working toward a ban on what the United State Constitution calls "cruel and unusual punishments." How these insights are to be squared with Kant's support of castration as a punishment is a mystery to me.

[8]   There is a certain ambiguity in the concept of proportionality as applied to the theory of punishment. It can mean either (a) doing to the criminal something of equal gravity to what he has done to his victim or (b) making sure that the most serious punishments are applied to the most serious offenses, etc. So if the most serious punishment in a particular legal system is 20 years in prison and if this punishment is applied to the crime of murder, it could plausibly be argued that the proportionality demand stated in (b) has been satisfied, but not that stated in (a). And my argument thus far has been that (b) is the most that can reasonably be derived from Kant's theory. The decision to allow or not to allow (say) *death* to remain as a system's most severe punishment, then, cannot be based simply on considerations of fairness but must be based on some other morally relevant properties of death.

[9]   Letter to J. B. Erhard, December 21, 1792, translated by Arnulf Zweig in his *Kant: Philosophical Correspondence* (Chicago: University of Chicago Press, 1967) p. 199.

[10]   Throughout most of his writings on moral philosophy, Kant *promises* (but does not ever totally deliver) an argument of the following form: that the preferability of a morálity of justice over a morality of utility can be established by the derivability of the former from the concept of *rationality*. Perhaps this promise is finally kept by John Rawls. See *A Theory of Justice, op. cit.*

[11]   *Religion Within the Limits of Reason Alone*, translated by Theodore M. Greene and Hoyt H. Hudson (New York: Harper, 1960), p. 33. This sounds very much like John Rawls' suggestion that certain of our abilities are morally arbitrary because their presence or absence is simply a matter of our "luck on a natural and social lottery." See *A Theory of Justice, op. cit.*

[12]   For an excellent discussion of these issues, see Joel Feinberg's 'Justice and Personal Desert' in *Nomos VI: Justice*, edited by Carl J. Friedrich and John W. Chapman (New York: Atherton Press, 1963), pp. 69–97.

[13] Plato's myth of Gyges' Ring, Jesus' caution "Let him who is without sin cast the first stone," and Shakespeare's drama *Measure for Measure* all force us to reflect upon the possible hypocrisy behind our demands that the guilty be held responsible and punished. What if we are among the non-guilty, not because of moral restraint, but because of fear of being caught, or attempting to do evil but failing through a fortuity, or – like Shakespeare's Angelo – simply being lucky enough never to have been adequately tempted? What then? It would be hasty to open the doors of all jails because of this reflection, for there is still an important social distinction between actually doing something and not. "Thoughts are no subjects." However, even though we shall still continue to punish in spite of the reflection, it should at least change our *attitude* to what we are doing. We should do it with regret and humility and not with an attitude of smug righteousness; we should not view the punishment of criminals as a drama in which the good people of the world are pitted against the bad people. For, as Bishop Creighton once remarked, "the good are not so good as they think themselves; the wicked are not so bad as the good think them." If our attitude toward punishment softened in this way, we might be less inclined to make prisons into the inhuman pestholes that they are today.

MARXISM AND RETRIBUTION*

Punishment in general has been defended as a means either of ameliorating or of intimidating. Now what right have you to punish me for the amelioration or intimidation of others? And besides there is history — there is such a thing as statistics — which prove with the most complete evidence that since Cain the world has been neither intimidated nor ameliorated by punishment. Quite the contrary. From the point of view of abstract right, there is only one theory of punishment which recognizes human dignity in the abstract, and that is the theory of Kant, especially in the more rigid formula given to it by Hegel. Hegel says: "Punishment is the *right* of the criminal. It is an act of his own will. The violation of right has been proclaimed by the criminal as his own right. His crime is the negation of right. Punishment is the negation of this negation, and consequently an affirmation of right, solicited and forced upon the criminal by himself."

There is no doubt something specious in this formula, inasmuch as Hegel, instead of looking upon the criminal as the mere object, the slave of justice, elevates him to the position of a free and self-determined being. Looking, however, more closely into the matter, we discover that German idealism here, as in most other instances, has but given a transcendental sanction to the rules of existing society. Is it not a delusion to substitute for the individual with his real motives, with multifarious social circumstances pressing upon him, the abstraction of "free will" — one among the many qualities of man for man himself? ... Is there not a necessity for deeply reflecting upon an alteration of the system that breeds these crimes, instead of glorifying the hangman who executes a lot of criminals to make room only for the supply of new ones?

Karl Marx, 'Capital Punishment'
New York Daily Tribune (18 February 1853)[1]

Philosophers have written at great length about the moral problems involved in punishing the innocent — particularly as these problems raise obstacles to an acceptance of the moral theory of Utilitarianism. Punishment of an innocent man in order to bring about good social consequences is, at the very least, not always clearly wrong on utilitarian principles. This being so, utilitarian principles are then to be condemned by any morality that may be called Kantian in character. For punishing an innocent man, in Kantian language, involves using that man as a mere means or instrument to some social good and is thus not to treat him as an end in himself, in accord with his dignity or worth as a person.

The Kantian position on the issue of punishing the innocent, and the many ways in which the utilitarian might try to accommodate that position, constitute extremely well-worn ground in contemporary moral and legal philosophy.[2] I do not propose to wear the ground further by adding additional comments on the issue here. What I do want to point out, however, is something which seems to me quite obvious but which philosophical commentators on punishment have almost universally failed to see — namely, that problems of the very same kind and seriousness arise for the utilitarian theory with respect to the punishment of the *guilty*. For a utilitarian theory of punishment (Bentham's is a paradigm) must involve justifying punishment in terms of its social results — e.g., deterrence, incapacitation, and rehabilitation. And thus even a guilty man is, on this theory, being punished because of the instrumental value the action of punishment will have in the future. He is being used as a means to some future good — e.g., the deterrence of others. Thus those of a Kantian persuasion, who see the importance of worrying about the treatment of persons as mere means, must, it would seem, object just as strenuously to the punishment of the guilty on utilitarian grounds as to the punishment of the innocent. Indeed the former worry, in some respects, seems more serious. For a utilitarian can perhaps refine his theory in such a way that it does not commit him to the punishment of the innocent. However, if he is to approve of punishment at all, he must approve of punishing the guilty in at least some cases. This makes the worry about punishing the guilty formidable indeed, and it is odd that this has gone generally unnoticed.[3] It has generally been assumed that if the utilitarian theory can just avoid entailing the permissibility of punishing the innocent, then all objections of a Kantian character to the theory will have been met. This seems to me simply not to be the case.

What the utilitarian theory really cannot capture, I would suggest, is the notion of persons having rights. And it is just this notion that is central to any Kantian outlook on morality. Any Kantian can certainly agree that punishing persons (guilty or innocent) may have either good or bad or indifferent consequences and that insofar as the consequences (whether in a particular case or for an institution) are good, this is something in favor of punishment. But the Kantian will maintain that this consequential outlook, important as it may be, leaves out of consideration entirely that which is most morally crucial — namely, the question of rights. Even if punishment of a person would have good consequences, what gives us (i.e., society) the moral right to inflict it? If we have such a right, what is its origin or derivation? What social circumstances must be present for it to be applicable? What does this right to punish tell us about the status of the person to be punished — e.g., how are we to analyze his rights, the sense in which he must deserve to be punished, his obligations in the matter? It is this family of questions which any Kantian must regard as morally central and which the utilitarian cannot easily accommodate into his theory. And it is surely this aspect of Kant's and Hegel's retributivism, this seeing of rights as basic, which appeals to Marx in the quoted passage. As Marx himself puts it: "What right have you to punish me for the amelioration or intimidation of others?" And he further praises Hegel for seeing that punishment, if justified, must involve respecting the rights of the person to be punished.[4] Thus Marx, like Kant, seems prepared to draw the important distinction between (a) what it would be good to do on grounds of utility and (b) what we have a right to do. Since we do not always have the right to do what it would be good to do, this distinction is of the greatest moral importance; and missing the distinction is the Achilles heel of all forms of Utilitarianism. For consider the following example: A Jehovah's Witness needs a blood transfusion in order to live; but, because of his (we can agree absurd) religious belief that such transfusions are against God's commands, he instructs his doctor not to give him one. Here is a case where it would seem to be good or for the best to give the transfusion and yet, at the very least, it is highly doubtful that the doctor has a right to give it. This kind of distinction is elementary, and any theory which misses it is morally degenerate.[5]

To move specifically to the topic of punishment: How exactly does retributivism (of a Kantian or Hegelian variety) respect the rights of persons? Is Marx really correct on this? I believe that he is. I believe that retributivism can be formulated in such a way that it is the only morally defensible theory of punishment. I also believe that arguments, which may be regarded as Marxist at least in spirit, can be formulated which show that social conditions as they obtain in most societies make this form of retributivism largely inapplicable within those societies. As Marx says, in those societies retributivism functions merely to provide a "transcendental sanction" for the status quo. If this is so, then the only morally defensible theory of punishment is largely inapplicable in modern societies. The consequence: modern societies largely lack the moral right to punish.[6] The upshot is that a Kantian moral theory (which in general seems to me correct) and a Marxist analysis of crime (which, if properly qualified, also seems to me correct) produces a radical and not merely reformist attack not merely on the scope and manner of punishment in our society but on the institution of punishment itself. Institutions of punishment constitute what Bernard Harrison has called structural injustices[7] and are, in the absence of a major social change, to be resisted by all who take human rights to be morally serious — i.e., regard them as genuine action guides and not merely as rhetorical devices which allow people to morally sanctify institutions which in fact can only be defended on grounds of social expediency.

Stating all of this is one thing and proving it, of course, is another. Whether I can ever do this is doubtful. That I cannot do it in one brief article is certain. I cannot, for example, here defend in detail my belief that a generally Kantian outlook on moral matters is correct.[8] Thus I shall content myself for the present with attempting to render at least plausible two major claims involved in the view that I have outlined thus far: (1) that a retributive theory, in spite of the bad press that it has received, is a morally credible theory of punishment — that it can be, H. L. A. Hart to the contrary,[9] a reasonable general justifying aim of punishment; and (2) that a Marxist analysis of crime can undercut the practical applicability of that theory.

THE RIGHT OF THE STATE TO PUNISH

It is strong evidence of the influence of a utilitarian outlook in moral and legal matters that discussions of punishment no longer involve a consideration of the right of anyone to inflict it. Yet in the eighteenth and nineteenth centuries, this tended to be regarded as the central aspect of the problem meriting philosophical consideration. Kant, Hegel, Bosanquet, Green — all tended to entitle their chapters on punishment along the lines explicitly used by Green: "The Right of the State to Punish."[10] This is not just a matter of terminology but reflects, I think, something of deeper philosophical substance. These theories, unlike the utilitarian, did not view man as primarily a maximizer of personal satisfactions — a maximizer of individual utilities. They were inclined, in various ways, to adopt a different model of man — man as a free or spontaneous creator, man as autonomous. (Marx, it may be noted, is much more in line with this tradition than with the utilitarian outlook.)[11] This being so, these theorists were inclined to view punishment (a certain kind of coercion by the state) as not merely a causal contributor to pain and suffering, but rather as presenting at least a *prima facie* challenge to the values of autonomy and personal dignity and self-realization — the very values which, in their view, the state existed to nurture. The problem as they saw it, therefore, was that of reconciling punishment as state coercion with the value of individual autonomy. (This is an instance of the more general problem which Robert Paul Wolff has called the central problem of political philosophy — namely, how is individual moral autonomy to be reconciled with legitimate political authority?)[12] This kind of problem, which I am inclined to agree is quite basic, cannot even be formulated intelligibly from a utilitarian perspective. Thus the utilitarian cannot even see the relevance of Marx's charge: Even if punishment has wonderful social consequences, what gives anyone the right to inflict it on me?

Now one fairly typical way in which others acquire rights over us is by our own consent. If a neighbor locks up my liquor cabinet to protect me against my tendencies to drink too heavily, I might well regard this as a presumptuous interference with my own freedom, no matter how good the result intended or accomplished. He had no right to do it and indeed violated my rights in doing it. If, on the other hand, I had asked him to do this or had given my free consent to his suggestion that he do it, the same sort of objection on my part would be quite out of order. I had given him the right to do it, and he had the right to do it. In doing it, he violated no rights of mine — even if, at the time of his doing it, I did not desire or want the action to be performed. Here then we seem to have a case where my autonomy may be regarded as intact even though a desire of mine is thwarted. For there is a sense in which the thwarting of the desire can be imputed to me (my choice or decision) and not to the arbitrary intervention of another.

How does this apply to our problem? The answer, I think, is obvious. What is needed, in order to reconcile my undesired suffering of punishment at the hands of the state with my autonomy (and thus with the state's right to punish me), is a political theory which makes the state's decision to punish me in some sense my own decision. If I have willed my own punishment (consented to it, agreed to it) then — even if at the time I happen not to desire it — it can be said that my autonomy and dignity remain intact. Theories of the General Will and Social Contract theories are two such theories which attempt this reconciliation of autonomy with legitimate state authority (including the right or authority of the state to punish). Since Kant's theory happens to incorporate elements of both, it will be useful to take it for our sample.

MORAL RIGHTS AND THE RETRIBUTIVE THEORY OF PUNISHMENT

To justify government or the state is necessarily to justify at least some coercion.[13] This poses a problem for someone, like Kant, who maintains that human freedom is the ultimate or most sacred moral value. Kant's own attempt to justify the state, expressed in his doctrine of the *moral title* (*Befugnis*),[14] involves an argument that coercion is justified only in so far as it is used to prevent invasions against freedom. Freedom itself is the only value which can be used to limit freedom, for the appeal to any other value (e.g., utility) would undermine the ultimate status of the value of freedom. Thus Kant attempts to establish the claim that some forms of coercion (as opposed to violence) are morally permissible because, contrary to appearance, they are really consistent with rational freedom. The argument, in broad outline, goes in the following way. Coercion may keep people from doing what they desire or want to do on a particular occasion and is thus *prima facie* wrong. However, such coercion can be shown to be morally justified (and thus not absolutely wrong) if it can be established that the coercion is such that it could have been rationally willed even by the person whose desire is interfered with:

Accordingly, when it is said that a creditor has a right to demand from his debtor the payment of a debt, this does not mean that he can *persuade* the debtor that his own reason itself obligates him to this performance; on the contrary, to say that he has such a right means only that the use of coercion to make anyone do this is entirely compatible with everyone's freedom, *including the freedom of the debtor*, in accordance with universal laws.[15]

Like Rousseau, Kant thinks that it is only in a context governed by social practice (particularly civil government and its Rule of Law) that this can make sense. Laws may require of a person some action that he does not desire to perform. This is not a violent invasion of his freedom, however, if it can be shown that in some antecedent position of choice (what John Rawls calls "the original position"),[16] he would have been rational to adopt a Rule of Law (and thus run the risk of having some of his desires thwarted) rather than some other alternative arrangement such as the classical State of Nature. This is, indeed, the only sense that Kant is able to make of classical Social Contract theories. Such theories are to be viewed, not as historical fantasies, but as ideal models of rational decision. For what these theories actually claim is that the only coercive institutions that are morally justified are those which a group of rational beings could agree to adopt in a position of having to pick social institutions to govern their relations:

The contract, which is called *contractus originarius*, or *pactum sociale* . . . need not be assumed to be a fact, indeed it is not [even possible as such. To suppose that would be like insisting] that before anyone would be bound to respect such a civic constitution, it be proved first of all from history that a people, whose rights and obligations we have entered into as their descendants, had *once upon a time* executed such an act and had left a reliable document or instrument, either orally or in writing, concerning this contract. Instead, this contract is a *mere idea* of reason which has undoubted practical reality; namely, to oblige every legislator to give us laws in such a manner that the laws *could* have originated from the united will of the entire people and to regard every subject in so far as he is a citizen as though he had consented to such [an expression of the general] will. This is the testing stone of the rightness of every publicly-known law, for if a law were such that it was impossible for an entire people to give consent to it (as for example a law that a certain class of subjects, by inheritance, should have the privilege of the *status of lords*), then such a law is unjust. On the other hand, if there is a mere *possibility* that a people might consent to a (certain) law, then it is a duty to consider that the law is just even though at the moment the people might be in such a position or have a point of view that would result in their refusing to give their consent to it if asked.[17]

The problem of organizing a state, however hard it may seem, can be solved even for a race of devils, if only they are intelligent. The problem is: "Given a multiple of rational beings requiring universal laws for their preservation, but each of whom is secretly inclined to exempt himself from them, to establish a constitution in such a way that, although their private intentions conflict, they check each other, with the result that their public conduct is the same as if they had no such intentions."[18]

Though Kant's doctrine is superficially similar to Mill's later self-protection principle, the substance is really quite different. For though Kant in some general sense argues that coercion is justified only to prevent harm to others, he understands by "harm" only certain invasions of freedom and not simply disutility. Also, his defense of the principle is not grounded, as is Mill's, on its utility. Rather it is to be regarded as a principle of justice, by which Kant means a principle that rational beings could adopt in a situation of mutual choice:

The concept [of justice] applies only to the relationship of a will to another person's will, not to his wishes or desires (or even just his needs) which are the concern of acts of benevolence and charity . . . In applying the concept of justice we take into consideration only the form of the relationship between the wills insofar as they are regarded as free, and whether the action of one of them can be conjoined with the freedom of the other in accordance with universal law. Justice is therefore the aggregate of those conditions under which the will of one person can be conjoined with the will of another in accordance with a universal law of freedom.[19]

How does this bear specifically on punishment? Kant, as everyone knows, defends a strong form of a retributive theory of punishment. He holds that guilt merits, and is a sufficient condition for, the infliction of punishment. And this claim has been universally condemned — particularly by utilitarians — as primitive, unenlightened and barbaric.

But why is it so condemned? Typically, the charge is that infliction of punishment on such grounds is nothing but pointless vengeance. But what is meant by the claim that the infliction is "pointless"? If "pointless" is tacitly being analyzed as "disutilitarian," then the whole question is simply being begged. You cannot refute a retributive theory merely my noting that it is a retributive theory and not a utilitarian theory. This is to confuse redescription with refutation and involves an argument whose circularity is not even complicated enough to be interesting.

Why, then, might someone claim that guilt merits punishment? Such a claim might be made for either of two very different reasons. (1) Someone (e.g., a Moral Sense theorist) might maintain that the claim is a primitive and unanalyzable proposition that is morally ultimate — that we can just intuit the "fittingness" of guilt and punishment. (2) It might be maintained that the retributivist claim is demanded by a general theory of political obligation which is more plausible than any alternative theory. Such a theory will typically provide a technical analysis of such concepts as crime and punishment and will thus not regard the retributivist claim as an indisputable primitive. It will be argued for as a kind of theorem within the system.

Kant's theory is of the second sort. He does not opt for retributivism as a bit of intuitive moral knowledge. Rather he offers a theory of punishment that is based on his general view that political obligation is to be analyzed, quasi-contractually, in terms of reciprocity. If the law is to remain just, it is important to guarantee that those who disobey it will not gain an unfair advantage over those who do obey voluntarily. It is important that no man profit from his own criminal wrongdoing, and a certain kind of "profit" (i.e., not bearing the burden of self-restraint) is intrinsic to criminal wrongdoing. Criminal punishment, then, has as its object the restoration of a proper balance between benefit and obedience. The criminal himself has no complaint, because he has rationally consented to or willed his own punishment. That is, those very rules which he has broken work, when they are obeyed by others, to his own advantage as a citizen. He would have chosen such rules for himself and others in the original position of choice. And, since he derives and voluntarily accepts benefits from their operation, he owes his own obedience as a debt to his fellow-citizens for their sacrifices in maintaining them. If he chooses not to sacrifice by exercising self-restraint and obedience, this is tantamount to his choosing to sacrifice in another way — namely, by paying the prescribed penalty:

A transgression of the public law that makes him who commits it unfit to be a citizen is called . . . a crime . . .
   What kind and what degree of punishment does public legal justice adopt is its principle and standard? None other than the principle of equality (illustrated by the pointer of the scales of justice), that is, the principle of not treating one side more favorably than the other. Accordingly, any undeserved evil that you inflict on someone else among the people is one you do to yourself. If you vilify him, you vilify yourself;

if you steal from him, you steal from yourself; if you kill him, you kill yourself . . .

To say, "I will to be punished if I murder someone" can mean nothing more than, "I submit myself along with everyone else to those laws which, if there are any criminals among the people, will naturally include penal laws."[20]

This analysis of punishment regards it as a debt owed to the law-abiding members of one's community; and, once paid, it allows re-entry into the community of good citizens on equal status.

Now some of the foregoing no doubt sounds implausible or even obscurantist. Since criminals typically desire not to be punished, what can it really mean to say that they have, as rational men, really willed their own punishment? Or that, as Hegel says, they have a right to it? Perhaps a comparison of the traditional retributivist views with those of a contemporary Kantian — John Rawls — will help to make the points clearer.[21] Rawls (like Kant) does not regard the idea of the social contract as an historical fact. It is rather a model of rational decision. Respecting a man's autonomy, at least on one view, is not respecting what he now happens, however uncritically, to desire; rather it is to respect what he desires (or would desire) as a rational man. (On Rawls' view, for example, rational men are said to be unmoved by feelings of envy; and thus it is not regarded as unjust to a person or a violation of his rights, if he is placed in a situation where he will envy another's advantage or position. A rational man would object, and thus would never consent to, a practice where another might derive a benefit from a position at his expense. He would not, however, envy the position *simpliciter*, would not regard the position as itself a benefit.) Now on Kant's (and also, I think, on Rawls') view, a man is genuinely free or autonomous only in so far as he is rational. Thus it is man's rational will that is to be respected.

Now this idea of treating people, not as they in fact say that they want to be treated, but rather in terms of how you think they would, if rational, will to be treated, has obviously dangerous (indeed Fascistic) implications. Surely we want to avoid cramming indignities down the throats of people with the offhand observation that, no matter how much they scream, they are really rationally willing every bit of it. It would be particularly ironic for such arbitrary repression to come under the mask of respecting autonomy. And yet, most of us would agree, the general principle (though subject to abuse) also has important applications — for example, preventing the suicide of a person who, in a state of psychotic depression, wants to kill himself. What we need, then, to make the general view work, is a check on its arbitrary application; and a start toward providing such a check would be in the formulation of a public, objective theory of rationality and rational willing. It is just this, according to both Kant and Rawls, which the social contract theory can provide. On this theory, a man may be said to rationally will X if, and only if, X is called for by a rule that the man would necessarily have adopted in the original position of choice — i.e., in a position of coming together with others to pick rules for the regulation of their mutual affairs. This avoids arbitrariness because, according to Kant and Rawls at any rate, the question of whether such a rule would be picked in such a position is objectively determinable given certain (in their view) noncontroversial assumptions about human nature and rational calculation. Thus I can be said to will my own punishment if, in an antecedent position of choice, I and my fellows would have chosen institutions of punishment as the most rational means of dealing with those who might break the other generally beneficial social rules that had been adopted.

Let us take an analogous example: I may not, in our actual society, desire to treat a certain person fairly — e.g., I may not desire to honor a contract I have made with him because so doing would adversely affect my own self-interest. However, if I am forced to honor the contract by the state, I cannot charge (1) that the state has no right to do this, or (2) that my rights or dignity are being violated by my being coerced into doing it. Indeed, it can be said that I rationally will it since, in the original position, I would have chosen rules of justice (rather than rules of utility) and the principle, "contracts are to be honored," follows from the rules of justice.

Coercion and autonomy are thus reconciled, at least apparently. To use Marx's language, we may say (as Marx did in the quoted passage) that one virtue of the retributive theory, at least as expounded by Kant and Hegel on lines of the General Will and Social Contract theory, is that it manifests at least a formal or abstract respect for rights, dignity, and autonomy. For it at least recognizes the importance of attempting to construe state coercion in such a way that it is a product of each man's rational will. Utilitarian deterrence theory does not even satisfy this formal demand.

The question of primary interest to Marx, of course, is whether this formal respect also involves a material respect; i.e., does the theory have application in concrete fact in the actual social world in which we live? Marx is confident that it does not, and it is to this sort of consideration that I shall now pass.

ALIENATION AND PUNISHMENT

What can the the philosopher learn from Marx? This question is a part of a more general question: What can philosophy learn from social science?

Philosophers, it may be thought, are concerned to offer *a priori* theories, theories about how certain concepts are to be analyzed and their application justified. And what can the mundane facts that are the object of behavioral science have to do with exalted theories of this sort?

The answer, I think, is that philosophical theories, though not themselves empirical, often have such a character that their intelligibility depends upon certain empirical presuppositions. For example, our moral language presupposes, as Hart has argued,[22] that we are vulnerable creatures — creatures who can harm and be harmed by each other. Also, as I have argued elsewhere,[23] our moral language presupposes that we all share certain psychological characteristics — e.g., sympathy, a sense of justice, and the capacity to feel guilt, shame, regret, and remorse. If these facts were radically different (if, as Hart imagines for example, we all developed crustaceanlike exoskeletons and thus could not harm each other), the old moral language, and the moral theories which employ it, would lack application to the world in which we live. To use a crude example, moral prohibitions against killing presuppose that it is in fact possible for us to kill each other.

Now one of Marx's most important contributions to social philosophy, in my judgment, is simply his insight that philosophical theories are in peril if they are constructed in disregard of the nature of the empirical world to which they are supposed to apply.[24] A theory may be formally correct (i.e., coherent, or true for some possible world) but materially incorrect (i.e., inapplicable to the actual world in which we live). This insight, then, establishes the relevance of empirical research to philosophical theory and is a part, I think, of what Marx meant by "the union of theory and practice." Specifically relevant to the argument I want to develop are the following two related points:

(1) The theories of moral, social, political and legal philosophy presuppose certain empirical propositions about man and society. If these propositions are false, then the theory (even if coherent or formally correct) is materially defective and practically inapplicable. (For example, if persons tempted to engage in criminal conduct do not in fact tend to calculate carefully the consequences of their actions, this renders much of deterrence theory suspect.)

(2) Philosophical theories may put forth as a necessary truth that which is in fact merely an historically conditioned contingency. (For example, Hobbes argued that all men are necessarily selfish and competitive. It is possible, as many Marxists have argued, that Hobbes was really doing nothing more than elevating to the status of a necessary truth the contingent fact that the people around him in the capitalistic society in which he lived were in fact selfish and competitive.)[25]

In outline, then, I want to argue the following: that when Marx challenges the material adequacy of the retributive theory of punishment, he is suggesting (a) that it presupposes a certain view of man and society that is false and (b) that key concepts involved in the support of the theory (e.g., the concept of "rationality" in Social Contract theory) are given analyses which, though they purport to be necessary truths, are in fact mere reflections of certain historical circumstances.

In trying to develop this case, I shall draw primarily upon Willem Bonger's *Criminality and Economic Conditions* (1916), one of the few sustained Marxist analyses of crime and punishment.[26] Though I shall not have time here to qualify my support of Bonger in certain necessary ways, let me make clear that I am perfectly aware that his analysis is not the whole story. (No monolithic theory of anything so diverse as criminal behavior could be the whole story.) However, I am convinced that he has discovered part of the story. And my point is simply that insofar as Bonger's Marxist analysis is correct, then to that same degree is the retributive theory of punishment inapplicable in modern societies. (Let me emphasize again exactly how this objection to retributivism differs from those traditionally offered. Traditionally, retributivism has been rejected because it conflicts with the moral theory of its opponent, usually a utilitarian. This is not the kind of objection I want to develop. Indeed, with Marx, I have argued that the retributive theory of punishment grows out of the moral theory — Kantianism — which seems to me generally correct. The objection I want to pursue concerns the empirical falsity of the factual presuppositions of the theory. If the empirical presuppositions of the theory are false, this does indeed render its application immoral. But the immorality consists, not in a conflict with some other moral theory, but immorality in terms of a moral theory that is at least close in spirit to the very moral theory which generates retributivism itself — i.e., a theory of justice.)[27]

To return to Bonger. Put bluntly, his theory is as follows. Criminality has two primary sources: (1) need and deprivation on the part of disadvantaged members of society, and (2) motives of greed and selfishness that are generated and reinforced in competitive capitalistic societies. Thus criminality is economically based — either directly in the case of crimes from need, or indirectly in the case of crimes growing out of motives or psychological states that are encouraged and developed in capitalistic society. In Marx's own language, such an economic system alienates men from themselves and from each other. It alienates men from themselves by creating motives and needs that are not "truly human." It alienates men from their fellows by encouraging a kind of competitiveness that forms an obstacle to the development of genuine communities to replace mere social aggregates.[28] And in Bonger's thought, the concept of community is central. He argues that moral relations and moral restraint are possible only in genuine communities characterized by bonds of sympathetic identification and mutual aid resting upon a perception of common humanity. All this he includes under the general rubric of reciprocity.[29] In the absence of reciprocity in this rich sense, moral relations among men will break down and criminality will increase.[30] Within bourgeois society, then, crimes are to be regarded as normal, and not psychopathological, acts. That is, they grow out of need, greed, indifference to others, and sometimes even a sense of indignation — all, alas, perfectly typical human motives.

To appreciate the force of Bonger's analysis, it is necessary to read his books and grasp the richness and detail of the evidence he provides for his claims. Here I can but quote a few passages at random to give the reader a tantalizing sample in the hope that he will be encouraged to read further into Bonger's own text:

The abnormal element in crime is a social, not a biological, element. With the exception of a few special cases, crime lies within the boundaries of normal psychology and psysiology . . .

We clearly see that [the egoistic tendencies of the present economic system and of its consequences] are very strong. Because of these tendencies the social instinct of man is not greatly developed; they have weakened the moral force in man which combats the inclination towards egoistic acts, and hence toward the crimes which are one form of these acts — Compassion for the misfortunes of others inevitably becomes blunted, and a great part of morality consequently disappears . . .

As a consequence of the present environment, man has become very egoistic and hence more *capable of crime*, than if the environment had developed the germs of altruism . . .

There can be no doubt that one of the factors of criminality among the bourgeoisie is bad [moral] education . . . The children — speaking of course in a general way — are brought up with the idea that they must succeed, no matter how; the aim of life is presented to them as getting money and shining in the world . . .

Poverty (taken in the sense of absolute want) kills the social sentiments in man, destroys in fact all relations between men. He who is abandoned by all can no longer have any feelings for those who have left him to his fate . . .

[Upon perception that the system tends to legalize the egoistic actions of the bourgeoisie and to penalize those of the proletariat], the oppressed resort to means which they would otherwise scorn. As we have seen above, the basis of the social feeling is reciprocity. As soon as this is trodden under foot by the ruling class the social sentiments of the oppressed become weak towards them . . .[31]

The essence of this theory has been summed up by Austin J. Turk. "Criminal behavior," he says, "is almost entirely attributable to the combination of egoism and an environment in which opportunities are not equitably distributed."[32]

No doubt this claim will strike many as extreme and intemperate — a sample of the old-fashioned Marxist rhetoric that sophisticated intellectuals have outgrown. Those who are inclined to react in this way might consider just one sobering fact: of the 1.3 million criminal offenders handled each day by some agency of the United States correctional system, the vast majority (80 percent on some estimates) are members of the lowest 15-percent income level — that percent which is below the "poverty level" as defined by the Social Security Administration.[33] Unless one wants to embrace the belief that all these people are poor because they are bad, it might be well to reconsider Bonger's suggestion that many of them are "bad" because they are poor.[34] At any rate, let us suppose for purposes of discussion that Bonger's picture of the relation between crime and economic conditions is generally accurate. At what points will this challenge the credentials of the contractarian retributive theory as outlined above? I should like to organize my answer to this question around three basic topics:

(1) *Rational Choice*. The model of rational choice found in Social Contract theory is egoistic — rational institutions are those that would be agreed to by calculating egoists ("devils" in Kant's more colorful terminology). The obvious question that would be raised by any Marxist is: Why give egoism this special status such that it is built, *a priori*, into the analysis of the concept of rationality? Is this not simply to regard as necessary that which may be only contingently found in the society around us? Starting from such an analysis, a certain result is inevitable — namely, a transcendental sanction for the status quo. Start with a bourgeois model of rationality and you will, of course, wind up defending a bourgeois theory of consent, a bourgeois theory of justice, and a bourgeois theory of punishment.

Though I cannot explore the point in detail here, it seems to me that this Marxist claim may cause some serious problems for Rawls' well-known theory of justice, a theory which I have already used to unpack some of the evaluative support for the retributive theory of punishment. One cannot help suspecting that there is a certain sterility in Rawls' entire project of providing a rational proof for the preferability of a certain conception of justice over all possible alternative evaluative principles, for the description which he gives of the rational contractors in the original position is such as to guarantee that they will come up with his two principles. This would be acceptable if the analysis of rationality presupposed were intuitively obvious or argued for on independent grounds. But it is not. Why, to take just one example, is a desire for wealth a rational trait whereas envy is not? One cannot help feeling that the desired result dictates the premises.[35]

(2) *Justice, Benefits, and Community*. The retributive theory claims to be grounded on justice; but is it just to punish people who act out of those very motives that society encourages and reinforces? If Bonger is correct, much criminality is motivated by greed, selfishness, and indifference to one's fellows; but does not the whole society encourage motives of greed and selfishness ("making it," "getting ahead"), and does not the competitive nature of the society alienate men from each other and thereby encourage indifference — even, perhaps, what psychiatrists call psychopathy? The moral problem here is similar to one that arises with respect to some war crimes. When you have trained a man to believe that the enemy is not a genuine human person (but only a gook, or a chink), it does not seem quite fair to punish the man if, in a war situation, he kills indiscriminately. For the psychological trait you have conditioned him to have, like greed, is not one that invites fine moral and legal distinctions. There is something perverse in applying principles that presuppose a sense of community in a society which is structured to destroy genuine community.[36]

Related to this is the whole allocation of benefits in contemporary society. The retributive theory really presupposes what might be called a "gentlemen's club" picture of the relation between man and society — i.e., men are viewed as being part of a community of shared values and rules. The rules benefit all concerned and, as a kind of debt for the benefits derived, each man owes obedience to the rules. In the absence of such obedience, he deserves punishment in the sense that he owes payment for the benefits. For, as a rational man, he can see that the rules benefit everyone (himself included) and that he would have selected them in the original position of choice.

Now this may not be too far off for certain kinds of criminals — e.g., business executives guilty of tax fraud. (Though even here we might regard their motives of greed to be a function of societal reinforcement.) But to think that it applies to the typical criminal, from the poorer classes, is to live in a world of social and political fantasy. Criminals typically are not members of a shared community of values with their jailers; they suffer from what Marx calls alienation. And they certainly would be hard-pressed to name the benefits for which they are supposed to owe obedience. If justice, as both Kant and Rawls suggest, is based on reciprocity, it is hard to see what these persons are supposed to reciprocate for. Bonger addresses this point in a passage quoted earlier: "The oppressed resort to means which they would otherwise scorn . . . The basis of social feelings is reciprocity. As soon as this is trodden under foot by the ruling class, the social sentiments of the oppressed become weak towards them."

(3) *Voluntary Acceptance*. Central to the Social Contract idea is the claim that we owe allegiance to the law because the benefits we have derived have been voluntarily accepted. This is one place where our autonomy is supposed to come in. That is, having benefited from the Rule of Law when it was possible to leave, I have in a sense consented to it and to its consequences — even my own punishment if I violate the rules. To see how silly the factual presuppositions of this account are, we can do no better than quote a famous passage from David Hume's essay "Of the Original Contract":

Can we seriously say that a poor peasant or artisan has a free choice to leave his country — when he knows no foreign language or manners, and lives from day to day by the small wages which he acquires? We may as well assert that a man, by remaining in a vessel, freely consents to the dominion of the master, though he was carried on board while asleep, and must leap into the ocean and perish the moment he leaves her.

A banal empirical observation, one may say. But it is through ignoring such banalities that philosophers generate theories which allow them to spread iniquity in the ignorant belief that they are spreading righteousness.

It does, then, seem as if there may be some truth in Marx's claim that the retributive theory, though formally correct, is materially inadequate. At root, the retributive theory fails to acknowledge that criminality is, to a large extent, a phenomenon of economic class. To acknowledge this is to challenge the empirical presupposition of the retributive theory — the presupposition that all men, including criminals, are voluntary participants in a reciprocal system of benefits and that the justice of this arrangement can be derived from some eternal and ahistorical concept of rationality.

The upshot of all this seems rather upsetting, as indeed it is. How can it be the case that everything we are ordinarily inclined to say about punishment (in terms of utility and retribution) can be quite beside the point? To anyone with ordinary language sympathies (one who is inclined to maintain that what is correct to say is a function of what we do say), this will seem madness. Marx will agree that there is madness, all right, but in his view the madness will lie in what we do say — what we say only because of our massive (and often self-deceiving and self-serving) factual ignorance or indifference to the circumstances of the social world in which we live. Just as our whole way of talking about mental phenomena hardened before we knew any neurophysiology — and this leads us astray, so Marx would argue that our whole way of talking about moral and political phenomena hardened before we knew any of the relevant empirical facts about man and society — and this, too, leads us astray. We all suffer from what might be called the *embourgeoisment* of language, and thus part of any revolution will be a linguistic or conceptual revolution. We have grown accustomed to modifying our language or conceptual structures under the impact of empirical discoveries in physics. There is no reason why discoveries in sociology, economics, or psychology could not and should not have the same effect on entrenched patterns of thought and speech. It is important to remember, as Russell remarked, that our language sometimes enshrines the metaphysics of the Stone Age.

Consider one example: a man has been convicted of armed robbery. On investigation, we learn that he is an impoverished black whose whole life has been one of frustrating alienation from the prevailing socio-economic structure — no job, no transportation if he could get a job, substandard education for his children, terrible housing and inadequate health care for his whole family, condescending-tardy-inadequate welfare payments, harassment by the police but no real protection by them against the dangers in his community, and near total exclusion from the political process. Learning all this, would we still want to talk — as many do — of his suffering punishment under the rubric of "paying a debt to society"? Surely not. Debt for what? I do not, of course, pretend that all criminals can be so described. But I do think that this is a closer picture of the typical criminal than the picture that is presupposed in the retributive theory — i.e., the picture of an evil person who, of his own free will, intentionally acts against those just rules of society which he knows, as a rational man, benefit everyone including himself.

But what practical help does all this offer, one may ask. How should we design our punitive practices in the society in which we now live? This is the question we want to ask, and it does not seem to help simply to say that our society is built on deception and inequity. How can Marx help us with our real practical problem? The answer, I think, is that he cannot and obviously does not desire to do so. For Marx would say that we have not focused (as all piecemeal reform fails to focus) on what is truly the real problem. And this is changing the basic social relations. Marx is the last person from whom we can expect advice on how to make our intellectual and moral peace with bourgeois society. And this is surely his attraction and his value.

What does Bonger offer? He suggests, near the end of his book, that in a properly designed society all criminality would be a problem "for the physician rather than the judge." But this surely will not do. The therapeutic state, where prisons are called hospitals and jailers are called psychiatrists, simply raises again all the old problems about the justification of coercion and its reconciliation with autonomy that we faced in worrying about punishment. The only difference is that our coercive practices are now surrounded with a benevolent rhetoric which makes it even harder to raise the important issues. Thus the move to therapy, in my judgment, is only an illusory solution — alienation remains and the problem of reconciling coercion with autonomy remains unsolved. Indeed, if the alternative is having our personalities involuntarily restructured by some state psychiatrist, we might well want to claim the "right to be punished" that Hegel spoke of.[37]

Perhaps, then, we may really be forced seriously to consider a radical proposal. If we think that institutions of punishment are necessary and desirable, and if we are morally sensitive enough to want to be sure that we have the moral right to punish before we inflict it, then we had better first make sure that we have restructured society in such a way that criminals genuinely do correspond to the only model that will render punishment permissible — i.e., make sure that they are autonomous and that they do benefit in the requisite sense. Of course, if we did this then — if Marx and Bonger are right — crime itself and the need to punish would radically decrease if not disappear entirely.

NOTES

* An earlier version of this essay was delivered to the Third Annual Colloquium in Philosophy ("The Philosophy of Punishment") at the University of Dayton in October, 1972. I am grateful to the Department of Philosophy at the University of Dayton for inviting me to participate and to a number of persons at the Colloquium for the useful discussion on my paper at the time. I am also grateful to Anthony D. Woozley of the University of Virginia and to two of my colleagues, Robert M. Harnish and Francis V. Raab, for helping me to clarify the expression of my views.

[1] In a sense, my paper may be viewed as an elaborate commentary on this one passage, excerpted from a discussion generally concerned with the efficacy of capital punishment in eliminating crime. For in this passage, Marx (to the surprise of many I should think) expresses a certain admiration for the classical retributive theory of punishment. Also (again surprisingly) he expresses this admiration in a kind of language he normally avoids — i.e., the moral language of rights and justice. He then, of course, goes on to reject the applicability of that theory. But the question that initially perplexed me is the following: what is the explanation of Marx's ambivalence concerning the retributive theory; why is he both attracted and repelled by it? (This ambivalence is not shared, for example, by utilitarians — who feel nothing but repulsion when the retributive theory is mentioned.) Now except for some very brief passages in *The Holy Family*, Marx himself has nothing more to say on the topic of punishment beyond what is contained in this brief *Daily Tribune* article. Thus my essay is in no sense an exercise in textual scholarship (there are not enough texts) but is rather an attempt to construct an assessment of punishment,

Marxist at least in spirit, that might account for the ambivalence found in the quoted passage. My main outside help comes, not from Marx himself, but from the writings of the Marxist criminologist Willem Bonger.

[2] Many of the leading articles on this topic have been reprinted in *The Philosophy of Punishment*, ed. H. B. Acton (New York: St. Martin's Press, 1969). Those papers not included are cited in Acton's excellent bibliography.

[3] One writer who has noticed this is Richard Wasserstrom. See his 'Why Punish the Guilty?' *Princeton University Magazine* 20 (1964) 14−19.

[4] Marx normally avoids the language of rights and justice because he regards such language to be corrupted by bourgeois ideology. However, if we think very broadly of what an appeal to rights involves − namely, a protest against unjustified coercion − there is no reason why Marx may not legitimately avail himself on occasion of this way of speaking. For there is surely at least some moral overlap between Marx's protests against exploitation and the evils of a division of labor, for example, and the claims that people have a right not to be used solely for the benefit of others and a right to self-determination.

[5] I do not mean to suggest that under no conceivable circumstances would the doctor be justified in giving the transfusion even though, in one clear sense, he had no right to do it. If, for example, the Jehovah's Witness was a key man whose survival was necessary to prevent the outbreak of a destructive war, we might well regard the transfusion as on the whole justified. However, even in such a case, a morally sensitive man would have to regretfully realize that he was sacrificing an important principle. Such a realization would be impossible (because inconsistent) for a utilitarian, for his theory admits only one principle − namely, do that which on the whole maximizes utility. An occupational disease of utilitarians is a blindness to the possibility of genuine moral dilemmas − i.e., a blindness to the possibility that important moral principles can conflict in ways that are not obviously resolvable by a rational decision procedure.

[6] I qualify my thesis by the word "largely" to show at this point my realization, explored in more detail later, that no single theory can account for all criminal behavior.

[7] Bernard Harrison, 'Violence and the Rule of Law', in *Violence*, ed. Jerome A. Shaffer (New York: McKay, 1971), pp. 139−176.

[8] I have made a start toward such a defense in my 'The Killing of the Innocent,' *The Monist* 57, No. 4 (October 1973). (Included in the present collection.)

[9] H. L. A. Hart, 'Prolegomenon to the Principles of Punishment', from *Punishment and Responsibility* (Oxford: Oxford University Press, 1968), pp. 1−27.

[10] Thomas Hill Green, *Lectures on the Principles of Political Obligation* (1885), (Ann Arbor: University of Michigan Press, 1967), pp. 180−205.

[11] For an elaboration of this point, see Steven Lukes, "Alienation and Anomie," in *Philosophy, Politics and Society* (Third Series), ed. Peter Laslett and W. G. Runciman (Oxford: B. H. Blackwell, 1967), pp. 134−156.

[12] Robert Paul Wolff, *In Defense of Anarchism* (New York: Harper, 1970).

[13] In this section, I have adapted some of my previously published material: *Kant: The Philosophy of Right* (London: Macmillan, 1970), pp. 109−112 and 140−144; 'Three Mistakes About Retributivism', *Analysis* 31 (April 1971), pp. 166−169; and 'Kant's Theory of Criminal Punishment', in *Proceedings of the Third International Kant Congress*, ed. Lewis White Beck (Dordrecht: D. Reidel, 1972), pp. 434−441. I am perfectly aware that Kant's views on the issues to be considered here are often obscure and inconsistent

– e.g., the analysis of "willing one's own punishment" which I shall later quote from Kant occurs in a passage the primary purpose of which is to argue that the idea of "willing one's own punishment" makes no sense! My present objective, however, is not to attempt accurate Kant scholarship. My goal is rather is build upon some remarks of Kant's which I find philosophically suggestive.

[14] Immanuel Kant, *The Metaphysical Elements of Justice* (1797), trans. John Ladd (Indianapolis: Bobbs-Merrill, 1965), pp. 35ff.

[15] *Ibid.*, p. 37.

[16] John Rawls, 'Justice as Fairness', *The Philosophical Review* 67 (1958), pp. 164–197; and *A Theory of Justice* (Cambridge, Mass.: Harvard University Press, 1971), especially pp. 17–22.

[17] Immanuel Kant, 'Concerning the Common Saying: This May be True in Theory but Does not Apply in Practice (1793)', in *The Philosophy of Kant*, ed. and trans. Carl J. Friedrich (New York: Random House, 1949), pp. 421–422.

[18] Immanuel Kant, *Perpetual Peace* (1795), trans. by Lewis White Beck in the Kant anthology *On History* (Indianapolis: Bobbs-Merrill, 1963), p. 112.

[19] Immanuel Kant, *The Metaphysical Elements of Justice*, p. 34.

[20] *Ibid.*, pp. 99, 101, and 105, in the order quoted.

[21] In addition to the works on justice by Rawls previously cited, the reader should consult the following for Rawls' application of his general theory to the problem of political obligation: John Rawls, 'Legal Obligation and the Duty of Fair Play', in *Law and Philosophy*, ed. Sidney Hook (New York: New York University Press, 1964), pp. 3–18. This has been reprinted in my anthology *Civil Disobedience and Violence* (Belmont, Cal.: Wadsworth Publishing Company, 1971), pp. 39–52. For a direct application of a similar theory to the problem of punishment, see Herbert Morris, "Persons and Punishment," *The Monist* 52, No. 4 (October 1968) 475–501.

[22] H. L. A. Hart, *The Concept of Law* (Oxford: Oxford University Press, 1961), pp. 189–195.

[23] Jeffrie G. Murphy, 'Moral Death: A Kantian Essay on Psychopathy', *Ethics* 82, No. 4 (July 1972) 284–298.

[24] Banal as this point may seem, it could be persuasively argued that all Enlightenment political theory (e.g., that of Hobbes, Locke and Kant) is built upon ignoring it. For example, once we have substantial empirical evidence concerning how democracies really work in fact, how sympathetic can we really be to classical theories for the justification of democracy? For more on this, see C. B. Macpherson, 'The Maximization of Democracy', in *Philosophy, Politics and Society* (Third Series), ed. Peter Laslett and W. G. Runciman (Oxford: B. H. Blackwell), pp. 83–103. This article is also relevant to the point raised in note 11 above.

[25] This point is well developed in C. B. Macpherson, *The Political Theory of Possessive Individualism* (Oxford: Oxford University Press, 1962). In a sense, this point affects even the formal correctness of a theory. For it demonstrates an empirical source of corruption in the analyses of the very concepts in the theory.

[26] The writings of Willem Adriaan Bonger (1876–1940), a Dutch criminologist, have fallen into totally unjustified neglect in recent years. Anticipating contemporary sociological theories of crime, he was insisting that criminal behavior is in the province of normal psychology (though abnormal society) at a time when most other writers were viewing criminality as a sympton of psychopathology. His major works are: *Criminality and*

Economic Conditions (Boston: Little, Brown, 1916); *An Introduction tc Criminology* (London: Methuen, 1936); and *Race and Crime* (New York: Columbia University Press, 1943).

[27] I say "at least in spirit" to avoid begging the controversial question of whether Marx can be said to embrace a theory of justice. Though (as I suggested in note 4) much of Marx's own evaluative rhetoric seems to overlap more traditional appeals to rights and justice (and a total lack of sympathy with anything like Utilitarianism), it must be admitted that he also frequently ridicules at least the terms "rights" and "justice" because of their apparent entrenchment in bourgeois ethics. For an interesting discussion of this issue, see Allen W. Wood, 'The Marxian Critique of Justice', *Philosophy and Public Affairs* 1, No. 3 (Spring 1972), pp. 244–282.

[28] The importance of community is also, I think, recognized in Gabriel de Tarde's notion of "social similarity" as a condition of criminal responsibility. See his *Penal Philosophy* (Boston: Little Brown, 1912). I have drawn on de Tarde's general account in my 'Moral Death: A Kantian Essay on Psychopathy'.

[29] By "reciprocity" Bonger intends something which includes, but is much richer than, a notion of "fair trading or bargaining" that might initially be read into the term. He also has in mind such things as sympathetic identification with others and tendencies to provide mutual aid. Thus, for Bonger, reciprocity and egoism have a strong tendency to conflict. I mention this lest Bonger's notion of reciprocity be too quickly identified with the more restricted notion found in, for example, Kant and Rawls.

[30] It is interesting how greatly Bonger's analysis differs from classical deterrence theory – e.g., that of Bentham. Bentham, who views men as machines driven by desires to attain pleasure and avoid pain, tends to regard terror as the primary restraint against crime. Bonger believes that, at least in a healthy society, moral motives would function as a major restraint against crime. When an environment that destroys moral motivation is created, even terror (as statistics tend to confirm) will not eradicate crime.

[31] *Introduction to Criminology*, pp. 75–76, and *Criminality and Economic Conditions*, pp. 532, 402, 483–484, 436, and 407, in the order quoted. Bonger explicitly attacks Hobbes: "The adherents of [Hobbes' theory] have studied principally men who live under capitalism, or under civilization; their correct conclusion has been that egoism is the predominant characteristic of these men, and they have adopted the simplest explanation of the phenomenon and say that this trait is inborn." If Hobbists can cite Freud for modern support, Bonger can cite Darwin. For, as Darwin had argued in the *Descent of Man*, men would not have survived as a species if they had not initially had considerably greater social sentiments than Hobbes allows them.

[32] Austin J. Turk, in the Introduction to his abridged edition of Bonger's *Criminality and Economic Conditions* (Bloomington: Indiana University Press, 1969), p. 14.

[33] Statistical data on characteristics of offenders in America are drawn primarily from surveys by the Bureau of Census and the National Council on Crime and Delinquency. While there is of course wide disagreement on how such data are to be interpreted, there is no serious disagreement concerning at least the general accuracy of statistics such as the one I have cited. Even government publications openly acknowledge a high correlation between crime and socio-economic disadvantages: "From arrest records, probation reports, and prison statistics a 'portrait' of the offender emerges that progressively highlights the disadvantaged character of his life. The offender at the end of the road in prison is likely to be a member of the lowest social and economic groups in the country,

poorly educated and perhaps unemployed . . . Material failure, then, in a culture firm-
ly oriented toward material success, is the most common denominator of offenders"
(*The Challenge of Crime in a Free Society, A Report by the President's Commission
on Law Enforcement and Administration of Justice*, U.S. Government Printing Office,
Washington, D.C., 1967, pp. 44 and 160). The Marxist implications of this admission
have not gone unnoticed by prisoners. See Samuel Jorden, 'Prison Reform: In Whose
Interest?' *Criminal Law Bulletin* 7, No. 9 (November 1971), pp. 779–787.

[34] There are, of course, other factors which enter into an explanation of this statistic.
One of them is the fact that economically disadvantaged guilty persons are more likely
to wind up arrested or in prison (and thus be reflected in this statistic) than are economically advantaged guilty persons. Thus economic conditions enter into the explanation,
not just of criminal behavior, but of society's response to criminal behavior. For a
general discussion on the many ways in which crime and poverty are related, see Patricia
M. Wald, 'Poverty and Criminal Justice,' *Task Force Report: The Courts*, U.S. Government Printing Office, Washington, D.C., 1967, pp. 139–151.

[35] The idea that the principles of justice could be proved as a kind of theorem (Rawls'
claim in "Justice as Fairness") seems to be absent, if I understand the work correctly,
in Rawls' recent *A Theory of Justice*. In this book, Rawls seems to be content with
something less than a decision procedure. He is no longer trying to pull his theory
of justice up by its own bootstraps, but now seems concerned simply to *exhibit* a certain
elaborate conception of justice in the belief that it will do a good job of systematizing
and ordering most of our considered and reflective intuitions about moral matters. To
this, of course, the Marxist will want to say something like the following: "The considered and reflective intuitions current in our society are a product of bourgeois culture,
and thus any theory based upon them begs the question against us and in favor of the
status quo." I am not sure that this charge cannot be answered, but I am sure that it
deserves an answer. Someday Rawls may be remembered, to paraphrase Georg Lukacs'
description of Thomas Mann, as the last and greatest philosopher of bourgeois liberalism.
The virtue of this description is that it perceives the limitations of his outlook in a way
consistent with acknowledging his indisputable genius. (None of my remarks here, I
should point out, are to be interpreted as denying that our civilization derived major
moral benefits from the tradition of bourgeois liberalism. Just because the freedoms
and procedures we associate with bourgeois liberalism – speech, press, assembly, due
process of law, etc. – are not the only important freedoms and procedures, we are not
to conclude with some witless radicals that these freedoms are not terribly important
and that the victories of bourgeois revolutions are not worth preserving. My point is
much more modest and noncontroversial – namely, that even bourgeois liberalism
requires a critique. It is not self-justifying and, in certain very important respects, is not
justified at all).

[36] Kant has some doubts about punishing bastard infanticide and duelling on similar
grounds. Given the stigma that Kant's society attached to illegitimacy and the halo that
the same society placed around military honor, it did not seem totally fair to punish
those whose criminality in part grew out of such approved motives. See *Metaphysical
Elements of Justice*, pp. 106–107.

[37] This point is pursued in Herbert Morris, 'Persons and Punishment'. Bonger did
not appreciate that "mental illness," like criminality, may also be a phenomenon of
social class. On this, see August B. Hollingshead and Frederick C. Redlich, *Social Class*

and Mental Illness (New York: Wiley, 1958). On the general issue of punishment versus therapy, see my *Punishment and Rehabilitation* (Belmont, Cal.: Wadsworth Publishing Company, 1973).

INVOLUNTARY ACTS AND CRIMINAL LIABILITY

> What is action? What is inaction? About this even the
> wise are confused.
>
> *Bhagavad-Gita*

INTRODUCTION

Human actions may misfire or reveal defects in a variety of ways. They may be done in ignorance, accidentally, compulsively, or under duress. And when we note the presence of such qualifications, our tendency is to mitigate the agent's responsibility for the action or to excuse its performance entirely. But when actions misfire in some even more basic way (as a result of an epileptic seizure, say) we are tempted not just to mitigate or excuse, but to say that no true human action has been performed at all. We appear to be confronted with nothing more than an event or a mere happening, and talk of excuse here seems to make no more sense than would talk of excusing a rock for falling on one's head.

Such basic pathologies are said, in the criminal law, to result in *involuntary* acts or omissions and to thus fail to satisfy the law's minimal condition for liability − the requirement of an *actus reus*. The practical importance (such as there is) of such a classification of acts and omissions into voluntary and involuntary arises primarily in the area of strict liability offenses − offenses where, roughly, absence of *mens rea* (even absence of negligence) is not allowed as an excuse if the defendant has in fact performed the proscribed act or has in fact omitted to perform that act which was his legal duty.[1] Some motoring offences may be construed in this way. But, if the behavior was involuntary, we are tempted to say that even the action itself was not performed. As Judge Desmond remarked (dissenting) in *People v. Decina*, "One cannot while unconscious 'operate' a car in a culpably negligent manner or in any other manner".[2]

Now some generally agreed cases of involuntary acts in the criminal law are the following: (1) seizures and convulsions (for example, epilepsy); (2) reflex movements (for example, reaction to attack by a swarm of bees); (3)

116

certain forms of drug- or alcohol-induced behavior (for example, behavior resulting from a drug administered to Jones without his knowledge or from his highly atypical reaction to alcohol); and (4) behavior engaged in while asleep or unconscious or (although this is controversial) while under post-hypnotic suggestion.

The uniting principle here, as most texts on the criminal law would state it, is "lack of control over one's movements." But this, of course, is not in itself very philosophically illuminating. Exactly in what does this lack of control consist? How, for example, does it differ from the lack of control over consequences which one failed, nonnegligently, to foresee — consequences which may, according to the criminal law, count as a part of a voluntary act?[3]

THE CLASSICAL ANALYSIS (JOHN AUSTIN)

The classical account on this question, expressed most clearly by John Austin and adopted by such writers as Holmes and Salmond, is *causal* in character. Voluntary acts are acts which have certain kinds of causes (volitions or desires), whereas involuntary acts (or non-acts) have other sorts of causes. And how should we describe the acts so caused? Acoording to the classical account, we should describe them as "muscular contractions". And thus we get the claim that a voluntary act (or act proper) is a "willed muscular contraction" whereas an involuntary act (or non-act) is an "unwilled muscular contraction." Austin puts the point as follows:

It will be admitted on the mere statement, that the only objects which can be called acts, are consequences of Volitions. A voluntary movement of my body, or a movement which follows a volition, is an *act*. The *in*voluntary movements which are the consequences of certain diseases, are *not* acts. But as the bodily movements which immediately follow volitions, are the only ends of volition, it follows that these bodily movements are the only objects to which the term 'acts' can be applied with perfect precision and propriety.[4]

To those whose philosophical nurturing is post-Wittgenstein, these assertions will seem strange. We seem to have a paradigm here of that metaphysical idiocy which is politely called "dualistic interactionism" and has been called by Gilbert Ryle (not so politely) "the dogma of the Ghost in the Machine".[5] The picture conjured up is of a spiritual mind pulling (in some causally mysterious way) the levers which run the body. Indeed, Holmes was inclined to marvel at the "mysterious accuracy with which the adult, who is master of himself, foresees the outward adjustment which would follow the inward effort".[6] If made with respect to a master sculptor or ballet dancer, this has some sense. But with respect to ordinary actions, this sort of remark now strikes us as just extremely funny.

Thus, it is not in the least surprising that the classical analysis of the voluntary-involuntary distinction has fallen upon hard times among contemporary legal philosophers. For example, H. L. A. Hart claims that the classical account of human action "is really nothing more than an out-dated fiction — a piece of eighteenth century psychology which has no real application to human conduct ... [It is] a misleading antiquated piece of philosophical psychology".[7]

Since my utimate purpose is to argue in defense of a form of the classical account, it will be instructive to examine Hart's objections to the Austinian analysis and the account which Hart would offer in its place. I shall argue that his objections misfire and that his own account is seriously defective. Thus, perhaps our only hope for philosophical clarity on this issue is through a resurrection (with some transformation) of the classical theory. This, at any rate, is what I shall attempt.

AN ALTERNATIVE ACCOUNT OF THE INVOLUNTARY (H.L.A. HART)

In his paper "Acts of Will and Responsibility" (n.7 herein), Hart develops two basic objections to the classical account of the involuntary. First, the account cannot plausibly be construed so as to cover involuntary *omissions*. Second, the analysis of action in terms of "muscular contraction" violates both our ordinary and our legal understanding of what an act is.

First, the problem of omissions: The switchman who fails to apply the lever is by no means typically a man whose muscular contractions result in injury. He may be asleep and thus contracting no muscles and making no bodily movements which have any causal connection with the resulting injury. When Prince Mishkin, is an epileptic seizure, flails his arms and breaks a valuable vase, it is not too implausible here to say that his body moved without a desire that it move or without any volition that it move. But this will not do for omissions. Here there is generally a failure to contract rather than any contraction, and it is only in the extremely rare case that a failure to contract certain muscles is to be explained by a desire not to contract them. Omissions are nondoings; and contractions, boring doings though they are, are doings nonetheless.

But if the classical account simply did not work for omissions, this might not be so bad. Perhaps we do need a different account of involuntary omissions than the one we give for involuntary acts. (Hart himself later comes to admit this.) But, Hart argues, the classical theory makes no sense even when applied solely to acts of positive intervention. Most obviously and most importantly, it goes against everything we want to say about acts in both ordinary life and the law. In no penal code, for example, will you find among the list of prohibited acts any prohibitions of muscular contractions — with a few possible exceptions, depending upon how we interpret some obscenity statutes. As P. J. Fitzgerald has put the point in a similar context:

Whatever an act is, both in and out of court, we use the term in a way quite different from Holmes' way. 'Caught in the act, ' for example, conjures up a picture of the burglar creeping away with the swag over his shoulder; of the murderer standing over his victim, bloody knife in hand: not of a criminal contracting various muscles.[8]

Of course, in certain rather esoteric circumstances, we might perform the act of contracting certain muscles. Strippers no doubt learn to do this, and they might be able to bump but not grind if the criminal law so instructed them. But the point here just is that these are esoteric cases. They can hardly be used as paradigms of the typical. The acts here are rarely performed, and most of them are rather difficult to perform. (Try wriggling your ears without moving your eyebrows, for example.) And some of these muscle-contracting acts can be performed only if we do another *kind* of act which cannot be so simply described. For example, the only way I know how to contract my muscles in just that way they are contracted when my arm is raised is to raise my arm. It does not go the other way around.

Thus, it begins to appear that the classical theory is something less than helpful on our question of how we distinguish the voluntary from the involuntary. If there were no other way to draw the distinction, then we might try to refine the theory and bolster it up against these objections. But this, argues Hart, is unnecessary. For there is a simple and plausible alternative account that accords with our ordinary and legal usage of the term "act". This account is in terms not of different sorts of *causes* (volitions, desires) for movements, but rather in terms of some *cognitive states* (being aware of what I am doing, having a reason) which *accompany* the movements. This is, for a variety of reasons, a "more adequate" account.

By a 'more adequate' account I mean one which involves no fictions; which is better fitted to the facts of ordinary experience; and which could be used by the courts in order to identify a range of cases where the requirement of a minimum mental element of responsibility is not satisfied. Such an account could cover both the conscious and unconscious examples suggested in the books, and it would necessarily differ from the kind of general explanation given there in two main ways. First, it would be disassociated from any claim that the ordinary way of talking about actions was inferior to, or less accurate than, the definition of acts as muscular contractions. Secondly, omissions would have to be treated separately from positive interventions. Granted these two things, we could characterize the involuntary movements such as those made in epilepsy, or in a stroke, or mere reflex actions to blows or stings, as *movements of the body which occurred although they were not appropriate, i.e. required for any action (in the ordinary sense of action) which the agent believed himself to be doing.* This, I think, reproduces what is in fact meant by ordinary people when they say a man's bodily movements are 'wild' or 'not governed by the will' in the sense that they are *not subordinated to the agent's conscious plans of action; they do not occur as part of anything the agent takes himself to be doing.*[9]

Here the voluntary is analyzed in terms of "what is appropriate," "what the agent takes himself to be doing," "what his plans are," "what his reasons are,"[10] and "bodily movements which occur as parts of plan". But unfortunately, this analysis simply will not do. As a minimal objection, it should be noted that Hart's statement of his position has been incautious. For example, is the notion of *appropriateness* really appropriate here? Surely not all eccentric actions (for example, a basketball player's "style" in shooting) are involuntary. Also, it is odd to say that bodily movements can or cannot occur as parts of plans. Is this not a simple category mistake? These objections are not too serious, however, for I think that Hart's thesis can easily be doctored up to avoid them (for example, drop "appropriateness," and talk instead of *thoughts* of bodily movements or *intended* bodily movements as parts of plans). I want to pursue more serious objections — objections serious enough to be fatal. For the conditions Hart lists are neither necessary nor sufficient for drawing the voluntary-involuntary act distinction. I can take myself to be doing A as a part of some reasoned plan of action and still be doing A involuntarily; and I can fail to take myself to be so doing A and still be acting voluntarily (in the law's sense in which, for example, negligent acts are voluntary acts — that is, not like strokes, convulsions, etc.).

Consider the following case: Suppose I am seriously playing a game of chess and my finger is close to a piece on the chessboard. In order to further my game plan, I decide at time t to advance the queen's pawn one square. At exactly time t, I have a finger spasm (I am just coming down with Saint Vitus' dance) and the piece moves forward in just the way I intended that it move. I believe that I have moved the piece and, perhaps because the movement is a part of something I take myself to be doing, that I have done so voluntarily. But I am *wrong*! What we have here is a possibility that Hart has quite overlooked — namely, the possibility that one may (a) believe that one is doing something voluntarily and (b) believe this *falsely*. One may have mistaken beliefs or be ignorant about one's capacities or about what movements are in one's control. Thus, here we have an act which satisfies Hart's criterion (occurs as a part of something I take myself to be doing) but which is still surely *involuntary*. This sort of case is going to be difficult (perhaps impossible) to verify with any certainty; but its possibility can be meaningfully described. And this is all we need to attack Hart's analysis of the *concept* of the voluntary. I do not think that Hart wants to save his theory by resorting to the verifiability criterion of meaning.

But Hart's analysis has another defect — one which is, from a legal point of view, even more grave: at least some *negligent* acts are now, on Hart's criterion, going to count as involuntary. But this is just what we do not want. We want to hold people responsible for negligence but not for involuntary acts. And we also want an explanation of how absence of *mens rea* (especially absence of negligence) is different from absence of *actus reus*. For in a strict liability case, we will want to hold a man liable even if he was not negligent — but *not* if his act was caused by stroke, attack by a swarm of bees, etc. Thus, if Hart's analysis does not sharply distinguish involuntariness from negligence, it is legally useless.

Consider then, with this in mind, another kind of case: Suppose I have been shingling my roof and am resting with the hammer in my hand — idly dreaming until my wife calls me for lunch. When she calls I get up to go down and *quite without thinking* I toss the hammer down. As it happens, the hammer is tossed too close to the edge of the roof, slips over, falls, and kills a passerby below. This has happened not as a part of anything I took myself to be doing. (I either did not take myself to be doing anything or took myself to be going down to lunch; and killing the man below was not a contemplated part of either.) Yet my act — from a legal point of view — was voluntary. It was not like having a stroke, etc.; and in fact, I am likely to be guilty of criminal manslaughter — causing death to another human being through negligence. Thus, Hart has manifestly failed to zero in on the problem of involuntary acts in the criminal law — on the problem of how having a stroke, for example, differs from just being grossly careless.

In view of the failure of Hart's analysis, it might be worth taking a fresh look at the classical account once agsin. There might be something in it worth saving after all.

THE CLASSICAL ANALYSIS RECONSIDERED
(CAUSATION AND MEANING)

Given the devastating appearance of Hart's attack on the classical theory, any attempt at its resurrection may seem doomed from the outset. I would suggest, however, that the devastating appearance of Hart's attack is just appearance and nothing more. Indeed, his whole case rests upon the commission of an *ignoratio elenchi*. The classical theory in fact contains *two distinct claims* which Hart fails to distinguish. Thus, in refuting the one, he believes (quite wrongly) that he has refuted the other. The two claims are the following: (1) the difference between a voluntary act and an involuntary act is a *causal* difference, and (2) acts are to be analyzed as movements of the body or as muscular contractions.

Claim (1) is a causal theory of the involuntary-voluntary distinction, whereas (2) is an attempted analysis of the meaning of the concept *act*. And Hart's case against (2) is in fact quite devastating. His error, however, is the failure to come to grips with (1). Either he believes (falsely) that a refutation of (2) counts as a refutation of (1) or he just overlooks (1) entirely. At any rate, he gives us no developed case against it. And therefore he fails to come to grips with what is surely the *most important* claim made in the classical account. This is extremely odd, since one of Hart's major departures from the classical account is his replacement of causal talk with talk of accompanying cognitive states. Thus, it is odd that we do not get from him any substantial argument against the challenging alternative.

Hart could, of course, stress his insistence that he is interested in an account which could be easily applied by the ordinary man in the jury box. But to insist on this is, of course, to beg one of the central questions at issue. For if the account that we give of the involuntary is causal in character, then (at least sometimes) it will be necessary to consider empirical scientific evidence with respect to the question, Was Jones' conduct voluntary or not? And this is not always the sort of evidence that the ordinary man, unaided, can grasp in a straightforward, commonsense way. He will need to rely on testimony of expert witnesses — particularly psychologists and neurophysiologists — concerning the mechanisms involved.

Thus, as I interpret the major thrust of the classical theory, it is an attempt to give an account of the voluntary-involuntary distinction in terms of causal factors — or, if one does not like the word "causal," in terms of scientific, law-like explanation. And this kind of account can be made out even if it is granted that the classical analysis of "act" (in terms of muscular contractions) is fatally defective. For we can modify the classical theory in the following way: Acts, of course, must sometimes be more broadly described than as mere muscular contractions. However, even given a broader decription (for example, "shooting Jones"), we can still raise the question of the action's *cause* — Why did it *occur*? and not just How do we analyze its *meaning*? If its causes are in terms of desires and volitions or reasons of the agent, then the act is voluntary. If the causes lie elsewhere (brain lesions, etc.), then the act is involuntary.[11]

Questions of the causal sort (Why did it occur?) seem to be the sort of questions on which scientific evidence is available and scientific testimony appropriate. This explains, I think, why the legal profession is still properly puzzled by actions performed under posthypnotic suggestion as candidates for involuntary acts. We simply do not have enough scientific evidence yet on just what the causal connections are. We do not fully understand the mechanisms involved. Our puzzlement, then, lies in the domain of the empirical, the scientific, the causal — *not the conceptual*. We are not puzzled about whether or not the man under posthypnotic suggestion takes or does not take what he does to be a part of some plan of his. Even if he does, we might want ultimately to say (given what we might come to know about such cases) that this does not matter, that his acts are involuntary *anyway*. This is why a reference to consciousness *simpliciter* cannot resolve our perplexities. Such a reference will be useful only if supplemented by a scientific theory which locates the role of consciousness in the mechanism. Otherwise, the reference will idle, will fail to explain.[12] Since Freud, we are used to talking beyond the conscious. This has almost become our *ordinary* way of talking.

Now in response to what I have argued thus far, Hart might reply as follows: It is a mistake to believe that your claims (1) and (2) are in fact logically independent. As soon as you analyze actions in terms broader than muscular contractions, you *logically* must make reference to the agent's mental states. Since certain desires and intentions will thus figure into the description of the action, they cannot also serve as causal explanations for the action. As Hume taught us, necessary connection precludes causal connection. Thus, motives, desires, reasons, and intentions are *not causes*; and the classical theory fails here.[13]

Can reasons be causes? To explore this dispute in any detail would involve us in a metaphysical excursion far beyond the scope of this paper. However, a few brief observations are in order. If we are reluctant to allow mental states to play a role in causal explanations, this might be for two reasons. First, we might have been persuaded by Ryle that mentalistic explanations are ghostly and Cartesian — that they commit us to a mind-body dualism. Or we might have been persuaded (by Melden, Peters, etc.) that, since mental states necessarily figure in the description of actions, they cannot causally explain actions. Against both these thrusts, it is worth noting the following:

(i) We need to distinguish the question Are mental states ghostly? from the question Are mental states capable of figuring in causal or scientific explanations? Surely we can, with Ryle, answer no to the first question without, on these grounds, answering no to the second question.

(ii) We have to question the intelligibility and truth of "Hume's law" that necessary connection precludes causal connection. For example, do not feet cause footprints?[14]

Let me elaborate: Might it not be the case that some form of the identity theory is true? Might not sensations or other mental states just be brain processes? Mental-state terms and brain-process terms do not of course *mean* the same thing, but might they not *name* the same things? That is, might not mental states and brain processes be *contingently identical*? If so, then explanations of actions in terms of mental states will not be in the least ghostly or dualistic. Also, even if "desire for *A*" is necessarily connected with "act *A*," it will not follow that brain-state *B* (contingently identical with the desire for *A*) is so connected; and it is perhaps *B* which explains the *occurrence* of act *A* though not, of course, the *meaning* of "act *A*" or the *meaning* of "desiring *A*." I am not proposing a defense for the identity theory. All I am suggesting is the following: If the truth of the identity theory is even a *possibility*, then we cannot rule out the classical account of the involuntary for purely *conceptual* reasons. Our language hardened before we knew any neurophysiology, and so it is not in the least surprising that mental-state talk does not find its meaning (use) in terms of brain-state talk. But this may just be one of those instances which Bertrand Russell described where our language encapsulates the metaphysics of the Stone Age.

When, then, is an act or omission involuntary? I tentatively propose the following: An act or omission is involuntary if and only if the behavior or the failure in question is explainable by factors which causally prevent the exercise of normal capacities of control or eliminate such capacities entirely. By "causally prevent" here I mean simply the following: that the factors and the incapacity can be related by subsumption under a scientific law.[15] Thus: Prince Mishkin acted involuntarily (or did not really act at all, if you prefer) in breaking the vase, because epilepsy is a factor which we know to be related (in a lawlike way) to capacities of control. The switchman who fails to pull the lever omitted to do so involuntarily if, for example, he was having a seizure at the time he was supposed to be pulling the lever. The merely negligent man, however, has the normal capacities. He simply did not exercise them.[16]

CONCLUDING REMARKS

Why do we feel a requirement to excuse the man whose actions are involuntary? Not merely for utilitarian reasons, surely. As Hart himself notes, a penal code so Draconian as to punish even epileptics might have high general deterrence and little disutility (as long as most of us could be fairly sure of not becoming epileptic.) So another important reason against holding liable here is justice or fairness. And we always feel the pressure to take account of justice or fairness — even in strict liability cases. We may hold a man liable without fault in some areas and thus punish him even if he was not negligent — even if he took all reasonable care. But we would surely object to this on grounds of justice (no matter how high the general utility) if the man did not have fair warning that this was an area of conduct in which he might have to expect this sort of thing.[17] A drug manufacturer is under danger of strict liability prosecution for any faultless adulteration in his product. But we do not object to this as much as we otherwise might as long as he is given fair warning to choose to do something else with his life if he is not willing to assume this kind of risk. If he does many things to protect his product and fails, then we can always say that he could have done more. A strict liability statute roughly tells you the following: Exercise your capacities to prevent injury; and the only way you can prove that you have exercised them sufficiently is to succeed in preventing injury.[18]

But compare strokes, seizures, and the like. We do not have any capacities to exercise when these are operative. And thus, by no stretch of the imagination can we regard their punishment as fair. When one is suffering a seizure, normal capacities just do not enter the picture. Of course, there may have been a *history* of such seizures. Then we might reasonably require that a man subject to seizures not put himself into a position (for example, driving a car) where having one is likely to result in harm. But even here, however, we should still have a separate offense so defined as, say, "operation by an epileptic of a motor vehicle." For it is unfair, if the recklessness consists in operating the vehicle at all, to get just those who happen to cause injury when they actually have a seizure — especially since at the time of the injury, the defendant (since busy with his seizure) can hardly be said to be *operating* a vehicle at all and thus not operating it recklessly.

When an act is involuntary, when it is explained by causal or lawlike reference to factors which eliminate normal capacities, the *agent* (the only intelligible object of act attribution) drops out. It is on its way out when we plead absence of *mens rea*. It is all the way out when we plead absence of a voluntary act (no *actus reus*). In the normal case, if asked what caused the injury, we shall reply that the agent caused it ("Jones did it"). If the defendant was having a seizure, however, our temptation will be to cite his seizure and not him as the cause. And it does not make sense to hold seizures criminally liable. Our ordinary notions of responsibility rest upon agent causation. When the causation is not agent causation, the ordinary notions have no application.

NOTES

[1] Some lawyers might not be happy with this characterization of strict liability, for they might argue that an offense is strict if it does not *mention* a specific mental state as one of the material or defining elements of the offense. But this is surely at least controversial. One might plausibly argue that a requirement of *mens rea* is a common-law presupposition and that if it is not explicitly ruled out in the statute, then the statute must not be construed as imposing strict liability (see *Morisette v. United States*, Supreme Court of the United States, 1952; 342 U.S. 246, 72 Sup. Ct. 240, 96 L. Ed. 288).

[2] New York Court of Appeals, 1956; 2 N.Y. 2d 133, 138 N.E. 2d 799.

[3] My concern in this paper is with the *legal* use of the involuntary-voluntary distinction, but it is important to see how this differs from our ordinary use. According to the law, we have a voluntary act whenever the *actus reus* requirement is satisfied, and only cases such as seizures and convulsions (negating *actus reus*) are called involuntary. This means that an act performed under duress, which we would ordinarily resist calling a voluntary act will be so called in the law, for it is surely not like a seizure or convulsion. This has little practical importance, of course, because actions performed under duress – though called voluntary and satisfying the legal requirements of an *actus reus* – will typically be excused on other grounds, for example, absence of *mens rea* or simply duress as a separate defense. It is particularly important to note, for reasons that will become clear later in the paper, that *negligent* acts and omissions satisfy the law's requirement of an *actus reus* and are thus not to be regarded as involuntary.

[4] John Austin, *Lectures on Jurisprudence* (London: John Murray, 1885), lecture 18, p. 414. See also Oliver Wendell Holmes, *The Common Law* (Boston: Little Brown, 1881); John Salmond, *Jurisprudence*, 11th edn. (London: Sweet & Maxwell, 1957); and Walter Wheeler Cook, 'Act, Intention and Motive', *Yale Law Journal* 26, (1917) 645–651.

[5] Gilbert Ryle, *The Concept of Mind* (London: Hutchinson, 1949).

[6] Holmes, p. 54.

[7] H. L. A. Hart, 'Acts of Will and Responsibility,' In *Punishment and Responsibility* (Oxford: Oxford University Press, 1968), p. 101; this originally appeared in *Jubilee Lectures of the Faculty of Law*, University of Sheffield, ed. O.R. Marshall (Sheffield: Sheffield University Press, 1960).

[8] P. J. Fitzgerald, 'Voluntary and Involuntary Acts', in *Oxford Essays in Jurisprudence*, ed. A. G. Guest (Oxford: Oxford University Press, 1961), p. 8.

[9] Hart, pp. 104–5; italics my own.

[10]   Hart adds the notion of *reasons* in his notes for the republication of this essay in *Punishment and Responsibility* (n. 7 above), pp. 255–56.

[11]   Recall the two cases I used against Hart. Regardless of how conscious the chess player was of what he believed he was doing, we want to say that his finger movement was involuntary (whether he knew it or not) because there was a flaw in his causal mechanism. Our negligent man's act, on the other hand, did not involve any foul-up in his causal mechanism and was thus voluntary – whether he was conscious of what he did or not. Thus, the analysis I propose in fact squares better than Hart's with ordinary and legal judgment here.

[12]   "A reference to consciousness, or perhaps to intention, in the conditions for ascribing knowledge to a person, merely sets the problem and does not solve it. For it is precisely those concepts which must be explained if we are to understand what it is to ascribe a capacity to a person rather than to his body or brain alone" (Thomas Nagel, 'The Boundaries of Inner Space', *Journal of Philosophy* 66, no. 14 [July 24, 1969], p. 456). Nagel is worried about the problem of tacit-knowledge claims as having explanatory value in psychology, but his skepticism about appeals to consciousness *simpliciter* has application to our present worry.

[13]   Several well-known recent books have argued that reasons cannot be causes or that reason explanations are incompatible with causal explantions (for example, G. E. M. Anscombe, *Intention* [Oxford: B. H. Blackwell, 1959]; A. I. Melden, *Free Action* [London: Routledge & Kegan Paul, 1961]; and R. S. Peters, *The Concept of Motivation* [London: Routledge & Kegan Paul, 1958]). In a footnote on p. 99 of *Punishment and Responsibility* (n. 7 above), Hart indicates sympathy with this general position.

[14]   See Donald Davidson, 'Actions, Reasons, and Causes', *Journal of Philosophy* 60, (1963) 685–700. In my judgment, Davidson has presented a nearly fatal case against the view that reasons cannot be causes. If Hart or anyone else proposes to assume that reasons, intentions, motives, desires, etc., cannot be causes, he *must* come to grips with Davidson's arguments.

[15]   Hart himself seems to subscribe to such a general view for omissions. Though he does not talk about relevant causes, he does rely on the notion of normal capacities. I do not see, and he does not explain, why this sort of account will not do for acts of positive intervention (see Hart, p. 106).

[16]   See Note 11 above.

[17]   "Engrained in our concept of due process is the requirment of notice" (Mr. Justice Douglas delivering the majority opinion in *Lambert v. California*, Supreme Court of the United States, 1957; 355 U.S. 225, 78 Sup. Ct. 240, 2 L. Ed. 2d 228).

[18]   For a general discussion of strict criminal liability, see Richard A. Wasserstrom, 'Strict Liability in the Criminal Law', *Stanford Law Review* 12, (1960) 730–45. I do not myself believe that strict criminal liability is morally justified even in cases where the defendant has been warned of the risk, but this is a topic for another paper.

MORAL DEATH: A KANTIAN ESSAY ON PSYCHOPATHY*

> No man is entirely without moral feeling, for were he completely lacking in capacity for it he would be morally dead. And if ... the moral life-force could no longer excite this feeling, then humanity would dissolve ... into mere animality and be mixed irrevocably with the mass of other natural beings.
>
> Immanuel Kant[1]

> The psychopath ... is incapable of kindness and consideration for the rights of others, and he is lacking in gratitude, affection, or compassion .... Whether judged in the light of his conduct, of his attitude, or of material elicited in psychiatric examination, he shows almost no sense of shame. ... He does not ... show the slightest evidence of major humiliation or regret. This is true of matters pertaining to his personal and selfish pride and to esthetic standards that he avows as well as to moral or humanitarian matters. If Santayana is correct in saying that "perhaps the true dignity of man is his ability to despise himself," the psychopath is without a means to acquire true dignity.
>
> Hervey Cleckley[2]

INTRODUCTION

This paper is concerned with an examination of the rights and responsibilities of those individuals having what psychoanalysts, psychiatrists, and psychologists call *psychopathic*, *sociopathic*, or *antisocial* personalities.[3] But it is also what Wilfrid Sellars has called a set of "variations on a Kantian theme." For in coming to terms with the concept of psychopathy, one is also forced to come to terms with the question of what it is to be a *person* – an individual having the value which Kant calls "dignity" (*Würde*) and thereby meriting that special kind of respect which in entailed by a moral commitment to justice rather than mere utility. I developed some thoughts on this in my book *Kant: The Philosophy of Right*, and this paper represents further thinking on the issue and a substantial rejection of much that I said in the book. In the book I argued (against H. J. Paton, primarily) that it is *Willkür* (capacity to choose) and not *Wille* (moral autonomy) which confers dignity or worth upon persons. In thinking about the psychopath, however, and in trying to develop a rational defense for my intuition that any such individuals would lack dignity or worth as persons, I have come to think that Paton was right after all — that it is *Wille* or moral autonomy, and not merely the capacity to choose, which makes the moral difference. Paton, however, had never been successful in articulating a theoretical defense for his correct intuition; and filling this theoretical gap will be one of my primary tasks in what follows.[4]

THE CONCEPT OF PSYCHOPATHY

A problem of growing concern, particularly in the criminal law, is the existence of psychopaths — a class which, according to some researchers, is on the increase in our highly fragmented and alienated society. Psychopaths constitute the class of so-called habitual criminals, and the law is becoming more and more concerned with what to do to, with, or for them. Should they, for example, be excused from criminal responsibility on the grounds that psychopathy is a mental disease? This single question poses serious problems of great difficulty. For unlike the psychotic, the psychopath seems to suffer from no obvious cognitive or volitional impairments. He knows what he is doing (he has no delusions); and, since he typically does just what he wants to do, it would be odd to call him compulsive or to claim that he acts on irresistible impulses. Thus, he is by no means clearly "insane" by currently accepted medical or legal standards. We seem simply left, then, with the fact of his continual wrongdoing; and yet surely we do not want to let acts of wrongdoing be their own excuse. Thus, some criteria for the identification of psychopathy, independent of wrongdoing itself, must be located before one can be in a position to assess the responsibility of the psychopath.

Now some writers on this topic, Baroness Wootton, for example,[5] argue that any criterion will ultimately be circular — will ultimately boil down simply to wrongdoing, which can hardly itself be an excuse for wrongdoing. What always happens, according to Wootton, is the following: A man is charged with a crime, and his lawyer argues that he should be excused from responsibility for the crime on the grounds that he is a psychopath or suffers from some related mental aberration. When one then wants to know what evidence there is that the individual charged does in fact so suffer, the "evidence" produced consists largely of his history of wrongdoing and perhaps even of a description of the very act he is at present charged with! The circle here is obvious; and, if psychiatrists could do no better in formulating criteria for the disorder, Wootton's skepticism would be quite in order.

Some psychiatrists, however, though they would agree with Wootton's description of what often goes on in the courtroom, would also argue that a better and threfore noncircular criterion for psychopathy can be formulated. For example, Cleckley[6] and the McCords[7] maintain that there are clinically identifiable criteria for psychopathy that are independent (both causally and logically) from criminal wrongdoing. Indeed, some prominent politicians and industrialists (even, I am sure, some academics), though not legally criminals, may satisfy these criteria.

What are the criteria? In general, these clinicians want to argue that the psychopath is to be identified as an individual who lacks what in the eighteenth century was generally called *moral feeling* or a *moral sense*, what Kant also called *respect for duty*, and what we all ordinarily call a *conscience*. It is significant and illuminating, I think, that the disorder, first noted clinically in the nineteenth century, was initially called "moral insanity." Though psychopaths know, in some sense, what it means to wrong people, to act immorally, this kind of judgment has for them no motivational component at all. They do not *care* about others or their duties to them; have no *concern* for others' rights and feelings, do not *accept responsibility*, and do not know what it is like to defer one's own gratifications out of *respect* for the dignity of another human being. Quite significantly, they feel no *guilt, regret, shame,* or *remorse* (though they may superficially fake these feelings) when they have engaged in harmful conduct. They are paradigms of individuals whom Kant would call "morally dead."

Now the notions of moral feeling and moral sense obviously stand in need of philosophical, not merely psychological, explication.[8] For example, can a man who feels no motivation to do *A* really be said to have made the judgment that *A* is morally right? Writers such as R. M. Hare, who believe that moral judgments are to be analyzed as prescriptions entailing imperatives, would answer this question in the negative. Though I believe that Hare is wrong on this, it is not this aspect of the issue that I want to pursue in this paper.[9] Neither am I concerned to argue about the clinical criteria *as* clinical criteria — that is, I have no interest here in discussing any of the empirical issues concerning psychopathy (e.g., are there now adequate diagnostic techniques for clinically recognizing all psychopaths and distinguishing them from individuals suffering from psychotic and neurotic disorders?). What I am interested in is the following: Supposing there are such individuals as described above — individuals who are morally dead in that they lack care, concern, respect, guilt. How should we respond to them? Are they responsible? Do they have rights? In answering no to both of these questions, I hope to illuminate the ideas of responsibility and rights. Thus, my interest here is primarily philosophical rather than practical; and the ideas I shall develop, for reasons I shall note at the conclusion of the paper, may have very limited or no legitimate application in legal reform.

RIGHTS, OBLIGATIONS, AND RESPONSIBILITY

It has been common for moral philosophers to approach the issue of moral and legal responsibility in terms of the free will-determinism controversy. Some, however, have wanted to go via different routes; and it is with one such different route that I shall be concerned here. I want to explore and develop the theory of responsibility sketched in the early part of this century by the eminent French penologist and legal philosopher Gabriel de Tarde in his book *Penal Philosophy*.[10] De Tarde's conviction is that the free will-determinism controversy is a red herring in disputes about responsibility. Determinism, he maintains, is obviously and universally true. It is true, without exception, of the criminal, the saint, and of each one of us that there are sufficient antecedent causal conditions that explain the occurrence of any action any of these persons performs. Thus, if we want to draw a responsible-nonresponsible distinction, this will have to be drawn *within* the class of determined actions. For the class of metaphysically (or, as C. A. Campbell would say, "contra-causally")[11] free actions is empty.

How might such a distinction be drawn? How can a theory of excuses or responsibility be formulated consistent with determinism? (A theory of excuses must be able to draw a distinction between responsibility and non-responsibility. And, as Clarence Darrow clearly saw, if one tries to build such a theory on any distinction between determinism and metaphysical freedom, the emptiness of the second class will dictate that the theory of excuses take the form so often used by Darrow in court: Determinism is true; therefore everyone should be excused for everything. But this — as Darrow clearly *failed* to see — is not a theory of excusing at all, for it necessarily fails to draw for us any of the relevant sorts of distinction that we would expect from such a theory.) Now de Tarde suggests that our criterion of responsibility should be based on two notions: *social similarity* and *personal identity*. What we really want to know about a man in judging his responsibility is (1) if he is sufficiently like his fellows in certain relevant respects and (2) if he has a sufficiently continuous conscious history to count as a person. I want here to ignore (2) — primarily relevant for the case of psychotics — and concentrate on (1).

What de Tarde is getting at, and this view would be at least partly shared by other compatibilists such as Hume and H. L. A. Hart, is that a responsible man is not one whose behavior was uncaused but, rather, one whose behavior was caused by normal or typical causes of behavior (desires, volitions, beliefs, etc.) and not by abnormal or atypical causes (epileptic seizures, blows on the head, etc.). To punish men in the latter class would be like punishing strangers or foreigners to the community. (This theory of responsibility, by the way, may help us make some sense of the title of Camus' famous novel *L'Etranger* — a novel about a criminal psychopath.)[12]

Why the emphasis on normality? De Tarde is inclined to let his theory rest upon an institutional fact — namely, that for all our talk about free will, it is really the notion of social similarity which operates in our actual practical judgments of excuse. Indeed, when a law court inquires into whether a confession, say, was freely signed, it is pretty clear that the inquiry is into the *kind of cause* (did the prisoner desire to sign it, was he coerced under threats, etc.) and *not*, surely, into whether it was signed as a result of the prisoner's "contra-causal freedom." Very well. This is, at least latently, our ordinary practice. But is our ordinary practice reasonable? This worry de Tarde leaves practically untouched.

Now I should like to suggest that no theory of responsibility can be developed in the abstract — in isolation from a theory of obligation. Thus, I shall here sketch a theory of obligation, a Kantian quasi-social-contract theory,[13] which in my judgment lends great plausibility to de Tarde's intuitions about responsibility and social similarity. I do not know (or at this point care) if it will work for all kinds of cases; but it does, I think allow us to say something plausible about the psychopath.

Before passing to the theory of obligation, however, it is important to note at the outset that de Tarde's theory of responsibility has one grave defect which any acceptable development of the theory will have to patch up — namely, that social dissimilarity *simpliciter* will excuse not merely the psychopath, but the moral saint or hero as well. And this is surely an unacceptable consequence. For example, we surely do not want to regard principled civil disobedients such as Gandhi and Martin Luther King, Jr., as nonresponsible for their actions simply because they differ from the rest of us in the makeup of their characters. I shall argue, however, that this defect in de Tarde's account is remediable. For what needs to be done is to develop the theory not just in terms of similarity or dissimilarity *simpliciter* but, rather, in terms of similarity or dissimilarity with regard to *certain specific charac-teristics* — for example, moral motivation, capacity to conform one's conduct to rules, and the like. If this is done, then we may be able to show that persons such as Gandhi, though dissimilar from the general community in terms of the *courage* of their convictions, are not different (as is the psychopath) in terms of the relevant characteristic of having a *moral sense*. The difficulty, of course, is in showing just what characteristics are conceptually tied to obliga-tion and responsibility (why moral sense is relevant, for example, and courage is not); and it is to this task that I shall now pass.

I should argue that talk about *obligation* (as opposed to talk merely about what we *ought* to do or what would be *good* to do on grounds of utility) is necessarily tied down to social practices or institutions.[14] Obligations are necessarily institutional in character, arising with respect to, and only with respect to, social practices — for example, legal systems, the promising "game," and the like. For example, I ought to be kind to any child, but I am *obligated* to be kind only to *my* child — because of the institution of parenthood. Also, I should argue that the notion of *a right* (though not, of course, the notion of what it *is right* to do) is similarly institutional in character.[15] I ought to be benevolent, it would be good for me to be benevolent, but no one (barring some special institutional arrangement such as marriage) can demand my benevolence as a right. I am *obligated* to keep my promises, however, and others can legitimately demand this by *right*. Kant was, I think, working toward this point in his distinction between perfect duties (duties of respect) and imperfect duties (duties of love). Perfect duties, resting on rights, may be legitimately coerced. Not so with imperfect duties. To violate an imperfect duty is to do something wrong, but it is not to wrong anyone. For imperfect duties rest not upon rights, but primarily upon the goodness of satisfying desires.

To neglect mere duties of love is *lack of virtue*. But to neglect duty that proceeds from the *respect* due to every man as such is *vice*. For no one is wronged when we neglect duties of love; but if we fail in a duty of respect, then a man is deprived of his lawful claim ... Violation of a duty of respect is not only a want of moral embellishment; it even removes the value of the respect that would otherwise *stand* the subject *in good stead*, and is therefore vice. For this reason, too, duties to one's fellow-men which arise from the respect due them are expressed only negatively ... by the prohibition of the opposite.[16]

Now what are the presuppositions of the intelligibility of the obligation-rights body of moral discourse? To put the question in a Kantian transcendental way: What is required to make obligation- and rights-creating institutions possible? I should argue, with Kant and John Rawls,[17] that one important condition is that of *reciprocity* or *fairness*. That is, the very possibility of institutions (as systems of rules) rests upon the general willingness of those persons involved in them to defer the gratification of their desires by recognizing and respecting the (at least *prima facie*) obligations that they have, to their fellows, to abide by the demands of the practice — *particularly* when these demands conflict with their desires. A practice which allowed the violation of its rules in all cases where the individuals bound *simply desired* such violation could not (*logically* could not) truly count as a practice or system of *rules* at all. Such reciprocity (self-restraint on the assumption that others will exercise comparable restraint in similar circumstances) is thus a presupposition for the very intelligibility of obligation-rights talk. Jones, in claiming a right (and thereby noting someone else's obligation) under a practice, speaks legitimately only insofar as he is prepared to recognize *and respect* his obligation to defer to others' rights in similar kinds of circumstances. Justice, to put it briefly, can apply only to those having a sense of justice.

We are now in a position to return to the psychopath. He is socially dissimilar from the majority of his fellows in his lack of moral feeling, by his failure to be motivated by a recognition of the rights of others and the obligations he has to them. *Thus, he is in no position to claim rights for himself.* He violates a condition for the possibility of reciprocity which is, I have argued, in turn a presupposition for the intelligibility of the whole obligation-rights language game. And this explains (in a way which should not please the psychopath) why he *may* (though not necessarily must) be excused from responsibility and punishment — namely, punishment may be regarded as a *right*, and he is in no position to claim rights.[18]

But who would want to claim such a painful right? This is an obvious question, but one susceptible to an obvious answer. The right to be punished and regarded as a responsible agent, though sometimes painful when honored, at least leaves one's status as a moral person intact. One here gets what he has a right to in the sense that he deserves it, having brought it on himself by his choices. Thus, practices of punishment and responsibility are compatible with a recognition of human dignity in that they place a premium upon the status of persons as choosing beings. One alternative to this is *coercive therapy*. One here gets not what one deserves but, rather, what one (in some paternalistic sense) *needs* — perhaps a total restructuring of one's personality. (Two novels which would give the reader some idea of what this may amount to are Anthony Burgess' *A Clockwork Orange* and Ken Kesey's *One Flew over the Cuckoo's Nest*.)[19] When one sees that this is a possible alternative to responsibility and punishment, one might very well want to insist on one's right to be punished — one's right to be taken seriously as a person.

Now before developing further thoughts on the psychopath, I should like to pause in anticipation of one objection that the reader may want to raise against what I have said thus far. It might be thought that, by conceptually linking rights with social institutions or practices, I am ruling out the possibility of there being what some philosophers have called *natural* rights, rights that persons may have antecedent to their participation in any social institutions. But this thought is mistaken. Natural rights, I should agree, do differ from conventional (e.g., legal) rights in that they may not be recognized within some particular practice or institution. However, I should argue that they are still conceptually linked to the idea of institutions in the following way: that natural rights, whatever else they may be, are rights a person may claim only insofar as he possesses those characteristics (particularly a sense of justice) which would make his membership in some institution or other *possible*. A man does not lack natural rights simply in virtue of the fact that he *actually* fails to participate in a social institution that recognizes them, but he cannot be said to have natural rights if he is the sort of being who is constitutionally *incapable of real participation* in cooperative social institutions or practices of any kind. For such incapacity would surely be sufficient to block the primary kind of argument in which natural rights talk is employed: "Jones has a *natural* right to *P*; therefore, we should modify our institutions in such a way that Jones can participate sufficiently to enjoy a *legal* right to *P*." Such an argument is in place in many cases (e.g., with respect to slaves and the right to liberty), but it is quite out of place when its potential beneficiary is a psychopath.

Indeed, the psychopath seems in a *worse* position with respect to claiming natural rights than he might be in claiming legal or conventional rights. We might continue to recognize the legal or conventional rights of a psychopath, of a man without a sense of justice, not because they are *owed to him* or because he *deserves* then personally, but because we have loyalty to the institution or practice itself and want to preserve it — even at the expense of some pretense about a few of the individuals who benefit from the institution. That is, we might (for example) keep our promises even to psychopaths because we (i) value the institution of promising and (ii) believe that our opting out —

even when we have judged that we are dealing with a psychopath – would damage the institution. In other words, Kant's first formulation of the Categorical Imperative ("Act only on that Maxim which you could simultaneously will to be a universal law") may give us good *prima facie* grounds for keeping our promises even to psychopaths. For we may not be willing to universalize the maxim "I shall opt out of my promise whenever I judge that I am dealing with a psychopath." (The worry here, which I shall explore further in the final section of the paper, concerns the legitimacy of extending a liberty of *judgment* which would invite substantial abuse and self-deception on grounds of self-interest.) When we consider Kant's second formulation of the Categorical Imperative ("Act so as to treat humanity always as an end in itself and never as a means only"), however, it seems singularly inapplicable to the psychopath. For reasons already hinted at, and to be elaborated in the next section, it is difficult to make any sense of the notion of a psychopath as an end in himself, as a creature having the value Kant calls "dignity." If this is so, of course, then the psychopath cannot be wronged, can be done no moral injury.

This, then, completes the point about natural rights: Since with respect to natural rights there is (by definition) no practice or institution to be preserved, any argument based on an analogy with the promising game for treating the psychopath as if he had rights will misfire. Thus, the only possible argument for regarding the psychopath as having natural rights would have to be based upon his dignity or worth as a person. But this is just what he does not have! Indeed, as I shall later argue, he is more profitably pictured – from the moral point of view – as an *animal*.

Before exploring this tendentious point, I should like to note in passing that the machinery developed thus far in the paper is sufficient to show why any political theory that is Hobbesian in character is doomed to failure. The men he imagines in a natural state (motivated solely by the egoistic desire for personal satisfaction and the preservation of their own lives) are *all psychopaths*. Thus, lacking a sense of justice, they do not satisfy the necessary conditions for the possibility of social institutions; and thus on this basis no theory of political obligation (dictating the necessity of civil government and the moral obligation to obey the law) can be generated. This becomes immediately apparent when we notice (i) that Hobbes' third Law of Nature – *justice* or the *obligation to honor covenants* – is absolutely required to justify on social-contract theory the passage from a state of nature to civil society an (ii) that this third law cannot be generated from purely egoistic premises, the only kind of premises Hobbes' theory allows.[20] From purely egoistic premises, one can generate only the *prudential maxim* to "honor covenants only so long as it is in my interest to do so" and never the *moral obligation* to "honor my covenants, because justice demands it, even when so doing may interfere with my self-interest." A man (such as the psychopath) who could never sincerely avow the latter principle is a man uniquely *un*qualified for membership in civil society, for he is a man in whose life obligation *cannot matter*.

PSYCHOPATHY AND MORAL PERSONALITY

Psychopaths, I have argued, are in no position to claim any rights on grounds of moral merit or desert. We can act wrongly with respect to them, but they cannot be wronged. They can be injured, but they can be done no moral injury. This indicates to me that, from the moral point of view, it is very implausible to regard them as *persons* at all.[21] For it seems to me that it is the possession of rights that morally distinguishes *persons* (objects of respect and dignity in Kant's sense) from *animals*.[22] Because animals are sentient creatures, there are things — on grounds of utility — that we ought not to do to them. But it makes little sense to worry about the *rights* of animals, for they do not satisfy the presuppositions for the intelligibility of this kind of talk.[23] Thus, the psychopath, by his failure to care about his own moral responsibilities, his failure to accept them even if he recognizes them,[24] becomes morally dead — an animal rather than a person. He has no rights to stand on when, for example, he wants to oppose a certain kind of therapeutic or medicinal treatment that may be mandated for him. All he can legitimately demand is that, since he is a sentient animal, we ought not — at least *prima facie* — cause him suffering. The man who, when told that his conduct harms the rights of others, sincerely responds "Who cares?" is hardly in any position to demand that others recognize and respect any rights that he might want to claim.[25]

Now many of my readers are inclined to think, I am sure, that this position is too harsh — that it is indeed the harshest possible position one could hold. But it may be too weak; for there is, it would seem, an even stronger position:

If there *could* be an instance of *sheer* corruption the individual concerned would *not* retain the status of a moral being, with all the practical implications of that status. It would, of course, still be true that we ought not to speak of him as 'merely an animal': we should do better to call him a monster. And as a monster (it might be held) not only would he not require to be treated with more respect than a brute, but he would lose his title even to such consideration as the brutes deserve.[26]

My thesis, however, is more charitable and can now be summarized as follows: *If* there are psychopaths as have been described above, they have no rights as persons (because they fail to satisfy a necessary presupposition of such rights), we have no moral obligations to them, and thus our moral response to them is to be on a par with our moral response to animals. We shall not hold them morally responsible; but neither shall we accord them moral respect.

It is worth noting that I have been able to deal with the rights and responsibilities of psychopaths without ever once considering the question of whether psychopathy is a "mental disease" or symptomatic of "insanity." And this seems to me a virtue of my account. For I submit that whether it is labeled "insanity" or not is irrelevant to moral responsibility and should be irrelevant to legal responsibility. What matters are the factors present in the syndrome itself and whether or not these factors come into conflict with the presuppositions of morality. Whether such factors *also* call for the name "insane" or "mentally ill" is, so far as I can tell, solely a matter of useful and economical medical taxonomy and therefore can have no important bearing on issues of rights and responsibilities. Indeed, I am inclined to suspect that the judgment that an individual lacks responsibility and is a defective person leads to the judgment that he is insane — not the other way around.

PSYCHOPATHY AND THE LAW

The practical implications of my argument thus far might seem to consist of something like the following principle: When an individual has been diagnosed a psychopath, his "rights" may be suspended and he may be subjected to involuntary indefinite preventive detention and therapy and perhaps even (if his case is hopeless) to painless extermination. There are, however, very grave objections to the adoption of any such practical principle; and I should like to conclude the paper by briefly elaborating these objections.

(1) It may be impossible to diagnose, on impeccable clinical grounds freed from ideology, any clear cases of psychopathy as herein defined. We all have our psychopathic tendencies, and so all the actual cases may be neither black nor white but various shades of gray. And surely, considering the gravity of denying an individual the status of a person, the burden of proof must lie on those who seek this denial. One grave temptation, one inviting substantial self-deception, is the tendency to regard a man who simply morally disagrees with us (or who does not share our political ideology) as lacking a moral sense.

(2) There are obvious and grave dangers, calling to mind Nazi Germany, in creating any political or legal authority to decide who is and who is not a person or to count as a person. This is not because, as may be supposed, that judgments of this sort are never true or reasonable. It is, rather, that political authorities could hardly be trusted to confine their actions to cases where they were true or reasonable. For this sort of political power immediately invites abuse and corruption of the very worst sort. I am sure, for example, that even in the United States Justice Department there are those who would be delighted if they could have all longhairs, SDS members, and Black Panthers diagnosed as psychopaths and treated accordingly.[27]

(3) There is the important problem of shared or collective social guilt. In many ways we may all be responsible, at least by omission, for allowing the kind of society to develop which produces psychopaths. Every time we vote for "law and order" over social justice and the elimination of poverty, for example, we may be voting unintentionally for an increase of the number of psychopaths in our society. For psychopathy may be bred in impoverished and malnourished conditions. As John Stuart Mill wrote, "If society lets any considerable number of its members grow up mere children, incapable of being acted on by rational considerations of distant motives, society has only itself to blame for the consequences".[28] Since, as in paragraph 1 above, the possibilities for self-deception here are enormous, any hasty self-righteousness about how psychopaths should be treated is quited out of order — another theme of Camus' L'Etranger.

(4) Finally, and perhaps most important, psychopaths may be like infants or the senile — not now persons, but potential or former persons. And thus they may deserve some respect on these grounds alone, respect for what they were or what they might be able to become.

I am not saying psychopaths should never, in practice, be treated in line with the thesis of this paper. But I am saying that, given the four points noted above, such cases may be so rare as to be without major legal or practical importance.[29]

Though a philosopher hates to admit it, the integrity of social and legal institutions may depend upon the maintenance of certain fictions — particularly fictions about the characters of the individuals involved in these institutions. For once we begin to entertain practical proposals which involve considering individuals as less than persons, we help to perpetuate a way of thinking about man and society which, via social engineering and management, approaches — at best — Brave New World and — at worst — 1984.[30]

NOTES

   I should like to express my gratitude to the National Endowment for the Humanities and to the Graduate College of the University of Arizona for grants which made possible the free time used in researching and writing this paper.
1   Immanuel Kant, *The Doctrine of Virtue*, trans. Mary J. Gregor (New York: Harper, 1964), p. 60; p. 399 of the Berlin Academy edition of *Metaphysische Anfangsgründe der Tugendlehre* (vol. 4 of the *Gesammelte Schriften*).
2   Hervey Cleckley, *The Mask of Sanity*, 4th edn. (Saint Louis: Mosby, 1964), pp. 306, 372. The first edition of this work, published in 1941, soon established itself as the best psychological and psychiatric study of psychopathy.
3   These names all pick out approximately the same syndrome and thus represent little more than differing fashions in medical taxonomy — the latter two serving at most to emphasize the fact that the syndrome typically manifests itself in socially undesirable actions. Since such differences in nomenclature have little to do with the inquiry of this paper, I shall henceforth simply refer to "psychopathy" and "the psychopath".
4   Jeffrie G. Murphy, *Kant: The Philosophy of Right* (London: Macmillan, 1970), esp. pp. 65–86 and 161. H. J. Paton, *The Categorical Imperative*, 4 th edn. (London: Hutchinson, 1963), esp. pp. 168–169. Though the psychopathic syndrome was not clinically noted until the nineteenth century, it can be very illuminating to read classical moral philosophers (particularly Kant and Aristotle) with such cases in mind. See particularly Vinit Haksar's 'Aristotle and the Punishment of Psychopaths,' in *Aristotle's Ethics*, ed. James J. Walsh and Henry L. Shapiro (Belmont, Calif.: Wadsworth Publishing Company, 1967), pp. 80–101.
5   Barbara Wootton, *Social Science and Social Pathology* (London: Allen & Unwin, 1959) and *Crime and the Criminal Law* (London: Stevens, 1963).
6   See n. 2 above.
7   William McCord and Joan McCord, *The Psychopath: An Essay on the Criminal Mind* (Princeton, N. J.: Van Nostrand, 1964).
8   Guilt, for example, cannot be identified as a feeling and distinguished from other feelings solely in terms of how, subjectively, it *feels*. There must also be public criteria in the language, criteria which will necessarily make reference to guilt as, for example, the feeling *appropriate* to the doing of moral injury.
9   R. M. Hare, *The Language of Morals* (Oxford: Oxford University Press, 1952) and *Freedom and Reason* (Oxford: Oxford University Press, 1963). Hare argues that a judgment of the form "*A* ought to be done," if having no motivational component for the man who utters it, is not really a moral judgment at all but is rather what he calls an "inverted commas" use of the word "ought." When ought judgments are used in an inverted-commas way, they are really nothing but reports on other people's moral beliefs and can be rewritten without loss of meaning in the following way: "*A* 'ought' to be done" means "People in a certain society believe that *A* ought to be done." Thus, Hare would have to say that the psychopath, like an anthropologist studying another society, must use his "moral" judgments simply to describe the practices of others. But I see no reason why this must necessarily be the case, for it is intelligible to imagine a psychopath arguing in the following way: "People in my society believe that *A* morally ought to be done; but I, having studied moral philosophy and having been persuaded of the truth of the Principle of Utility, believe that not-*A* should be done since *A* is

disutilitarian – but I still don't really *care* and do not propose to base my life on the principle." Even if one agrees with Hare, however, my argument can be rewritten in his language – that is, the psychopath can be defined as one who never really makes moral judgments; and my later arguments will still hold for the psychopath so defined.

[10]   Gabriel de Tarde, *Penal Philosophy* (Boston: Little, Brown, 1912). A brief excerpt from de Tarde's book may be found in *Freedom and Responsibility*, ed. Herbert Morris (Stanford, Calif.: Stanford University Press, 1961).

[11]   C. A. Campbell, *On Selfhood and Godhood* (London: Allen & Unwin, 1957), pt. 1.

[12]   I am not suggesting that Camus himself intended that the novel be taken in this way – only that this way of taking it is philosophically illuminating.

[13]   This theory is more fully developed in my book *Kant: The Philosophy of Right*. See also John Rawls' 'Legal Obligation and the Duty of Fair Play', in *Law and Philosophy*, ed. Sidney Hook (New York: New York University Press, 1964), pp. 3–18. Rawls' essay has been reprinted in my *Civil Disobedience and Violence* (Belmont, Calif.: Wadsworth Publishing Co., 1971).

[14]   For further development of this and related ideas, see the following: A. I. Melden, *Rights and Right Conduct* (Oxford: B. H. Blackwell, 1959); H. L. A. Hart, 'Legal and Moral Obligation,' in *Essays in Moral Philosophy*, ed. A. I. Melden (Seattle: University of Washington Press, 1958), and 'Are There Any Natural Rights?' in *Philosophical Review* **64**, (1955) 175–91; and John Rawls, 'Two Concepts of Rules', in *Philosophical Review* **64**, (1955) 3–22.

[15]   Because I want to leave room for the possibility of *natural* rights, I am here speaking of rights and obligations as "related to institutions" and as "institutional in character" rather than as necessarily being *within* institutions. This point will be developed later in the paper.

[16]   *The Doctrine of Virtue* (Note 1 above), pp. 134–35 (p. 463 of the Academy edition).

[17]   See, in addition to other works by Rawls already cited, his 'Justice as Fairness,' *Philosophical Review* **67**, (1958) 164–94, and particularly 'The Sense of Justice', *Philosophical Review* **72**, (1963) 281–305.

[18]   The notion of punishment as a right may be found in Kant, Hegel, and Hartmann. For a contemporary and very sophisticated elaboration of this view, see Herbert Morris' 'Persons and Punishment,' *Monist* **52**, (1968) 475–501. The plausibility, in some circumstances, of claiming punishment as a right is illustrated by the central character in Friedrich Duerrenmatt's novel *Traps*.

[19]   Of course, institutions of punishment may *in fact* be administered in such a way as to be just as dehumanizing as institutions of coercive therapy, and that is why I made my point in as weak a way as I did – namely that institutions of punishment are *compatible* with human dignity. Since coercive therapeutic institutions are, by definition, going to be paternalistic in that they exist to restructure a man's personality, they are not even compatible with a respect for the autonomy and integrity of persons. The limitations of punishing institutions are contingent; those of coercive therapeutic institutions are necessary. This is not, of course, to say that coercive therapy is always wrong. Of course, it is not. Indeed, as I am arguing in the paper, the status of the psychopath as a being without rights invites the appropriateness of a coercive therapeutic response. But it is important to see what values are lost in such a response – something often not seen by the ideologists of social psychiatry. For more on this, see my 'Criminal Punishment and Psychiatric Fallacies,' *Law and Society Review* **4**, (August 1969) 111–22, and my

collection of essays, *Punishment and Rehabilitation* (Belmont, Calif., Wadsworth Publishing Company, 1972).

[20]   See chapters 14 and 15 of *Leviathan.*

[21]   I include the phrase "from a moral point of view" because it is not solely within a moral context that we find it worthwhile to draw a person-non-person distinction. Intelligence or rationality, often cited as distinguishing marks of persons, may function in these other contexts; but they will hardly do the job in morality — not, at any rate, unless one seriously wants to entertain the possibility of someday having to accord computers greater moral respect than one accords one's fellow human beings. If any kind of rationality is to be the criterion of the dignity of persons, it will have to be what Kant calls *practical reason.* And that would be just another way of putting the point I am making in this paper.

[22]   This certainly seems to have been Kant's view, as the passage initially quoted (no. 1 above) from the *Tugendlehre* makes clear.

[23]   Professor Lewis Beck has pointed out to me in discussion that we sometimes do speak of the rights of animals and of obligations we have toward them. We might say, for example, that I have an obligation to take my cat (though not any other cat) to the vet when it is sick and that this obligation cannot be analyzed solely in terms of not causing unnecessary suffering to the cat as a sentient creature. Similarly, we might sometimes speak of a horse's right to spend its declining years in a pleasant pasture after years of faithful service. Now I believe that I can account for our practices here in a way compatible with my general thesis. For I should argue that this way of speaking is intelligible only insofar as we regard our animals as in some (perhaps metaphorical) sense *persons*, as beings capable of moral feeling. If we are not regarding them in this way, how could we make any sense of talk about their being faithful, feeling guilty for breaking rules, and the like? We may be utterly deluding ourselves in thinking of our pets in this way, but the fact that we do so is further evidence of the conceptual link between rights and obligations, on the one hand, and personality and moral feelings, on the other. When it is just obviously absurd to attribute any moral qualities to our animals, then we should hardly want to speak — even in a highly metaphorical sense — of their rights and our obligations. With dogs and cats and horses, things go pretty well. But would anyone feel comfortable in speaking of his obligation to take his goldfish to the vet; or of the right of his salamander to spend its declining years in comfort?

[24]   For a probing discussion of the acceptance of responsibility, with specific application to the psychopath, see Herbert Fingarette's 'The Acceptance of Responsibility', in his *On Responsibility* (New York: Basic Books, 1967), pp. 17–45.

[25]   In their book *Sense and Delusion* (London: Routledge & Kegan Paul, 1971), Ilham Dilman and D. Z. Phillips ponder the character of Ivan Ilych in Tolstoy's story *The Death of Ivan Ilych.* Ivan Ilych, by Tolstoy's standards and by Ivan's own deathbed standards, is judged to have lead a *meaningless* life because it was an utterly selfish life, devoid of any care and concern for persons or his moral responsibilities to them. All he had cared about was obedience to conventional expectations as a vehicle for increase of his own position and power. The question worrying Dilman and Philips is the following: Is the judgment of meaninglessness here purely emotive, reflecting merely a subjective attitude toward Ivan's life, or can the judgment in some sense be said to be objective? The thesis I have developed in this paper provides, I think, a *start* toward securing its objectivity. For Ivan, by living a life with at least a strongly psychopathic tendency, can be said to have

cut himself off from what it means fully to be a person, to be human.

26 W. G. Maclagan, 'How Important is Moral Goodness,' in *Ethics*, ed. Judith J. Thomson and Gerald Dworkin (New York: Harper, 1968), p. 521; the essay originally appeared in *Mind* **64**, (1955) 213–25. By speaking of "corruption" and "monsters," Maclagan would seem to be morally *condemning* individuals such as the psychopath, saying that they are morally *evil* in some fundamental way. My thesis, however, is that such individuals stand totally outside the domain of moral discourse employing such concepts as *desert, responsibility, blameworthiness*, and the like.

27 For a fuller development of these worries, see my 'Criminal Punishment and Psychiatric Fallacies' (n. 19 above) and my 'Preventive Detention and Psychiatry,' *Dissent* (September–October 1970), pp. 448–460. In both articles I explore the actual and potential dangers of social psychiatry. (Both are reprinted in the present collection.)

28 *On Liberty*, chap. 4. The following kind of case, though no doubt too simple to be true, illustrates the worry here: Suppose it were discovered that there is a high correlation between psychopathy and a chemical deficiency in the brain related to very low protein diets — the kind of diets forced by economic necessity upon a substantial portion of the population. Who would be responsible for the social consequences of psychopathy then? By introducing these kinds of consideration, it may seem that the free will-determinism issue is creeping back into the discussion. But this is all right. The fact that certain kinds of causal discoveries provide an *additional* reason for excusing the psychopath does not show that psychopathy by itself is not also sufficient.

29 I do submit that, in thankfully extreme and rare cases, we may in fact respond justifiably to certain individuals as animals. Suppose we are living in a society where psychopaths are in control and where there are thus, as in the state of nature, no institutions of integrity that we have to worry about preserving. Karl Jaspers, living in Nazi Germany, lived in such a society; and he responded, quite rightly in my judgment, to the psychopaths running his society as though they were animals: "To me there seemed nothing left beyond at least being at all times clear about what I was doing and intending to do, and to act accordingly. What we had to do was to act naïvely, to pretend no interest in the affairs of the world, to preserve a natural dignity . . . , and if need be to lie *without scruples*. For beasts in possession of an absolute power to destroy must be treated with cunning and not as men and rational beings" (Karl Jaspers, epilogue to *Philosophy of Existence*, trans. Richard F. Grabau [Philadelphia: University of Pennylvania Press, 1971], p. 97. I have italicized the phrase "without scruples" to stress Jaspers' realization that his situation was not one where the normal obligation to tell the truth is overridden by even more important moral requirements but, rather, one where he was dealing with beings of a nature that precluded their imposing any moral requirements on him at all.) I am grateful to my colleague, Prof. Charles F. Wallraff, for calling this passage in Jaspers to my attention.

30 Since writing this paper, I have come to think that there are really two concepts of rights. Some rights (which I call autonomy rights) are claims for the protection of the special moral status of persons. Other rights (which I call social contract rights) are standards of treatment that any decent society would legally guarantee for all creatures (including animals) under its jurisdiction. Psychopaths and animals can have rights of the latter sort, but not of the former sort. This distinction is explored in detail in my 'Rights and Borderline Cases,' *Arizona Law Review* **19**, No. 1 (1977), pp. 228–241, and reprinted in the present volume.

PART THREE

THERAPEUTIC INTERVENTION

There is a reason for the general deterioration as regards liberty. This reason is the increased power of organizations and the increasing degree to which men's actions are controlled by this or that large body. In every organization there are two purposes: one, the ostensible purpose for which the organization exists; the other, the increase in the power of its officials. This second purpose is very likely to make a stronger appeal to the officials concerned than the general public purpose that they are expected to serve.

Bertrand Russell
'Symptoms of Orwell's 1984' in
Portraits from Memory and Other Essays

CRIMINAL PUNISHMENT AND PSYCHIATRIC FALLACIES

> Experience should teach us to be most on our guard to protect liberty when the government's purposes are beneficent. Men born to freedom are naturally alert to repel invasions of their liberty by evil-minded rulers. The greatest dangers to liberty lurk in insidious encroachment by men of zeal, well meaning but without understanding.
>
> Louis D. Brandeis
> *Olmstead v. United States* (1928)

Nowhere is this general tendency expressed by Brandeis more prominent than in the area of criminal law. In spite of the reasoned warnings of some writers, we are greeted by a continuous stream of books and articles from psychiatrists and psychoanalysts (and their judicial followers) with one common theme: Criminal punishment is an unscientific survival of barbarism and must be replaced by a system of individual and social therapy.[1] To believe otherwise is to be unscientific and (if the distinction is recognized) immoral.

The most recent attempt to argue this position comes from the pen of Dr. Karl Menninger. In his Isaac Ray Award book, *The Crime of Punishment*,[2] Dr. Menninger launches (in the name of scientific psychiatry) a radical attack on the institution of criminal punishment as it operates in the context of the Anglo-American legal system. He does not wish merely to change parts of the existing system (e.g., the insanity defense) but wants, as an ideal, the elimination of that system entirely. The idea is then to replace this system with a more "scientific" system of social control. With sentencing largely in the control of psychiatrists and other health workers, and increased use of preventive detention, the new system would not be subject to the inefficiencies in controlling crime that characterize our present judicial adversary system.

The juridical system seems to the doctor to be an unscientific jumble based on clumsy and often self-defeating precedents. Psychiatrists cannot understand why the legal profession continues to lend its support to such a system after the scientific discoveries of the past century have become common knowledge. That this knowledge is cooly ignored

147

and flouted by the system is not so much an affront to the scientists as it is a denial of what was once mystery and is now common sense . . . .

Being against punishment is not a sentimental conviction. It is a logical conclusion drawn from scientific experience.

The criminal court should cease with the findings of guilt and innocence, and the "procedure thereafter should be guided by a professional treatment tribunal composed, say, of a psychiatrist, a psychologist, a sociologist or cultural anthropologist, an educator, and a judge with long experience in criminal trials and with special interest in the protection of the rights of those charged with crime".[3]

Why not a large number of *community safety centers* or crime prevention centers? Such a center would be concerned far more with the prevention of crime than with the arrest and mop-up. Offenders or supposed offenders upon capture would be conveyed immediately to the proper center for identification and examination, and then, if indicated, transferred to a central court and/or diagnostic center. Later — if the judge so desires — a program for continuing correction and/or parole could be assigned, again to the officers of the local center. [pp. 91–92; 204; 139; 268][4]

It is my view that Menninger's position is totally and systematically wrong — that its defense is fabricated solely upon confusions and fallacies (e.g., that moral conclusions can be drawn from scientific premises). And thus, in this brief essay, I should like to expose these confusions and fallacies. This task is important for three main reasons. First, though his book is in many ways erroneous, Dr. Menninger is a popular and widely influential practitioner in his field; and thus it is important to show that he is wrong and to point out the implications of his positions.[5] Second, if my reading constitutes a fair sample, his views are representative of what is a common position among psychiatrists, psychoanalysts, and social scientists in general. Third, and perhaps most important, his views are not merely incorrect, but are of a kind that is socially and political dangerous.

Enough by way of introduction. I should now like to pass to a consideration of the argument itself and the character of the confusions and fallacies it exhibits. These are of three main kinds: moral, legal, and (ironically) scientific.

VALUES, COMPETING VALUES, AND JUSTICE

When we speak of moral values we can mean either of two very different things. First, we can mean those moral beliefs which, as a matter of fact, people or groups of people have. The term "mores" is sometimes used for values in this sense. Second, we can mean those values which ought to be promoted — regardless of whether or not they are in fact promoted or believed valuable. This is the sphere, not of mores, but of ethics or morality proper. And quite clearly the two spheres are different. No one, for example, really believes that it was morally right for the Nazis to persecute the Jews (or that they ought to have done it) just because they believed it was right. One holding such a view would be committed to the proposition that the Nazis were subject to no moral criticism for what they did, and this is absurd. Being wrong about morality may, under some circumstances, excuse; but it can never justify. For example, we may absolve from moral blame the Jehovah's Witness who lets her child die for lack of a transfusion without thereby agreeing that the action performed was really right and ought to be recommended to others.

Now it should be fairly clear that it is only values in the first sense (mores) which can be regarded as discoverable by empirical science. Beliefs about values are not themselves values; they are facts. And thus, like all facts, they are open to the expert analysis of the behavioral scientists. But we must not be deceived into thinking that this expert authority about beliefs or mores extends to pronouncements about what really ought to be done. The scientist, like any other rational and informed man, may certainly be competent in moral discussion; but (and this is crucial) he is not *professionally* competent. Though his studies may give him access to facts relevant in moral argument, they do not give him special insight into moral conclusions. To put the point in another and perhaps even more obvious way: Scientists are professionally competent to tell us the most efficient means for the technical attainment of our goals; but they are not competent *qua* scientists to set those goals or to morally assess the means. Efficiency is not be be identified with morality.

These points are often forgotten when important decisions of social policy are being made. Menninger ignores them entirely:

The very word *justice* irritates scientists. Now surgeon expects to be asked if an operation for cancer is just or not. No doctor will be reproached on the grounds that the dose of penicillin he has prescribed is less or more than *justice* would stipulate. Behavioral scientists regard it as equally absurd to invoke the question to justice in deciding what to do with a woman who cannot resist her propensity to shoplift, or with a man who cannot repress an impulse to assault somebody. This sort of behavior has to be controlled; it has to be discouraged; it has to be *stopped*. This (to the scientist) is a matter of public safety and amicable coexistence, not of justice . . . .

Being against punishment is not a sentimental conviction. It is a logical conclusion drawn from scientific experience. [pp. 17; 204]

It is almost impossible to believe that Menninger intends that we take these remarks seriously. How in the world is "being against" anything logically derivable from scientific premises? (I would love to see such an argument formalized.) And what moral are we supposed to draw from the remarks about the surgeon? It is, of course, true that no surgeon expects to be asked if an operation is just. But neither does he expect to be asked if an operation is hexagonal, approaches middle C, or tastes good. Are we thus to conclude that hexagonality, middle C, and good taste are meaningless concepts?

Of course, Menninger's thesis may be restricted solely to moral values, and the argument may be that their inaccessibility to scientific procedures renders them meaningless. But there is not a single reason to hold such a view (to hold that "meaningful" means "scientifically useful"); and, in fact, I do not think that Menninger himself really holds such a view — even if he does espouse it in theory. To say that a concept is meaningless and to really believe this are two different things. For example: Does Menninger really believe that, if police broke into his home and detained him for months without trial because some psychiatrist thought he was dangerous, he would be talking nonsense if he described his treatment as unjust? I seriously doubt it.

What is really going on in the quoted passage is, I think, the following: Menninger has noted that science, as a social institution,[6] has incarnate in it certain mores. And it is Menninger's view that these mores ought to be elevated to a more influential place in our moral decisions than they now occupy. But this is itself a piece of moral advice — a judgment of value priority and not of fact — and so it is open to the same kinds of standards we use in evaluating any moral recommendation. No matter how much Menninger propagandizes for the scientific status of his recommendations, the fact remains that they are recommendations and not findings. Thus with respect to them he has no professional competence. We must, therefore, evaluate his proposals in the light of all those considerations which are relevant from the moral point of view.

What are these considerations? To avoid starting a treatise in moral philosophy, I shall state rather dogmatically that there are two main kinds of considerations relevant to moral evaluation: considerations of utility; and considerations of justice. Utilitarian considerations are concerned with promoting the greatest amount of happiness and well-being in the world as possible. Considerations of justice function as checks on social utility, weighing against promoting happiness if in so doing some people must be treated unfairly in the process. These considerations compete and often have to be weighed against each other. But it is just this competitive nature of basic moral values that Menninger fails to appreciate. In effect, he opts for considerations of utility (e.g., health and public safely) to the exclusion of considerations of justice. And he does this with a vengeance:

Eliminating one offender who happens to get caught *weakens* public security by creating a false sense of diminished danger through a definite remedial measure. Actually, it does not remedy anything, and it bypasses completely the real and unsolved problem of how to *identify, detect, and detain potentially dangerous citizens.* [p. 108]

The argument here seems to be that since health is the predominant value in psychiatry, its social analogue (public safety) ought to be the predominant political value. What is being suggested is that we deprive people of their liberty as a kind of preventive medicine, and this is clearly to choose social utility over one of the mainstays of criminal justice: procedural due process.

Our system of criminal due process involves such guarantees as the following: (1) No man is to be deprived of his liberty for what he is or what he might do, but only because he has in fact violated some legal prohibition. This is the traditional requirement for an overt act. (2) A man is to be presumed innocent. This means that the state must prove its case beyond a reasonable doubt to a jury of the defendant's peers and that the defendant may exploit the adversary system to its full to make such proof impossible. (3) A man is to be responsible only for what he has done as an individual. He is not to be held guilty because others like him often commit crimes.[7] (4) A man is not to be forced to testify against himself, to help the state in its attempt to deprive him of his liberty.

Such guarantees would have no place in a purely therapeutic or preventive context, and Menninger quite correctly argues that the procedures they involve are not the best way to arrive at truth and thus that they interfere with the efficiency of securing public safety (pp. 53 ff.). But of course they do; *that is their very function*! They aim, not at the discovery of truth, but at the protection of the defendant in his otherwise unequal battle with the state. And our employment of these procedures tests the sincerity of our commitment to what is often claimed as the basic moral value in our system of criminal justice — namely, the belief that it is better to free some guilty persons than to convict some innocent ones.

We can begin to understand the tensions inherent in the criminal process only if we realize how the values of justice and due process compete with the utilitarian value of public safety.[8] If we were only interested in public safety, we would let the police coerce confessions, deny any excuses for wrongdoing, and even punish some innocent people to keep everyone else careful. One only has to call to mind Nazi Germany, Soviet Russia, and present-day South Africa and Greece for a picture of the logical outcome of a society which places order or public safety over all values of justice. (Almost unbelievably, from a man famous for his liberal and benevolent humanism, Menninger looks with wistful longing at the security provided by the legal systems of Greece and China!) [p. 277]

Being involuntarily deprived of our liberty (even by a benevolent Dr. Menninger who calls it therapy rather than punishment) is an evil most of us would like to avoid — particularly if we have done nothing wrong, but only appear to have "dangerous tendencies." Thus we should be quite stupid to take steps that would involve giving up the guarantees which help us avoid this evil. Menninger, of course, does not explicitly say that he is against due process (who would?); but if he is not against it, then his set of proposals involves a fundamental paradox. For if his proposed system is to retain all present guarantees to preserve fairly the freedom of each individual, why suppose that it will be any more efficient than present practices? To make it more efficient, some due process will necessarily have to be sacrificed.

THE SCIENTIFIC EXAMINATION OF DETERRENCE THEORY

It is absurd to characterize public safety as the *real* problem of criminal law (as though other issues, such as due process, are illusions), but surely such safety is admittedly one of the important values that any system of criminal law must seek to promote. And so it is worth inquiring if it is even true that, as a matter of fact, our present system of criminal punishment fails to work in providing for our security. Here we are dealing with an empirical scientific issue, and one would think that Menninger would be on safe ground. But he is not. He tells us that we must replace punishment with therapy because the only possible defense for punishment is deterrence theory; and this theory is known to be false.[9] But he is quite wrong here. Deterrence theory is not known to be false, and Menninger fails to show that it is false. His whole case is one of ridicule supported by no evidence whatsoever. Here is all that he says to support his attack on deterrence theory:

["Brushes" with the law] are dreary, repetitious crises in the dismal, dreary life of one of the miserable ones. They are signals of distress, signals of failure, signals of crises which society sees primarily in terms of *its* annoyance, *its* irritation, *its* injury. They are the spasms and struggles and convulsions of a submarginal human being trying to make it in our complex society with inadequate equipment and inadequate preparations.

[We have described] a man who seemed to have spent his life going from one difficulty into another, into the jail and out of it, only to get back in again, like one caught in a revolving door. It ended in death. The grinding mills of the law did nothing for Crow; they cost Kansas City a lot of money, mostly wasted. It gave a score of people something to do, mostly useless. One might wonder what could have been done early in this chap's life to have protected his victims better. [pp. 19; 21–22]

It is almost impossible to know what Menninger expects us to conclude from these passages, for they appear to involve at least two gross confusions. First, as a psychiatrist, Menninger has perhaps seen a limited number of criminals who really are compulsive and thus are nondeterrable. And the existence of such people certainly points up a distinct failure within our system of criminal punishment. But they will indict the system *as a whole* only if they can be regarded as representative of criminality in general. But this is just the conclusion we may not draw on the basis of so limited a sample. What about the college student who smokes marijuana, or the Martin Luther King, Jr., who engages in civil disobedience, or the university professor who omits some lecture fees on his tax return? These are all legally criminals, but are their actions "the spasms and struggles and convulsions of a submarginal human being"? Note what Menninger says:

"Ah," the reader will say, "perhaps what you say is true in those violent rape and murder cases, but take everyday bank robbing and check forging and stealing – you cannot tell me that these people are not out for the money!"

I would not deny that money is desired and obtained, but I would also say that the *taking* of money from the victim by these devices means something special, and something quite different from what you think it does. [p. 183]

Here we enter the world of apparent fantasy. The actions of our pot smoker, our civil disobedient, and our tax evader are all symbolic of something unconscious. (It requires, I should think, a rather smug view of our society to regard all those who break any of its rules as crazy.) But, even if this is true, just how is it relevant? It will, presumably, be relevant only if it is the case that these unconscious motives can be said to compel the agent in such a way that he is not responsible and thus not a proper object for punishment. But, having ridiculed the notions of fault and responsibility, and having modestly declared the inability of the psychiatrist in a courtroom ever to say with any certainty that an action of a particular man was compulsive (and thus nonresponsible) because of mental disorder (pp. 312 ff.), Menninger can hardly go forth and present a perfectly general theory of determinism for all human action. A general theory of determinism, if it rests on no inductive basis of established particular cases, is a metaphysical theory and not a scientific conclusion. And if, as a metaphysical theory, it requires that we stop distinguishing the actions of a Martin Luther King, Jr., from those of a Daniel M'Nagthen, then it is a useless bit of stipulation.

The second confusion in Menninger's rejection of deterrence theory is related to the first. It is the failure to distinguish special from general deterrence.[10] He thus makes a quite misleading use of the facts of recidivism. Recidivism surely shows that criminal punishment does not deter many of the particular people who are caught up in the criminal process. But this fact is quite irrelevant to the claim that having a deterrence system has the general effect of keeping many members of society from ever engaging in criminal conduct and thus making themselves eligible for the process. It is not difficult to believe, for example, that one major reason why more of us do not smoke marijuana or submit fraudulent tax returns is that we are deterred by the criminal penalties. To scientifically refute deterrence theory, and thus provide a basis for replacing our entire system of punishment with something else, it would have to be shown that substantial numbers of those who do not now commit crimes would continue to be law-abiding if all criminal sanctions were abolished. But we have no evidence at all on this complex counterfactual. And, in the absence of any such evidence, it is irresponsible to ridicule and reject deterrence theory in the name of science.

LAW AND PSYCHIATRY

The psychiatrist, Menninger argues, should be removed from the courtroom entirely (p. 138). I have some sympathy with these sentiments, but not for the reasons Menninger offers. His suggestion (a not unfamiliar one) is that at most psychiatric testimony is relevant to establishing the *mens rea* of the offense — that is, the mental element which establishes the degree of personal responsibility or blameworthiness for what was done. But, with much invective and ridicule, Menninger says that we should drop inquiries into *mens rea* entirely. We should simply inquire if the offense was committed, regardless of the mental state with which it was committed. If we determine that the prisoner (patient?) did commit the offense, he should be turned over to a team of psychiatrists and other experts. They would then inquire into his mental state in order to determine how long to detain him for society's protection and his own rehabilitation (pp. 113 ff., 139).

Though this proposal has a plausible ring to it, it is in fact almost impossible to give it a coherent interpretation. How, for example, can one convict for the offense alone when a *mens rea* is typically a material (i.e., defining) element of the offense itself? Was the offense murder or manslaughter? The question cannot be answered without an inquiry into *mens rea* — i.e., did the actor have malice aforethought? The revisions and complexities that elimination of *mens rea* would introduce into our legal system are vast. If he is aware of such problems, Menninger totally ignores them.[11]

Suppose, however, we did eliminate *mens rea* at the trial and then had our fellow convicted for the offense of (say) "causally bringing about the death of another human being." And now he is turned over to psychiatrists. The kinds of problems that might arise become obvious. Suppose he caused the death by nonculpable accident (that is, he did not even have what we would now call the *mens rea* of negligence). Further suppose that, upon examination, he was found to be "potentially dangerous." Should he be locked up for a period of enforced therapy (perhaps for life) even though he had committed no wrong at all? Or consider trivial offenders. Should a man who compulsively cashes bad checks be sent to a mental institution for an indeterminate period because he is hopeless? The questions are not medical or scientific. They are question of *moral* and *political decision*, and we should be foolish to entrust our responsibility for them to a team of "experts." Criminal judges, whatever their weaknesses, are at least bound by the rules of our community. They may not, as may psychiatrists, act on their own personal conceptions of what is good for or dangerous to the community.

An actual example is illustrative here: The closest existing analogue to what Menninger advocates is to be found in the American juvenile courts. Here it has been traditional to suspend guarantees of due process because the state was presumably acting in the benevolent interest of the juvenile rather than as a punishing agent. (It is really astounding how we can deceive ourselves merely by changing the name of what we do.) A reading of the opinion of Justice Fortas in the 1967 *Gault* case (where some due process is finally guaranteed to juveniles) should give us pause before we hand over any other area of human liberty to benevolent experts.[12] Menninger is right in his premise that science and due process do not mix well. The moral to be drawn, however, is the following: Beware of psychiatrists bearing gifts.

Near the end of his argument, after dismissing the notions of blameworthiness and responsibility, Menninger suggests that instead of punishing people we might impose *penalties* on them:

If a burglar takes my property, I would like to have it returned or paid for by him if possible, and the state ought to be reimbursed for its costs, too. This could be forcibly required to come from the burglar. This would be equitable; it would be just, and it would not be "punitive." [p. 203]

Just how "punitive" this would be depends, I suppose, on just how rich the burglar is and on just what happens to him for nonpayment. But this is not the objection I want to pursue. What interests me is the suggestion that criminal law ought to move toward becoming a part of tort law — the law of damages for harms done not involving breach of contract. Does Menninger find damages attractive for any other reason than that they are not *called* "punishment"? After all, in tort law conditions of blameworthiness and responsibility are relevant. We do not normally make a man pay damages in the absence of any fault on his part. We rather, as the phrase goes, let the loss lie where it falls. If I am not negligent, then normally (though not always) I am not liable for damages. What if Menninger's burglar was a man who believed the property was his own, or who was sleepwalking, or caused damage in an epileptic seizure, or took it to use for his self-defense? Judgments of liability for damages might well differ in all these cases. And so even this move toward tort will not allow us to avoid something like the criminal law's *mens rea.*

CONCLUSION

Dr. Menninger is no doubt a decent and generous man, and I do not mean to charge that he intentionally advocates injustice. He has simply fallen victim to the trap which often leads benevolent men to pursue an unjust course: the single-minded pursuit of one social goal to the exclusion of all others. In addressing himself to the limited goals of public safety and rehabilitation, he does highlight some terrible abuses and inadequacies that exist within our present system of criminal punishment. What we do not get from him, however, is a persuasive case against that system itself.

I would not pose as a man devoted to our system of criminal punishment. It contains much hypocrisy and moral pretension and is, at best, a necessary evil. However, in spite of its admitted shortcomings, it does appear to do at least a tolerable job of balancing public safety against the often competing values of liberty and due process. And thus there is presumption in its favor. By this I mean nothing more than that the burden of proof lies on the man who would replace it to provide careful arguments which are conceptually clear, empirically well-founded, and morally cogent. It is just this burden which Dr. Menninger has failed totally to bear.

NOTES

[1] Standard sources for such a view are F. Alexander and H. Staub *The Criminal, the*

Judge and the Public: A Psychological Analysis (Glencoe: Free Press, 1956), and D. Abrahamsen, *The Psychology of Crime* (New York: Columbia University Press, 1960). This theme is also to be found throughout most of the books produced by winners of the Isaac Ray Award. The most detailed and persuasive case against this position has been made by Thomas Szasz in *Law, Liberty & Psychiatry* (New York: Macmillan, 1963). See also F. Wertham's 'Psychoauthoritarianism and the Law', *University of Chicago Law Review* **22** (Winter), pp. 336–338.

[2]   New York: The Viking Press, 1968.

[3]   It is significant that the judge is listed last, and that it is not specified whether or not he is to have a decisive veto power with respect to a violation of the prisoner's rights. The judge must simply be "interested" in these rights. The quoted portion of the extract is from S. Glueck's *Crime and Justice* (Boston: Little, Brown, 1936).

[4]   It is important to note that Menninger's recommendations range over *supposed* offenders. Nowhere does he suggest that the operations of these centers (including their detention powers) are to be restricted to those who have been convicted of some legal wrong.

[5]   Menninger is often called in for expert testimony at legislative hearings on criminal law reform, for he is taken to be a chief spokesman for a liberal and humane jurisprudence. Such a reputation accounts, I gather, for his selection for a feature interview in the issue of *Psychology Today* devoted to law and psychology (February 1969). Views like Menninger's are surely in part behind the pressure for sexual psychopath laws and other laws for the preventive detention of those (e.g., drug addicts, homosexuals, and drunks) who are judged to present a "potential danger" to the community.

[6]   For an elaboration of the institutional character of science, and of psychiatry in particular, see the material by Thomas Szasz in *Psychiatry and Responsibility*, ed. H. Schoeck and J. W. Wiggins (Princeton: Van Nostrand, 1962).

[7]   It is often not noticed that provisions for preventive detention (especially if they rest on statistical evidence) tend to involve *collective* rather than individual criteria for guilt. It is judged that Jones is to be detained because he is a member of some class (e.g., vagrants) which manifests a high crime rate. This point is totally missed in the otherwise excellent article on preventive detention by Alan Dershowitz in the *New York Review* (13 March 1969).

[8]   An important recent book, Herbert Packer's *The Limits of the Criminal Sanction* (Stanford: Stanford University Press, 1968), illuminates the tension inherent in our system of criminal punishment by contrasting the "crime control model" with the "due process model".

[9]   Menninger dismisses entirely the arguments of those who have advocated a retributive theory of punishment. For example, he fails to consider the possible alteration in our concept of a human being (and how we *treat* human beings) if we cease to regard people as agents of dignity and responsibility who are capable of being blameworthy for what they do. To see that one can offer a retributive theory which is something more than disguised vengeance, consult Herbert Morris, 'Persons and Punishment', *The Monist* **52**, (October 1968) 475–501.

[10]   For more on this distinction, see Packer, *supra* note 8.

[11]   Some psychiatrists try to meet this worry by advocating a *bifurcated* trial (something along the lines of the California practice). There is to be a guilt trial and a sanity trial. At the former, considerations of *mens rea* will be relevant and allowed. All questions

of sanity, however, will be reserved for the second trial; and thus it is only at this second trial that psychiatric testimony will be allowed. This system, however, will fail for the following reason: If a man is insane, he might be incapable of having the *mens rea* required for the commission of the offense. It would thus deny him due process to exclude psychiatric testimony from the first trial. See *People v. Wells* (1949) Cal. 2d33: 330; p. 2d. 202: 53.

[12] *In re Gault* (1967) U.S. 387:1. See also the horror stories of arbitrary mental commitment cited by Szasz *supra* note 1. Szasz has raised profound questions and deserves a serious answer. Menninger simply proposes to eliminate such abuses by training police and mental health workers with the proper *therapeutic attitude* (pp. 260; 271). But this misses the point entirely; benevolence is not justice, and therapeutic attitudes are not necessarily due process attitudes. Menninger might also recall Lord Acton's reminder about the corruptive nature of power. Or does he perhaps think that psychiatrists are immune from such corruption? Nice, benevolent people are perhaps preferable to mean, stubborn ones; but it does not follow from this that the former should be allowed to coerce and confine the latter.

PREVENTIVE DETENTION AND PSYCHIATRY

> They that can give up essential liberty to obtain a little
> temporary safety, deserve neither liberty nor safety.
>
> Benjamin Franklin

It is no surprise that our society contains people who support the idea of preventive detention. What is surprising is that this support cuts across the usual political ideologies and allegiances. Dr. Karl Menninger, a benevolent humanist, and Attorney General Mitchell, a law-and-order hard-liner, have both recently come out in support of the idea of preventive detention as a partial solution to the crime problem — Menninger in his *The Crime of Punishment* (New York: Viking, 1968) and Mitchell in proposed criminal legislation for the District of Columbia.[1]

Preventive detention, generally speaking, consists in locking people up for what they *might* do, rather than for what they have in fact done. It is generally taught that our legal system does not in theory countenance such proceedings. But, of course, it does countenance and even encourage them in fact — though generally under some euphemistic description. Obvious examples are status crimes (e.g. vagrancy), refusal of bail for those accused — though not convicted — of crime, involuntary commitment for the "insane," and wide judicial discretion in matters of parole and length of sentence. Such discretion might allow a judge to extend a man's sentence (for either punishment or therapy) if he believes the man is still prone to crime. The old retributive idea that a man, having paid the price, may regain his liberty is being replaced with the idea that liberty depends on something more — on his "rehabilitation".

Both the attractiveness and danger of these proposals lie in their scientific and even benevolent facade — especially if detention is coupled with therapy. Who could object to rehabilitation? It seems more sensible than traditional punishment. And even those too toughminded to object to vengeance *simpliciter* must admit that mere vengeance does not work. The poeple we put in prisons because they have harmed us get out, harm us again, and return to prison — a seemingly useless waste of time and resources. So, for once, it seems that the interests of benevolent men, prone to forgive the criminal,

159

and harsh men, whose only concern is to prevent crime, coincide. Once we have determined that a man is dangerous, why wait until he actually does harm? Why not *prevent* the harm by detaining him in advance? Objections we might feel to this can be dispelled if preventive detention is coupled with therapy and rehabilitation. Punishing a man for what he might do is admittedly bad; but, we are to be led to believe, rehabilitating a man for what he might do is not. We can help the man and society at the same time.

This rosy picture is too good to be true. Let me outline the most important, and in my judgment fatal, objections to preventive detention — whether punitive or therapeutic.

PREDICTION AND PRINCIPLE

One morally ineffectual way in which people sometimes seek to oppose preventive detention is to rest their case against it solely on the difficulty of prediction. This allows them to avoid the troublesome appeal to moral values. Professor Alan Dershowitz of the Harvard Law School, for example, has argued that no important issues of principle are involved in preventive detention. The important objection, in his judgment, is practical — the difficulty of accurate prediction and the institutional pressures that make a prediction of dangerousness much more likely than a prediction of non-dangerousness.

When we establish rules for convicting the guilty, we do not require certainty; we only require that guilt be proved "beyond a reasonable doubt." . . . What difference is there between imprisoning a man for past crimes on the basis of "statistical likelihood" and detaining him to prevent future crimes on the same kind of less-than-certain information? The important difference here may not be one of principle; it may be, as Justice Holmes said all legal issues are, one of degree.

The most serious danger inherent in any system of preventive detention is that it always seems to be working well, even when it is performing dismally; this is so because it is the nature of any system of preventive detention to display its meager successes in preventing crime while hiding its errors. One such area . . . is the confinement of the mentally ill on the basis of psychiatric prediction of injurious conduct. . . . The psychiatrist almost never learns about his erroneous predictions of violence. But he almost always learns about his erroneous predictions of non-violence — often from newspaper headlines announcing the crime. The fact that the errors of underestimating the possibilities of violence are more visible than errors of overestimating inclines the psychiatrist — whether consciously or unconsciously — to err on the side of confining rather than of releasing. His *modus operandi* becomes: When in doubt, don't let him out.[2]

Dershowitz's practical case is important. But surely he is wrong on the question of principle. First, it is important to see that the case for preventive detention is based on a kind of evidence that would be *constitutionally in-admissible in a criminal trial*. One may not, in a trial, introduce statistical evidence against the defendant — evidence that he is a member of a social group (say, vagrants) which manifests a high crime rate. Evidence at a criminal trial is, to be sure, less than certain, but this does not make it statistical evidence. To allow statistical evidence would represent a shift from an individualized conception of guilt to a collective or group criterion. This would seem a kind of guilt by association and would involve a moral regression of utmost gravity. It would represent a way of circumventing a basic rule of procedural due process and would surely, therefore, raise a vital issue of principle.[3]

Second, it is important to see that competing models of human nature are involved here. Traditionally, the criminal law has regarded men as agents of freedom and dignity — agents who, up to the very last minute, are capable of having changes of heart, of deciding *not* to perform a certain evil action in the face of even a very high probability that they will perform it. This is why the criminal law does not punish for merely intending, planning, and preparing for a crime. It also explains, in part, why the criminal law punishes less severely for attempts than for completed crimes. Preventive detention, of course, rests upon a totally different model: locate a man in a sociological framework and deal with him accordingly — deal with him, as you would with an object, solely in terms of prediction and control. As in so many other areas of contemporary life, an elevation of the importance of technology (especially that of the social sciences) results in the demotion of the importance of humanity, freedom, and dignity as these concepts have been traditionally understood.

THERAPY AND PUNISHMENT

If preventive detention is coupled with therapy, objections to the program tend to the blunted. But they should not be. We should delude ourselves neither about the efficacy of therapy nor about its benevolence and justice. Attempts at criminal rehabilitation have not been markedly successful. They represent the promises of psychology rather than a fulfillment. Also, it is dangerously simpleminded to assume the moral preferability of a therapy system to a punishing system. For the central and often ignored point is that common to both criminal punishment and preventive rehabilitation is the *involuntary deprivation of liberty*. It is at least *prima facie* wrong to do to a man what he does not want done to him, to confine him against his will, no matter whether you call what you do to him punishment or therapy, or whether you call where you put him a prison or a hospital. If therapy is so benevolent and glorious, and rehabilitation so desirable, how can we account for the fact that people resist it as much as (sometimes more than) punishment? When we are to be punished, we at least know what we are bargaining for. Not so when we believe that someone is going to attempt to restructure our personality against our will.

Now I am not, let me insist, an opponent of therapy or rehabilitation. Quite the contrary. It is a moral disgrace that neither our prisons nor our state mental hospitals provide decent opportunities for meaningful therapy — little more than monthly talks with a psychiatrist or a few electric shock treatments. What I do oppose is the *involuntary* deprivation of liberty for the purpose of therapy, for the attempt at rehabilitation *against the will* of the man to be rehabilitated. Punitive detention is at least honest. It is oppressive and cruel, and everyone knows it. Thus, we are alert to guard our liberty against it. Therapeutic detention, however, masks practically identical treatment with the slogans of benevolence. But Big Brother is Big Brother — even if he wears a Jesus costume.

IDEOLOGY AND REHABILITATION

Another important and seldom noted problem is the extent to which political preference and ideology may affect our application of a notion like "needs rehabilitation".[4] Consider, for example, the psychiatric concept of the *psychopathic* or *sociopathic* personality. Psychopaths are said to "lack a moral sense" and to "show no normal care and concern for the interests of others." But just imagine the political danger of setting up persons with the authority to deprive people of their liberty on such nebulous grounds. How would Martin Luther King, Jr., have fared at the hands of Southern state psychiatrists? How would the Black Panthers fare at the hands of some Northern state psychiatrists? Psychiatrists, especially state psychiatrists, are not immune from the tendency to project their own fears and hostilities onto the man they are evaluating.[5] What hope would any of us have under a system of preventive detention based on such criteria as "probably dangerous" or "lacks a moral sense?" This is not to say, of course, that all the people declared dangerous by judges and psychiatrists are in fact quite safe. Some of them are indeed frighteningly dangerous. But surely free men must have the courage to brave this sort of danger (the danger of waiting until the people actually commit a criminal act before detaining them) — at least if we consider the *1984* alternative.

Finally, we should take an honest look at what sometimes counts are rehabilitation in our state hospitals and prisons. We should not kid ourselves into believing that those pronounced rehabilitated have necessarily developed morally sensitive and highly principled characters. Quite the contrary may be the case. They may have simply learned to identify with the aggressor and adapt to repression, to have learned the dubious virtues of civility and conformity, to have learned to do what others want them to do rather than what their own characters dictate. Some immates will not so compromise, but they of course then pay the price of staying longer (in either prison or hospital) than their more pliable fellows.

It may be that I can harm myself by speaking frankly and directly, but I do not care about that at all. Of course I want to get out of prison, badly, but I shall get out some day. I am more concerned with what I am going to be after I get out. I know that by following the course which I have charted I will find my salvation. If I had followed the path laid down for me by the officials, I'd undoubtedly have long since been out of prison – but I'd be less of a man. I'd be weaker and less certain of where I want to go, what I want to do, and how to go about it.[6]

Here is a man holding on to his personal integrity against heavy odds, odds which are probably even greater in state mental hospitals than in state prisons.

The protagonist of Anthony Burgess' novel *A Clockwork Orange* acts on violent impulses. Diagnosed a criminal psychopath, he is subject to Ludovico's Technique – a refined Pavlovian technique that conditions in him utter revulsion to any form of violence. It also results, alas, in his being rendered incapable of appreciating the music of Beethoven – the one experience in his previous life that had any meaning or character. There is a lesson here.

NOTES

[1] For a discussion of Menninger's views, see my article 'Criminal Punishment and Psychiatric Fallacies,' In *Law and Society Review* (August 1969), pp. 111–122. Menninger would no doubt be an opponent of any preventive detention that would not provide for therapy.

[2] 'On Preventive Detention,' *New York Review*, (March 13, 1969) pp. 22–27.

[3] This circumvention would be purely linguistic. That is, we would not *call* the preventive detention hearing a trial. We could then claim that the constitutional bar on statistical evidence did not here apply since the proceedings did not constitute a criminal trial. But we would, of course, be doing substantively exactly the same thing to the defendant. This may sound outlandish, but intelligent men have been taken in by even less: Consider, by way of example, how the injustices of the juvenile court system were masked by benevolent rhetoric – rhetoric finally exploded by the Supreme Court's 1967 *Gault* decision.

4 Thomas Szasz makes a similar point about the concept "mentally ill" in his *The Myth of Mental Illness* (New York: Harper, 1961). Not being a trained psychiatrist, I am not competent to pronounce on his claim that *all* so-called "mental illness" may be so analyzed. Surely at least some cases may be, and this in itself is enough to raise substantial political worries.

5 *State* psychiatrists are particularly to be feared for the obvious reason that they act, not as the agent of the defendant, but as paid arm of the established political structure. Surely some of them will (as would some of us in similar roles) be corrupted away from objectivity. Indeed, labels such as "lacks a moral sense" invite such corruption.

6 Eldridge Cleaver, *Soul on Ice* (New York: Delta, 1968), p. 17.

INCOMPETENCE AND PATERNALISM

Paternalism is the coercing of people primarily for what is believed to be their own good. When, for example, a person is committed to a mental hospital, not because he is believed to be dangerous to others, but because he is believed to be dangerous to himself or at least in need of treatment, we have a clear example of paternalistic intervention. The coercion involved in such intervention comes into conflict with certain basic principles of political liberty, however, and is usually regarded as justified only if the individual in question is judged *incompetent* to make a certain class of decisions — e.g. to refuse treatment for supposed mental illness. John Stuart Mill's classic liberal limitation on coercion ("The only purpose for which power can be rightfully exercised over any member of a civilized community, against his will, is to prevent harm to others".[1]) is normally thought to apply only to persons who are competent — e.g. not to children or the insane.

To be judged incompetent often results in one's status as a full-fledged *person* being taken away or at least greatly attenuated. Basic human rights (including the right to do stupid and dangerous things if one so desires) may be set aside, and the incompetent person may simply be treated as the object of someone's (usually the state's) benevolent concern and management — a clear demotion from the status normally thought proper for an adult person. If, for example, a person is judged mentally ill and in need of treatment, his expressed desire not to go into the hospital may be ignored on the grounds that mentally ill persons are incompetent to make such decisions (the desire not to be admitted to the hosptial may itself be taken as evidence of incompetence) and that it is only the desires of competent people that deserve to be respected.

Given that so much of consequence can (for better or for worse) hang on the label "incompetent", it is important that we try to get as clear as possible about the meaning (or meanings) of this concept. Only then will we be in a position intelligently to consider the question of just how far, if at all, social policy ought to depend upon this concept — however analyzed.

After distinguishing several different (but related) senses of "incompetence", I shall argue that, however plausible it may be to regard a judgment of incompetence as a necessary condition for justified paternalistic intervention, a judgment of incompetence ought *never* to be regarded as a sufficient condition for such intervention.[2] The primary issues with respect to paternalism are moral and social and should be faced squarely as such — something which we shall fail to do if we let ourselves believe that the only important question is whether or not the label "incompetent" accurately describes the person with respect to whom paternalistic intervention is being considered. In this area we always run the risk of smuggling our moral judgments in under an apparently value-neutral description — e.g. calling Jones "incompetent" when what we really mean, but could not let ourselves explicitly say, is "Jones ought to be fixed — like it or not".[3] Such a risk is high because it is an extremely common temptation, one to which even very distinguished thinkers occasionally succumb, to believe or at least propound a false proposition because of a belief that the proposition is required by some moral principle that one holds dear. John Stuart Mill, terribly concerned to oppose paternalistic interventions, put forth as part of his case the obviously false claim that each man knows his own interests best. In a similar vein, as Thomas Szasz has repeatedly pointed out, persons often call some of their fellows mentally ill, and pretend to be stating facts, when they are really expressing the evaluative preference that these people should be interfered with in some way.[4] And ironically, Szasz himself comes dangerously close to succumbing to this very temptation — i.e. his refusal to accept that there is such a thing as mental illness often appears to be little more than his way of expressing the evaluative preference that society should not coerce people unless they are clearly criminals.[5]

Hopefully, in attempting to analyze the concept of incompetence, I shall be able at least to make a start toward sorting out and distinguishing the purely conceptual or descriptive issues from the moral principles with which they may easily be confused. This, at any rate, will be my primary task in what follows.

I

In this section, I propose to elaborate truth conditions for sentences of the form "Jones is incompetent to make decisions of type X".[6] The "type X" restriction is important, since it is fairly rare that people are incompetent across the board. Incompetence is usually limited to certain areas — e.g. inability to manage money. This fairly obvious point is, alas, ignored in many state mental commitment statutes. In many states, the judgment that Jones is mentally ill (and, if a danger to self or others, is committable) automatically carries with it the judgment that Jones is also incompetent to do such things as vote, manage his money, or get married.[7] But surely this is absurd. A compulsive child molester, for example, is someone who is perhaps not unreasonably regarded as mentally ill, a danger to others, and properly committable. But there is no reason at all to suppose that such a person necessarily (or even probably) will lack the competence to, say, manage his own checkbook or vote.[8] Thus to say that all mentally ill persons are necessarily incompetent is to fail to draw distinctions that any reasonable man would surely want to draw. (A comparable mistake is made when it is suggested that mentally ill persons are necessarily not responsible for what they do. A kleptomaniac may not be responsible for certain acts of theft, but should his kleptomania be accepted as an excuse for *any* offense he might commit — e.g. rape? Surely we should demand some fairly plausible causal link between the disorder and the act before making judgments about either incompetence or nonresponsibility.[9])

When is a person rightly to be judged incompetent to make decisions of a certain sort? Unfortunately, but not surprisingly, the concept of incompetence can mean several different (though related) things. In general, I shall argue, a person is to be regarded as incompetent to make decisions about X if he is *ignorant, compulsive*, or *devoid of reason* with respect to X.

Ignorance. Suppose the point at issue is whether or not a given patient in the hospital requires brain surgery. We would find it natural to say that the hospital janitor is incompetent to make this decision because he lacks the kind of knowledge that is relevant to making a decision of this sort. (Note that this is different from a lack of *authority*, or *legal* competence, to make the decision. The head of the hospital might have the authority but still be as incompetent in the cognitive sense as the janitor — e.g. suppose he has not kept up on recent medical developments and has forgotten, in the whirlwind of administration, most of what he once knew about brain physiology and brain pathology.[10]) Keeping the janitor (or the administrator) from making a decision about the appropriateness of brain surgery would not, of course, be an example of paternalism. But consider the following case: Jones is in the process of making a selection of items from the buffet table without knowing that some of the items have been poisoned. It would not be unreasonable for me, knowing that some of the items are poisoned, to regard Jones as incompetent (because of ignorance) to make the selection that he is involved in. I might stay his hand or knock his plate away and justify my paternalistic interference by citing his incompetence to make a responsible decision. If Jones, after learning that some of the food is poisoned, still wants to go ahead and make a selection and take his chances in spite of his newly acquired knowledge, we have an entirely new ballgame. If I still want to interfere paternalistically, I may not now cite his incompetence in terms of ignorance as a part of my justification. If I still want to regard Jones as incompetent, it will now have to be in *some other sense* — perahps one of those to be noted below.

Compulsion. I think we should regard a person as incompetent if we know that he is compelled to make a certain decision — i.e. given a choice between A and not-A, we know that Jones is compelled to "choose" A. Given the problems involved in analyzing the concept of compulsion, and given also the difficulty in acquiring conclusive evidence on which to base compulsion claims, we are usually going to fall short of certain knowledge in this area and are going to have to rely on more or less reasonable beliefs grounded on more or less clear analyses and more or less reliable evidence. The following, however, can surely be regarded as a reasonably clear case of compulsion undermining competence: Suppose we are considering whether or not to hire Jones to umpire a baseball game that we are sponsoring between teams A and B. We then learn that gamblers have kidnapped Jones's child and have told him that the child will be tortured to death if team A does not win. Knowing this, it would be reasonable for us to conclude that Jones is likely to be incompetent to umpire the game in a fair, unbiased way. Here some might even want to say that there is a sense in which Jones, under this kind of pressure, really has no choice or decision power at all. He certainly does not have a fair choice, and persons operating under such a demanding burden or unfairness are unlikely to be fully competent with respect to the choice involved.

Compulsion cases, the above being one of *duress* or *external compulsion,*[11] are of a kind where the attainment of certain knowledge is very difficult (perhaps impossible) to come by; and that is why we can at most speak of the extent to which a person is *likely* to be incompetent in such circumstances. Given certain general truths about the typical nature of human motivation, probabilities are clearly on the side of our judgment of incompetence in the above case. However, it is surely possible (though not likely) that Jones is highly atypical — e.g. so indifferent to the welfare of his child or so fanatically devoted to the integrity of the game of baseball (e.g. "Mike the Mouth" in Philip Roth's novel *The Great American Novel*[12]) that he could remain competent to make fair calls in the game even in the face of such threats.

Other interesting cases, at least some of which we might be inclined to call cases of *internal compulsion*, are the following: (a) Jones has a brain tumor or a brain dysfunction which, in any situation involving a choice between A and B, triggers a "choice" of A. (b) Jones has been put under post-hypnotic suggestion and told, when give a choice between A and B, to choose A. (c) Jones has a compulsion neurosis such that with respect to certain choices (keep the kitchen clean or feed his baby) he will inevitably choose the one (keep the kitchen clean) rather than the other. (d) Jones is an alcoholic or drug addict trying to decide whether or not to give up his habit. (e) Jones suffers from pathological jealousy and is trying to decide whether or not to sue his wife for divorce on grounds of adultery. (f) Jones is a judge trying to decide an important controversy between two corporations and he, being deeply involved in the financial affairs of one of them, has a personal stake in the outcome of the controversy.

These cases all involve some notion of internal or psychological pressure, but not all of them are equally plausible to regard as cases of compulsion. They move from cases which are as plausible as any we are likely to have in this area (a and b), through cases that are more uncertain for a variety of reasons (c and d), to the final cases (e and f) where we should be more inclined to speak of "very strong temptation" rather than compulsion.[13] Thus, when we ground our judgments of incompetence on judgments of compulsion, the cases — each requiring discussion in terms of its own particular combination of relevant conditions — can be thought of as descending in a continuum (with many borderline cases) from *well-confirmed* incompetence, through *probable* incompetence, so what I shall call a *real possibility* of incompetence — i.e. a possibility grave enough that a prudent man would certainly want to be on his guard against it. (For example: Even if 99 out of 100 judges could in fact resist the temptation noted in the final case described above, we might still want to adopt a general policy that barred such judges entirely just to protect ourselves from the injustices that those of weak will might cause and from the general suspicion and cynicism that the presence of such judges might breed).

Sometimes we speak of compulsion when we may, at least in part, really have something else in mind. We find it very natural to speak of the compulsive child molester, for example, even though it is by no means clear that his sexual impulses necessarily "drive" or "overpower" him to a greater extent than do those of persons who focus on more approved (and thus more easily available) objects for their gratification. Part of our thinking here may go as follows: "No one could naturally desire sexual relations with small children, and thus those who seek such relations must in some sense be forced or compelled to". We might reason in a similar way about a man who goes to great (perhaps even illegal) lengths to acquire women's panties and fondle them as his only means of sexual gratification. What we may really be saying about such people is that there is a sense in which we find their desires intrinsically unintelligible, not a meaningful part of anything that could count as a rational pattern of human motivation. Indeed, these people may be just as bewildered as we are about their behavior, may find their own desires and actions unintelligible. Such persons, though perhaps neither clearly ignorant nor clearly compulsive, may still be in some sense irrational and thus lack something basic to human competence and responsibility.[14]

There are, of course, a variety of ways of being irrational (some of these ways being manifested by all of us at one time or another) and we clearly do not want to regard as incompetent all persons whom, in some informal way, we might call irrational. We should not, for example, hold incompetent persons who are merely eccentric, have desires we happen not to share, and engage in practices of which we disapprove. The concept of irrationality must therefore be very carefully defined if it is not to lead to confusion and iniquity. I shall speak of persons whose rational failings render tham incompetent (and not, say, merely eccentric) as persons *devoid of reason*.

Devoid of Reason. Incompetent people may be people who are in a certain sense devoid of reason. What does this mean? I suggest that "Jones is devoid of reason" can mean any of the following:

(1) Jones is *nonrational* — i.e. like a stone or any other object Jones is such that it makes no sense even to attribute choice or decision power to him at all — e.g. Jones is in a deep coma, is catatonic etc.

(2) Jones is *irrational*. This notion can be broken down as follows:

(a) Jones believes things that are *intrinsically* irrational — i.e. believes propositions which, by their very nature, no rational man could believe.[15]

(b) Jones is *systematically* wrong in his judgments — i.e. he systematically weighs available evidence incorrectly.

(c) Jones *does not even appreciate what is relevant* to forming a judgment on the issue in question — i.e. he does not even *consider* relevant evidence.

Though these various kinds of irrationality have a tendency to merge into each other in actual cases, we can perhaps imagine cases where they may be isolated. (2 a) is easiest: Suppose Jone literally believes that he is an insect. We would not have to know anything else about Jones at all to correctly conclude that he is irrational.

Let us try to construct a case to illustrate (2 b). Suppose Jones is trying to determine the molecular structure of a certain substance. He draws upon some old, badly documented work by the late scientist Smith. It is the best work available, and worth considering, but it leaves a great deal to be desired.

Suppose Jones now sets up an excellent modern laboratory, staffs it with the best experts available, and begins to perform elaborate x-ray defraction crystallographic analysis on the substance. Smith had said that the structure of the substance was A, Jones's carefully controlled experiments show not-A, and Jones publishes paper in which he defends A and cites Smith's work as his main justification. And his whole scientific career (as long as it lasts) has a similar pattern. Here he knows what is relevant, and yet he seems unable to weigh it correctly − i.e. he gives a greater weight to old, badly documented studies than to controlled experiments carried out under the best conditions. Granting agencies, knowing this about him, would surely be reasonable in regarding him as incompetent to engage in this sort of research and correctly speak of him as irrational. Compare the case of the paranoid who agrees that certain compassionate behavior on the part of people is evidence that not everyone is out to get him but who systematically downplays and reinterprets that evidence in the light of anything, however slight, that seems persecutory in nature.

Let us move to case (2 c). Jones wants to discover the cure for a certain disease. He has access to the best available scientific findings concerning the disease and its cure − findings that strongly indicate that the disease can be cured by administration of drug D. Indifferent to all this, however, Jones visits a local guru. The guru touches him on the head, mumbles a few beatitudes of doubtful intelligibility, and then loudly proclaims that God has revealed to him in a vision that the disease is not to be cured by drug D. It is rather to be cured by having the patient stand on his head and recite his astrological chart backwards in Greek. Jones, not even surprised that God would concern himself with such matters, immediately believes all that he has been told by the guru. Here we do not have a case of weighing relevant evidence badly, but a case where the individual involved reveals that he does not have the slightest idea of what *counts* as relevant to determining the question at issue. This kind of case, unfortunately, is not at all unreal − e.g. it parallels almost exactly the recently publicized case of a child allowed to die of diabetes because his parents (paradigm examples of religious fanatics), in trying to determine how best to control their son's diabetes, accepted the counsel of a crackpot faith healer over that of expert doctors who had prescribed insulin.[16] This is a clear case of grotesque inattention to what is noncontroversially relevant; for any reasonable person knows that idle remarks from an ignorant faith healer can contribute absolutely *nothing* to the understanding and control of physical disease. Such remarks have *no weight*.[17] People who do not see this are incompetent and irrational with respect to medical matters.

At this point, someone will surely argue as follows: "There are no objective interpersonal standards — even for relevance. What is relevant for one person is not necessarily relevant for another, and it makes no sense to speak of objectivity in these matters. Where are the absolute standards supposed to come from — out of the sky? To talk of objectivity in these matters is just to be dogmatic, and thus it is wrong to regard people as incompetent and irrational for acting against these so-called objective considerations".

This very common way of thinking is very confused. Standards of objective relevance do not have to be plucked out of the sky. In general, *the character of the issue under dispute generates the criteria of relevance appropriate for its resolution.* If, for example, it is a scientific issue, it follows (as part of the meaning of "scientific issue") that controlled observations and experiments are relevant to its resolution and that other sorts of appeals — e.g. to visions — are not. If the issue is legal, then cases, statutes, etc. are relevant to its resolution. And so on.

Even if one accepts that there may be standards of objective relevance for factual issues, however, it might still be argued that we can generate nothing comparable when what is at stake is not facts but values. Here, it may be argued, subjectivism is the only acceptable view. This is a large issue,[18] but even here we can surely cite at least some considerations such that a person who ignored them would be regarded as incompetent to make decisions on the evaluative issue in question. Suppose we have a person (e.g. a psychopath) who sincerely says "I fail to see why the fact that my doing A will hurt people is a moral reason that counts against my doing A". Such a person reveals that he fails to see the relevance of something (causing harm to people) that is necessarily relevant to moral issues — fails indeed to see part of what it is that makes an issue moral at all. Either such a person does not even understand what "morality" means or, understanding what it means, he does not care in the least about the practices it describes. In either case, such a person could not take part in meaningful human relationships and is to be regarded as morally irrational and incompetent.[19] We do, of course, have the concept of areas in which reasonable men can disagree. But, even in morality, not all issues have this character. It is not every person who disagrees with us, or even every person we might regard as morally eccentric, whom we should regard as irrational and incompetent. It is only the person who is totally out of touch with those basic, noncontroversial matters which *must* be regarded as relevant who is to be considered irrational and incompetent. Herbert Fingarette has illuminatingly introduced the concept of *essential relevance* in a similar context:

What is at issue is the kind of patent, rudimentary, fundamental relevance without which ordinary human intercourse breaks down. We do not say that Jones throwing a rock at [a] snake, or Jones throwing [a] rock maliciously at Smith, is rational because of the wisdom or moral depth of vision displayed. Both actions might in fact be rather foolish and perhaps both even morally wrong. No matter: these acts are not irrational acts. Jones is not irrational so long as Jones is capable of grasping what is patently, rudimentarily, and fundamentally relevant − that thrown rocks can hurt people, that hurting people and causing people to suffer are of themselves bad, that willfully injuring people is generally a crime . . . This kind of relevance I shall call, for the sake of brevity, essential relevance − i.e. the relevance which constitutes the warp and woof of the fabric of ordinary human intercourse.[20]

Ironically, the attack against standards of objective relevance is often put forth as a confused and terribly misleading way of expressing a commitment to a (presumably objective!) moral principle which is, within limits, admirable − namely, a principle of *tolerance*. We must not, so the claim goes, persecute and coerce people solely because they seem irrational and incompetent to us. Very well. But accepting this moral injunction does *not* commit us to denying that some of those who seem irrational and incompetent to us *really are* irrational and incompetent. As I suggested at the outset of the paper, to judge a man incompetent at most should be allowed *sometimes* to remove *one obstacle* to justifiably coercing him. But this does not show that "incompetent" and "is rightly coerced" mean the same thing or even that it is ever justifiable, *all* things considered, to coerce incompetent people.[21] There is nothing linguistically, logically, or conceptually odd (though there may be something morally wrong) in saying "We should leave everyone alone − no matter how incompetent they are". Thus the issue of competence should be kept *conceptually distinct* from the question of coercion − paternalistic or nonpaternalistic.

Consider the following two cases: (1) A religious fanatic believes that God will cure his diabetes better than insulin and stops taking his insulin. (2) A religious fanatic believes that God will cure his child's diabetes better than insulin and refuses to let his child take insulin. Most of us would, I think, be inclined to be much more tolerant in case (1) than in case (2). But surely the man in case (2) is no more *incompetent* than the man in case (1). Both appeal to obviously irrelevant considerations with respect to health matters and are equally incompetent to make medical decisions. If we choose to intervene in case (2), therefore, but not in case (1), we should not confuse matters and justify our discriminatory intervention by saying that the man is competent is case (1) but not in case (2). We should bring the ethical issue clearly into the open (i.e. our judgment that self-destructive incompetence is more to be tolerated than other-destructive incompetence) and not pretend that such issues are always to be resolved simply by getting clear on how to apply correctly the description "incompetent". These cases surely show that the issue of who is irrational and incompetent must be separated from the issue of whom we may justifiably coerce. Once we do this, we can see clearly that tolerance of Jones is logically compatible with a belief that Jones is as stupid, irrational, and incompetent as they come. Surely only at most a subclass of incompetent and irrational people are properly to be coerced − even for their own good. The real problem of paternalism, then, is the attempt to identify − if possible − such a subclass. This is clearly a moral issue, one not to be completely resolved simply by analyzing the meaning of "incompetent" and then applying the concept to cases. If we think that this is all that is involved, we shall deceive ourselves into thinking we are reasoning "He is incompetent; therefore he should be coerced for this own good" when we are really reasoning "He should be coerced for this own good; therefore he is incompetent".

We have, as an ideal norm, the model of a fully competent agent as one who acquaints himself with all available relevant evidence, who is unmoved by emotional bias or internal or external compulsion, and who has all of his rational faculties intact. No existing person conforms fully to this model, and all of us have some areas in which we blatantly fail to conform − e.g. assessing the beauty of our own children. However, we do of course have cases of persons who blatantly fail to conform to this model in areas, unlike judging the beauty of children, so basic and important to human life that failure in these areas are likely to be irreversibly self-destructive. In these clear cases, there seems to be a good *prima facie* case for paternalistic intervention. But the vast majority of cases that confront us will be borderline − cases in that greyish area between full competence and obvious incompetence. The real problem that will face us, then, is what to do in the borderline cases. When in doubt, which way should we err − on the side of safety or on the side of liberty? It is vital that we do not adopt analyses of "incompetence" or patterns of argument that obscure the obviously moral nature of this question.[22]

II

My primary purpose in this paper has been to analyse the concept of incompetence and to distinguish questions concerning its analysis from the basic moral questions of paternalism. However, in closing, I should like briefly to address myself to these moral questions. I should like to outline what seems to me a reasonable way to establish a *prima facie* case for paternalism and then note certain important obstacles to this case which, if they prove insurmountable, may keep the *prima facie* case from ever being conclusive. In this brief discussion I shall only note the obstacles and shall not at this time consider in detail the very complex (and lengthy) question of whether or not ways can be devised to overcome them.

I shall propose the following as a principle that is at least *prima facie* reasonable: When a person is incompetent in any of the ways specified above, and if his incompetence is likely to result in major and not easily reversible harm to him, then paternalistic intervention is justified provided that it is carefully specified, limited, controlled, and explicitly tailored to the *kind* of incompetence manifested. Let me explain the rationale behind this moral principle and behind some of its qualifying clauses.

Defending the Principle. How are moral principles to be defended? I know of no better answer to this question than that provided by John Rawls.[23] According to Rawls's general theory, we may use the idea of a social contract as a model of rational decision. That is, we shall regard as rationally justified any moral principle (or any social practice) if that principle (or practice) would be unanimously agreed to, adopted, or contracted for by a group of rational agents[24] coming together, in what Rawls calls the "original position".[25] in order to pick principles and then practices to govern their relations with each other as members of a common community. An important restriction on Rawls's model of a rational being is that such a being is said to operate under a "veil of ignorance" − i.e. to know what in general can happen to persons in various positions in society but not to know what his own actual position is likely to be.[26] (So, for example, in trying to decide whether or not to adopt a practice of slavery, each agent would know in general what it is like to be a slave and what it is like to be a slaveholder; but none of the agents is allowed to know whether he is likely to be the one or the other). Rawls further suggests that each rational agent will value a set of primary goods (e.g. liberty, security, self-respect) and will always choose so as to minimize, as far as possible, threats to these goods.[27] (So, to continue the slavery example, rational agents would not be willing to risk the loss of primary goods involved in being a slave simply on the chance that they might enjoy the benefits of being a slaveholder − i.e. rational agents will not gamble with their primary goods. Rational agents therefore would not agree to adopt a practice of slavery.)

The reader must realize that the above is a very brief and inadequate outline of what is in fact an extremely complex, subtle, and sophisticated theory.[28] Hopefully, however, I have been able to sketch enough of Rawls's theory to at least indicate how it might be used in a defense of the principle of paternalism I have outlined. Basically, the argument would go as follows: Rational men, valuing primary goods, would see (a) that these goods could become compromised if a person became incompetent in any of the ways specified in this paper and (b) that no person has a guarantee that he will not become incompetent in any of the ways specified. Thus rational men, desiring above all else to protect themselves against such losses, might well agree to a principle which allowed a carefully limited paternalism — i.e. paternalism which would dictate interference in just those cases of incompetence in which primary goods were genuinely in grave and irreversible danger and in no other cases. Interference in other cases would, of course, represent threats to (and not protections of) primary goods and would of course be an object of avoidance by persons in the original position. They surely would not contract for any principle of paternalism countenancing a substantial risk to primary goods. Thus: If a paternalistic principle can be devised which would rule out interferences with primary goods, then it seems to me that parties in the original position would agree to such a principle.[29]

Let us now turn to some of the limits that rational persons might want to place on a paternalistic principle before they would adopt it — limits which would attempt to preclude the use of the principle to threaten rather than protect primary goods.

Major and Not Easily Reversed Harm. Liberty is too important a value, too primary a good, to be interferred with except in the clearest cases of major harm — i.e. harm that any human being could be presumed to want to avoid at nearly all costs. Harm this grave (loss of even more liberty, death, loss of mental powers, etc.) can be regarded as either a direct obstacle to liberty itself or an obstacle to a necessary condition for liberty or for the enjoyment of liberty. (Preventing this sort of harm is not to be thought of as on a par with, say, preventing tooth decay.) Extent of reversibility is also an important thing to consider, since the gravity of a harm is sometimes a function of its extent of reversibility — e.g. if LSD causes permanent brain damage the case for preventing its use is stronger than if it merely causes temporary incapacity.

Specification. Given the repugnant things that are sometimes done to people in the name of benevolence and therapy,[30] parties in the original position would surely want to know exactly what kind of treatment a person might receive if, after being judged incompetent, he was deprived of liberty on paternalistic grounds. A rational man wants to know exactly what *risks* he is running.

Limit and Control. Given the dangers of arbitrary coercion and repression flowing from paternalistic discretion, parties in the original position would surely want to agree to paternalistic measures only if they were able to know exactly the criteria to be used in defining such concepts as "dangerous" and "incompetent", the maximum extent (in time) of interventions, and the procedures for selecting and controlling those who are to have coercive power in the system. Rational agents would presumably want discretion kept at a minimum.

Tailoring to Kind. If (to modify an earlier example) I am ignorant that the substance in the glass I am about to drink is poison, and in that sense incompetent to decide whether to drink it, you (who know it is poison) might be justified in intervening and staying my hand until you can tell me that it contains poison. This kind of incompetence at most justifies a *short term* intervention. If, knowing that the drink is poisoned, I still want to consume it, you may still be justified in a paternalistic intervention — perhaps one of longer term. If so, however, you must shift to another conception of incompetence in your justification — one which may be much more difficult (perhaps impossible) for you to support. "If possible, a man should be stopped from dying through his own ignorance" is a fairly plausible claim. "If possible, a man should be stopped from risking his life or from intentionally killing himself" is much, much less plausible — i.e. much less likely to be accepted by parties in the original position.

Parties in the original position would, I think, agree to a paternalistic principle if it could be qualified as noted above. But (and herein lie the obstacles) it is by no means clear that these qualifications could ever in fact be specified exactly enough or — even more important — that any actual practice or human institution (necessarily staffed by fallible and often stupid and venal human beings) could be designed so as to guarantee the literal application of the principle. Such a principle, even if intrinsically reasonable, obviously could not apply itself. Making it socially operative would require the design and creation of an actual human institution and all of the problems such institutions are heir to. Thus, if these problems of qualification and design seemed insurmountable, parties in the original position might override their *prima facie* commitment to the *principle* of paternalism by their mistrust of all suggested *mechanisms* for implementing the principle — i.e. they might decide that they had rather take their chances of becoming incompetent and being left helpless than run the risk of suffering from an abuse of a paternalistic institution. They might reasonably judge that the former is not nearly as likely as the latter.

There is no *a priori* way of determining whether a paternalistic practice or institution can be designed that parties in the original position would agree to adopt, all things considered. The burden of proof is upon those who advocate paternalism seriously to attempt, in *detail*, to overcome problems in qualification and institutional design. Respect for human good demands nothing less.

NOTES

[1] *On Liberty*, 1859, Chapter 1. Mill stresses that the principle applies only to "civilized communities" and goes on to argue, in what appears to be a defense of imperialistic paternalism, that "despotism is a legitimate mode of government in dealing with barbarians, provided the end be their improvement and the means justified by actually effecting that end".

[2] I say that it is plausible to regard incompetence as a necessary condition for justified paternalistic coercion because I find plausible the general Millian position on the importance of human liberty. Persons unsympathetic to the Millian position, or unimpressed with the importance of human liberty for some other reason, might not want to regard incompetence as even a necessary condition for justified paternalistic coercion — e.g. they might argue that it is justified to coerce men for their own good *simpliciter*.

[3] See Livermore, Malmquist and Meehl, 'On the Justifications for Civil Commitment', *117 U. Pa. L. Rev.* (1968) 75.

[4] See, for example, *The Myth of Mental Illness* (New York: Harper and Row, 1961) and *The Manufacture of Madness* (New York: Harper and Row, 1970).

[5] See the review of Szasz, *The Manufacture of Madness*, by Herbert Morris, 18 *UCLA L. Rev.* 6 (1971).

[6] In this paper I am interested in decisions, not actions, and thus will not discuss incompetence that is solely relevant to actions. Frequently, of course, a man is incompetent to perform a certain action because he is incompetent to make the decisions the action requires. But not all cases are of this nature — e.g. the incompetent mechanic who, though making all the right decisions about what needs doing on my car, is negligent and clumsy in his execution.

[7] For a survey of various statutes, see S. Brakel and R. Rock (eds.), *The Mentally Disabled and the Law*, rev. ed. 1971 (Chicago: University of Chicago Press, 1971) pp. 250–256. Even in states where committability and incompetence are distinguished by statute, the two judgments are often confused in practice. See David B. Wexler, Stanley E. Scoville *et al.*, 'The Administration of Psychiatric Justice: Theory and Practice in Arizona', 13 *Ariz. L. Rev.* 1 (1971), esp. pp. 88–96.

[8] A recent study of voting behavior of mental patients (M. Klein and S. Grossman, 'Voting Competence and Mental Illness', *American Journal of Psychiatry 127*, (May 1971) 11), concludes that "the results of these studies appear to dispel any factual basis for the disenfranchisement of mental patients". There may, of course, be reasons of policy or therapy for withholding certain rights from mental patients (e.g. to make them earn them in a token economy setting). These policy arguments (no doubt difficult if not impossible to defend) should be put forth honestly as the policy arguments that they are, however, and not disguised under a judgment of incompetence. (Indeed a program

of token economy will presumably work only on persons who are *competent* with respect to managing their supply of tokens.)

[9] I am drawing here on some points made by Joel Feinberg in his 'What is So Special About Mental Illness?' in his collection of essays *Doing and Deserving* (Princeton, N.J.: Princeton University Press, 1970) pp. 272–292.

[10] There is, of course, usually a reasonably high correlation between authority or legal competence and cognitive competence – e.g. though a few children may be as cognitively competent as the average adult, the fact that the vast majority are not provides a basis for a general policy which makes children legal incompetents. In the absence of such a high correlation, such a general policy would presumably be unjustified. Even where such a general policy seems justified, however, it is important – in order to avoid injustice to those few who are cognitively competent – to have some procedure (e.g. becoming an emancipated minor) whereby they can establish legal competence if circumstances warrent and if they so desire.

[11] The "internal/external" contrast, though often used to talk about compulsion, is somewhat misleading. In the duress case, for example, what really compels Jones is presumably his very strong desire to save his child. In the absence of such a desire, the external threat would not compel him – indeed, would not even be seen as a genuine threat. But desires are just about as "internal" or "psychological" as any objects that can be named. What is really "external" in the case of duress is the *way* in which my desire has to be satisfied; *that* is what is imposed by the coercer. The desire to save my child from harm is normally fulfilled by doing such things as taking him to the doctor, making sure that he looks both ways before crossing a street, etc. – all things which, even if I have no strong direct desire to do them, do not seem repugnant to me as necessary conditions for doing what I really desire (i.e. protecting my child). However, when I am under duress, the *means* that I must follow to protect my child are repugnant to me and have been imposed from without. That is the "external" element in the case.

[12] New York: Random House, 1973.

[13] Even cases (a) and (b) are not without problems, for we still do not have complete knowledge of the requisite brain physiology and of the mechanisms of posthypnotic suggestion. (For a very instructive presentation of the difficulties, both conceptual and empirical, of establishing causal connections between neurophysiological phenomena, on the one hand, and decisions and actions on the other, see John Hodson, "Reflections Concerning Violence and the Brain", 9 *Crim. Law Bull.* 684, 1973.) Case (c) is difficult because it appels to the very vague concept of *neurosis* (and perhaps begs the causal and philosophical questions at issue by calling it a *compulsion* neurosis). With respect to so-called neurotic compulsion, can we distinguish impulses that are irresistible from those which simply have not been resisted but which could have been had the agent tried harder? Case (d) may involve genuine compulsive behavior (addiction), but it is not clear whether the compulsion involved interferes with faculties of *decision* and, if so, to what extent. A drug addict might be unable to choose a cure if all we can offer him is a lengthy period of painful withdrawal. But suppose we could cure addiction in five minutes with a pleasant tasting pill. Would addicts be unable to choose this kind of cure? (For more on this, see David Wexler, 'Therapeutic Justice', 57 *Minnesota L. Rev.* 2, 1972, esp. pp. 326ff.) Related problems arise in the question of whether or not prisoners are able to give informed consent to such things as psychosurgery. Does their desire to get out of prison somehow compel them to accept the surgery; or does it just strongly tempt them?

Those who claim that prisoners cannot give informed consent in such cases tend to suggest the former when the evidence may at most support the latter. And sometimes, succumbing to a temptation previously noted, they claim that informed consent for prisoners is impossible as their way of expressing the (perhaps correct) *moral* view that psychosurgery should never be done on prisoners *simpliciter*. (For a general discussion of some of these issues, see A. M. Capron, 'Medical Research in Prisons', *Hastings Center Report*, 3:3, June 1973; see also the opinion in the recent case *Kaimowitz v. Dept. Mental Health*, Mich. Cir. Ct., Wayne Cty., 7/10/73, 13 *Crim. L. Rep.* 2452 (8/22/73).)

[14]   I am here again drawing on Feinberg, *supra*, note 9.

[15]   One might supplement this principle, formulated in terms of belief, with one formulated in terms of desire: "Jones desires things that are intrinsically irrational – i.e. desires things which, by their very nature, no rational man could desire". Though it is going to be harder to get agreement on cases here, there are perhaps a few obvious ones that would not be controversial – e.g. a masochistic desire for intense pain. I should be strongly inclined to include the desires of the child molester and the fetishist with respect to women's panties (cases previously discussed), but I suspect that I might get some argument here.

[16]   An interesting thing about this case is that (according to news reports) the parents genuinely wanted to control the child's diabetes and were seeking the best way to do this. A more difficult case would be that of the religious fanatic who knows that a certain medical procedure (e.g. a transfusion) is the only way to save his child's life and yet does not want to save the child's life as much as he wants to do something else – e.g. to do "God's will". I am inclined to think that such a person would be *morally* incompetent; but demonstrating this would, I admit, be very difficult.

[17]   One might say that such persons suffer from a kind of ignorance, and this is certainly true. The ignorance is so basic, however, so out of touch with what is noncontroversially relevant to deciding medical matters, as to deserve special treatment as a kind of irrationality. It should not be confused with the kind of ignorance (e.g. not knowing that a glass contains poison) that is possible even for a rational person.

[18]   I have explored this issue in detail in my monograph *The Possibility of Moral Philosophy*, forthcoming.

[19]   For an elaboration of this point, see my "Moral Death: A Kantian Essay on Psychopathy", *Ethics* 82:4, July 1972. (Reprinted in the present collection.)

[20]   H. Fingarette, 'Insanity and Responsibility', *Inquiry* 15:1–2, Summer 1972, pp. 17–18.

[21]   At most, a judgment that Jones is incompetent may eliminate the relevance of some of Jones's desires in determining whether or not to coerce him. Even ignoring some of Jones's desires, however, there may be many other considerations which still justify not coercing him – e.g. his other desires, social costs, danger of setting up paternalistic institutions with discretionary authority, the belief that he might still be better off in the long run if left alone, etc.

[22]   A widely used introductory text on basic psychiatry puts forth the following as (presumably) a *psychiatric* judgment: "When there is significant doubt about the necessity for hospital protection, it is best to err on the side of safety" (Eric Pfeiffer, *Disordered Behavior* [Oxford: Oxford University Press, 1968] p. 123). Surely there can be no doubt that this is really a moral judgment.

[23]   *A Theory of Justice* (Cambridge, Mass.: Harvard University Press, 1971). This book

is an elaboration, with some important modifications, of some of Rawls's earlier articles – esp. "Outline of a Decision Procedure for Ethics", *Philosophical Review 66*, (1957) 177–197; and "Justice as Fairness", *Philosophical Review 67*, (1958) 164–194. Rawls briefly discusses paternalism in his *A Theory of Justice*, pp. 248–250.

[24] Rawls gives an elaborate specification of the concept of a rational agent, esp. at pages 142ff.

[25] The "original position" is simply a hypothetical situation in which (a) there are a group of rational agents desiring to agree to principles for the resolution of controversies, (b) there does not already exist a set of such principles, and (c) the rational agents operate under certain noncontroversial moral constraints – e.g. a willingness to live by the rules they agree to, an inability to decide moral questions on the basis of factors (e.g. skin color) that are obviously morally irrelevant, etc. Rawls does not, as has sometimes been charged, attempt to get moral principles out of totally nonmoral premises. Rather he attempts to get controversial moral principles out of a set of premises consisting of (i) nonmoral claims *and* (ii) moral claims that are considerably less controversial than those to be derived. (For a full explanation of the concept of the original position, see Chapter 3.)

[26] In a very brief (but extremely important) section (pp. 251–257) Rawls interprets the veil of ignorance in terms of Kant's concept of a person acting in an *autonomous* way, expressing his nature as a *free* and *rational* being, and respecting a comparable nature in others. At least for me, this section illuminated the entire theory and made it come to life. At least in part, the veil of ignorance is a way of keeping parties in the original position from choosing on the basis of *morally irrelevant* considerations (e.g. skin color) – considerations incompatible with moral autonomy.

[27] On page 62, Rawls defines primary goods as "things that every rational man is presumed to want. These goods normally have a use whatever a person's rational plan of life". One of the more controversial (but, I think, correct) elements in Rawls's theory is his claim that liberty normally has a priority over all other goods.

[28] The theory is also quite controversial and has been subjected to criticisms in articles far too numerous to list here. Some of the more basic of these criticisms, however, have been raised in the following review essays on *A Theory of Justice*: Joel Feinberg *81, Yale L. J.* 5 (1972), and Thomas Nagel, *Philosophical Review 82* (1973). See also Brian Barry's *The Liberal Theory of Justice* (Oxford: Oxford University Press, 1973). Rawls's theory is not without problems, but I know of no other moral theory even remotely comparable in terms of power or general plausibility.

[29] In his excellent article "Paternalism", from which I have learned a great deal, Gerald Dworkin argues as follows: "I suggest that since we are all aware of our irrational propensities, deficiencies in cognitive and emotional capacities, and avoidable and unavoidable ignorance it is rational and prudent for us to in effect take out "social insurance policies". We may argue for and against proposed paternalistic measures in terms of what fully rational individuals would accept as forms of protection. Now clearly, since the initial agreement is not about specific measures we are dealing with a more-or-less blank check and therefore there have to be certain kinds of conditions which make it plausible to suppose that rational men could reach agreement to limit their liberty even when other men's interests are not affected" (p. 120). Though Dworkin makes no reference to Rawls, I believe I am correct in interpreting this as an appeal to a Rawlsian social contract argument. This appeal is, in my judgment, far superior to the "future-oriented

consent" model which Dworkin also considers — superior in the sense that the social contract model captures the essential insight of the future-consent model without falling victim to its considerable weaknesses. Roughly, the future-oriented consent model justifying paternalism goes as follows: "Parental paternalism may be thought of as a wager by the parent on the child's subsequent recognition of the wisdom of the restrictions. There is an emphasis on what could be called future-oriented consent — on what the child will come to welcome, rather than on what he does welcome" (p. 119). There are two basic problems with this: (1) How can we be sure that we do not *manufacture* the consent in the paternalistic process? An example: Jones does not want to be hypnotized. In spite of his wishes, we finally get him hypnotized, place him under suggestion, and command that when he wakes up he will express gratitude that we hypnotized him. When he does this, does it follow that our coercing him was justified? (2) I suspect that some conception of what Rawls calls primary goods is going to condition what we would accept as a genuine case of future consent — i.e. we might never accept as a counter-example the case of someone, who, even after years of paternalistic intervention, still insisted that he preferred some obviously bad state (e.g. being a delusional drug addict) to what he now is (e.g. a successful college student). We should be strongly inclined to say here that he really has not been fully cured yet (using his lack of consent to what we know is reasonable as evidence for this) and insist that, if the cure is ever complete, we will indeed have his consent. This is self-deceptively circular; for we are using our conception of what really is good for a person as a criterion for what a person really consents to. Thus, in spite of all the roundabout talk of future consent, we are really intervening because we believe it is good for the person that we do so. Consider the following example: Suppose our child never comes to agree that those trips to the dentist were worth it. Would we then conclude that we acted wrongly in taking him to the dentist? Surely not. What this shows is that paternalistic intervention in this case is clearly something considerably more than a wager on future consent. The future-consent model's insight lies in its attempt to distinguish between what a man wills at a particular time and what he *would* will if he were only rational. This distinction is much better explicated in terms of what parties in the Rawlsian original position would adopt, and future consent can at most serve as *evidence* that this, the genuine criterion, has been satisfied. Future-consent cannot itself be the criterion. (Dworkin's article appears in *Morality and the Law*, ed. by Richard Wasserstrom [Belmont, Calif.: Wadsworth Publishing Company, 1971].)

[30] For example: Attempts have been made to condition alcoholics against drinking by the administration of anectine — a drug which produces paralysis and near suffocation. Such attempts move us into the world described by Anthony Burgess in his novel *A Clockwork Orange* (New York: Norton, 1963). For more details on this and related cases, see Wexler, *supra*, note 13.

TOTAL INSTITUTIONS AND THE POSSIBILITY
OF CONSENT TO ORGANIC THERAPIES*

Certain contemporary forms of organic therapy used in an attempt to correct or control deviance strike terror into the hearts of traditional liberals and humanists. In addition to radical forms to behavior modification therapy (*e.g.*, the use of "shock sticks" or "cattle prods" on autistic children and the administration of drugs which produce symptoms of suffocation in patients), psychosurgery has also experienced a resurgence of popularity. Its use has been advocated (and sometimes practiced) on impulsively violent persons and on so-called "hyperkinetic" children.

Concern over such dramatic interventions into people's lives is certainly understandable and justified, but reasonable persons presumably are not going to address themselves to this concern merely at the level of gut feeling. They are, of course, going to be alert to protect the rights of individuals against intrusions into important freedoms. But they are going to be equally diligent in attempting to insure that persons retain a right to avail themselves of new and possibly very beneficial forms of therapy or treatment that behavioral science may develop. They are, in other words, going to resist being drawn into some ignorant, anti-scientific movement and are going to expect something more than knee-jerk liberal sloganeering and romantic clichés about humanism, spiritual values, and autonomy.

Organic therapies, contrasted with more conventional psychotherapies, have been defined by Professor Michael Shapiro as "procedures which affect or alter through electrochemical or surgical means a person's thought patterns, sensations, feelings, perceptions, and mentation . . . or mental activity generally; or . . . *conditioning* techniques using the effects of electrical or chemical intervention into mental functioning [or severe physical pain] as part of the conditioning program."[1] Decisions on how to classify certain therapies will no doubt be difficult, and there will surely be some (*e.g.*, those using only moderately severe pain) which we shall have to regard as borderline cases. Given this, it will be useful if a discussion of organic therapies at least begins with what everyone would agree is a non-controversial example, an absolutely clear or paradigm case. *Psychosurgery* is such a case. Used to alter behavior and/or mental activity, it involves a direct physical intervention into and a change in the biological nature of the brain. Its contrast with traditional

183

psychotherapy could hardly be more dramatic, and thus it will be an extremely useful example upon which to build a discussion of organic therapies in general.

Psychosurgery is also a useful example for another reason: It is the therapy of primary focus in what is (in my judgment) the most important and interesting legal case bearing on the issues of organic therapy: *Kaimowitz v. Department of Mental Health.*[2] In this case, which I shall later discuss in detail, it was held that psychosurgery could not legally be performed on involuntarily confined inmates of prisons or mental hospitals ("total institutions," to use Erving Goffman's language[3]) because such inmates are incapable of giving informed, competent, and voluntary consent to such procedures.

Kaimowitz certainly focused upon some absolutely central issues. In the absence of an adequate analysis of the nature and importance of proper *consent*, it is impossible to develop reasonable criteria for evaluating the use of psychosurgery and other organic therapies. Professor Shapiro has put the point as follows:

Personal autonomy values (from which the presumption against substitution of judgment was originally derived) presumptively override the state's interests (and/or means) to the extent that these interests, as implemented by the means, contemplate coercion of the subject. If that is so, then presumptively the state can act in the way it proposes only by securing the informed consent of the subject. Therefore a doctrine of informed consent to organic therapy is constitutionally required.[4]

This, as it stands, strikes me as requiring two modifications. First, the consent requirement needs to be disjunctive, *i.e.*, not informed consent *simpliciter* but rather informed consent *or* a demonstration that the subject is incapable of giving informed consent. Professor Shapiro's statement is acceptable only on the assumption that we are dealing with *competent* subjects. If the subject is incompetent, we will presumably require informed consent — not from the subject — but from a competent surrogate. Second, and related, is the following point: Important as informed consent is as a necessary condition for proper (*i.e.*, morally and legally acceptable) consent, we also surely want to require and urge with equal vigor the following as necessary conditions: the consent must be *competent* and must be *voluntary*. We could, of course, attempt to build the competence and voluntariness requirements into the meaning of "informed consent" as was attempted in California Assembly Bill 2296:

For purposes of this Article, a person gives his "informed consent" if and only if he knowingly [rationally] and intelligently, without duress or coercion, and clearly and explicitly manifests his consent to the proposed organic therapy to the attending physician.[5]

Such is the attempt. However, if this linguistic and conceptual mess is the best that can be done, it does not appear to be a fruitful path to follow. In addition to appearing to suggest that the only knowledge required for informed consent is the knowledge that one is consenting, this passage also crams together a variety of elements of such diversity that — in the interests of clarity — every effort should be made to keep them distinct. For example, I can surely be fully informed on a given medical procedure and yet consent to it only because I was put under duress. Such consent is improper (because involuntary or coerced), but it would be bizarre to regard it as a case of consent that was not informed. And yet the above passage would invite us to do just that. Given such problems and confusions, the reasonable course is, in so far as possible, to keep the requirements of information, competence, and voluntariness conceptually distinct — three *different* but *equally important* necessary conditions for morally and legally proper consent.

In order to limit the number of issues discussed to a manageable set, I shall, even though I do not regard it as self-evident, make the following assumption for purposes of this paper: Psychosurgery (and probably other organic therapies) should be used only on persons who give *consent* that is *competent*, *informed*, and *voluntary* or whose surrogates give such consent. In order to confine discussion to reasonable limits, I shall not consider the special problems raised by the appointment of surrogates — *e.g.*, the special problems involved in using organic therapy on children or the whole complex issue of the nature and justification of paternalism.[6] Given the noted assumption made for purposes of the paper, I shall explore the following two issues: (1) How are the concepts of *competent consent, informed consent,* and *voluntary consent* to be analyzed? (2) Is it possible for such consent, with respect to psychosurgery and other organic therapies, to be given by those who (in some sense) may "need" the therapy the most — namely, involuntarily confined inmates of total institutions?

I shall begin my exploration of these issues by discussing the previously mentioned case of *Kaimowitz v. Department of Mental Health.*[7] This case illustrates the enormous practical importance of analysing the concepts of informed, competent and voluntary consent. It also illustrates the enormous moral and legal mischief that can be done when these concepts are used in a causal and ill-considered way.

KAIMOWITZ V. DEPARTMENT OF MENTAL HEALTH

The opinion in *Kaimowitz* contains a conclusion and a set of arguments in defense of that conclusion. The conclusion, that psychosurgery should not be performed upon prisoners or involuntarily confined inmates of mental hospitals, is one with which I am strongly inclined to agree. The primary argument given in defense of this conclusion, however, is that inmates of these total institutions are incapable of giving competent, informed, and voluntary consent to such surgery. In this section of the paper, I shall argue that the opinion fails utterly to provide a coherent and evidentially well-founded case for this claim and that the claim itself entails consequences that would probably be undesired by most of those who offer it.

The court gives only two arguments in support of the claim that an inmate of total institution cannot give consent that is truly *informed*. The first, that the very character of a total institution is such that it paralyzes the rational and cognitive faculties of inmates, is more relevant to competence and voluntariness than to knowledge; and I shall thus explore it at a later point. The second is that informed consent cannot be given to psychosurgery because psychosurgery is an experimental procedure which, at least at the present time, is not surrounded by a sufficient amount of empirical evidence to allow accurate predictions of probable risks and benefits; and it is to this argument that I shall now address myself.

I agree that psychosurgery is indeed *at best* experimental and tentative and that, given this, we now have no way accurately to assess probable risks and benefits. However, this has *absolutely nothing to do with informed consent* and *absolutely nothing to do with total institutions*! What is currently known about psychosurgery within the scientific community is totally independent of the location, institutional or otherwise, where a potential knowledge seeker resides. Thus if the present state of scientific knowledge concerning psychosurgery is such that it renders informed consent impossible, then *nobody* (in or out of an institution) can give informed consent to psychosurgery.

The above consequence need not worry us, however, since the antecedent of the hypothetical is false. Consent does not become uninformed, in any relevant sense, merely because there is a shortage of information. It is legally and morally important to secure informed consent as a way of respecting the subject's autonomy — which means in this context making sure that he is not merely *used* or *manipulated*. This is at least part of what it means to treat the subject as a person (rather than a thing) or what Kant would call "an end in himself."[8] Now surely I satisfy this demand with respect to a subject so long as I tell him *everything that is known* (little though this may be) about a given procedure, for I thereby eliminate the possibility of using what I know (but he does not) to manipulate him. When he learns that almost nothing is known and that risks and benefits cannot accurately be predicted, *he has been informed* of the information relevant to making an autonomous choice. Many persons, learning of the great uncertainty, might well back off. Others, thinking that a mere *chance* of an improved situation is worth a very high risk, might well proceed; it is difficult to see why such persons would necessarily fail to be autonomous or rational.

The court does not limit itself to an attempt to establish that consent to psychosurgery in total institutions cannot be informed. It also argues that such consent can be neither *competent* nor *voluntary* (concepts which, by the way, the court tends to conflate). Let me quote some of the stronger passages:

A patient is always under duress when hospitalized and . . . in a hospital or institutional setting there is no such thing as a volunteer.

Although an involuntarily detained patient may have a sufficient I.Q. to intellectually comprehend his circumstances . . . the very nature of his incarceration diminishes the capacity to consent to psychosurgery. He is particularly vulnerable as a result of his mental condition, the deprivation stemming from involuntary confinement, and the effects of the phenomenon of "institutionalization."

The inherently coercive atmosphere to which the voluntarily detained mental patient is subjected has bearing upon the voluntariness of his consent. . . . They are not able to voluntarily give informed consent because of the inherent inequality in their position.[9]

What is incredible is that the evidential case presented in defense of these extremely strong claims is hopelessly inadequate. How do we know that institutionalization has these consequences? When, how, and with what frequency do they occur? Does a person become incapable of competent and voluntary consent the moment he enters a total institution, or does this incapacity come about only after a certain amount of time? If the latter, how long? (This matter of temporal duration is of some practical importance. If the terrible effects of institutionalization set in only after a long period of incarceration, then presumably an inmate who has been in a total institution a reasonably short time might well be able to give competent and voluntary consent to psychosurgery.) However, such vital questions are not even *raised*, much less answered, by the court. What we have instead is the uncritical presentation of a certain currently fashionable ideology about institutions.

In order to give the court's opinion the most sympathetic interpretation possible, let us reflect on the nature of total institutions and what there might be about them which tempts the court to conclude that their inmates cannot give competent and voluntary consent. One likely possibility is that the *lure of release* could be used to coerce an inmate into surgery. For example, one would certainly want to guard against something like the following (addressed by a physician to an inmate): "Listen you: unless you submit to psychosurgery, I'll make sure you never get out of here!" Put so baldly, this does indeed look coercive. But because certain offers of psychosurgery in total institutions are coercive, we should not conclude that all offers necessarily are. Compare the following two cases:

(1) Jones is indefinitely confined because he has been held to be dangerous to others. The physician says to him: "It is up to me whether to recommend keeping you in or letting you out. If you go along with this surgery, I shall recommend letting you out. If you refuse to go along, however, I shall recommend keeping you in because of your refusal."

(2) Jones is indefinitely confined because he has been held to be dangerous to others. The physician says to him: "It is up to me whether to recommend keeping you in or letting you out. I cannot justifiably recommend release unless I am reasonably confident that you are no longer dangerous to others. You should consider (a) that traditional methods have failed to correct your dangerous impulses and are almost certain to continue to fail in the future and (b) that psychosurgery, though carrying high risks, *may* eliminate your dangerous tendencies and thus make your release reasonable. Unless you consent to psychosurgery, I do not think it at all likely that I can ever recommend your release. If you do consent, however, the chances of my someday being able to make such a recommendation are perhaps at least a little better."

Assuming that (a) and (b) are true, I see no reason for regarding the situation outlined in case (2) as necessarily an instance of coercion. Case (1) is objectionable in part because the release is being denied *because of the refusal simpliciter* and thus with no reference or relevance to the factors which supposedly justified Jones's incarceration in the first place. This is to take unfair advantage of the subject's vulnerability (a central feature, as I shall later argue, in the concept of coercion) and also involves ignoring a kind of promise to society, *i.e.*, a promise to withhold release until a judgment of nondangerousness is reasonable. (I am not here passing judgment on the question of whether institutions involving such promises are ever justified, all things considered.) In case (2), however, the criterion for justifiable release (in this case, freedom from dangerous impulses) is *independent* from the subject's decision on whether or not to agree to the procedure. If he is released, the reason will be that he is now judged safe — *not* that he consented. (There are various practical mechanisms whereby one might attempt to insure this. For example, the parole or release board might be allowed access only to behavioral information about the inmate and prevented from knowing if the inmate had ever undergone psychosurgery.) This independence tends to minimize the potential for unfair coercion and may reasonably be viewed as a step toward *expanding* the freedom or autonomy of the inmate by giving him an additional option that is *prima facie* reasonable. I seriously doubt that the court wishes to hold that offers to prison inmates of *parole* or reduced sentence for good behavior or for completing programs of vocational rehabilitation are impermissible because unfairly coercive, and yet these offers clearly introduce the lure of release as an incentive to prompt the inmate to improve himself and thus eliminate at least *some* of the reasons that supposedly justified the deprivation of his liberty in the first place.[10] Focusing on inmates of mental institutions, where none of the reasons justifying incarceration will be retributive, it could plausibly be argued that such inmates may have a constitutional *right* to elect even extreme and risky forms of treatment if such treatment offers them their only hope of getting out of society's institutional clutches. For consider the following two claims: (a) "You will remain in this terrible place for the rest of your life, *period*." (b) "You will remain in this terrible place for the rest of your life *unless* this surgical procedure succeeds in rendering you reasonably harmless to society." I could certainly sympathize with the claim (much more radical than any the court would want to make) that *both* (a) and (b) constitute coercive assaults on human rights, dignity, and autonomy. What I find bizarre, however, is the claim that (b) constitutes such an assault whereas (a) does not — that leaving the inmate to languish in some terrible place because of some terrible condition somehow preserves respect for his rights, dignity and autonomy.

Many of the remarks made by the court seem to make an even stronger claim than the one I have just discussed. It is not merely that the lure of release makes an offer of psychosurgery coercive, it is (so the argument now runs) that total institutions turn inmates into incompetent near-vegetables or automata. Their minds, having become a kind of spiritual jello, are no longer capable of the kinds of choices we think normal for autonomous persons. Having previously argued that inmates can give neither informed nor voluntary consent to psychosurgery, the court now argues that inmates are not even *competent*.

I have previously noted that the court gives almost nothing in the way of evidence to support its very strong claims, and so I should now like to concentrate on three additional (and related) points:

(i) If prisons and mental hospitals are in fact destroying the minds and wills of inmates, then I do not see how we can ever be justified in putting people into these cruel and unusual institutions in the first place *or* how psychosurgery is likely to be much worse. Why protect inmates against losing that which, according to this view, they have lost already? How can we be called upon to respect their rights as autonomous persons in institutions when, according to this theory of institutions, they do not have any autonomy within them?[11]

(ii) The court supplements its argument about consent with constitutional arguments to the effect: (a) there are constitutional rights to express and generate ideas and to maintain the privacy of the intellect, and (b) psychosurgery is likely to destroy a person's capacity to generate ideas and would interfere with the privacy of that person's intellect. Given this, psychosurgery should never be allowed in total institutions. I find this constitutional argument extremely plausible in its own terms; but it does not, in my judgment, sit at all well with the arguments previously given by the court in attempting to establish that consent to psychosurgery in total institutions could not be competent. According to the picture painted of total institutions when the court was trying to persuade us that consent to psychosurgery in such institutions could not be competent, inmates in total institutions *already* seem to have lost their capacity to generate ideas and no longer have any intellect to invade! I do not see how the court can easily have it both ways. It cannot be the case that, when attempting to consent to things, inmates in total institutions are incompetent, ignorant, irrational and coerced but that, when constitutional issues are raised, these same inmates are suddenly transformed into spontaneous, autonomous, enlightened generators of ideas.

(iii) The final point worth making about *Kaimowitz*, and the most important one from a practical standpoint, is that the main reasoning of the court quite ironically *goes against* a major thrust of liberal reform in the mental health-prison area in recent years. In trying to win for patients and/or prisoners the rights to do such things as vote, get married, manage their own money, consent (or refuse to consent) to *normal* medical procedures, etc., it has been necessary to insist again and again that one may not infer incompetence from the mere fact of institutionalization. A person might justifiably be committed to an institution and yet remain perfectly competent to manage — if not all — at least a very wide and complex range of his affairs; the mere fact of institutionalization, in other words, must not be allowed to demote an inmate from the status of an autonomous person and a bearer of rights. But now, in *Kaimowitz*, the court seems to be saying (by implication) that the above reform was all a mistake, that the mere fact of institutionalization *does* establish incompetence. The *Kaimowitz* decision was enthusiastically welcomed by liberals who seek to reduce the coercion experienced by inmates in total institutions. Ironically, the decision provides the basis for making the very coercion feared by liberals *easier* to justify!

It should be obvious from this discussion that *Kaimowitz* has certainly not cleared up the conceptual and moral problems surrounding consent to organic therapies in total institutions. It has, rather, shown just how badly such clarification is needed. In the remaining time, I should like to make a *start* toward such clarification.

INFORMATION, VOLUNTARINESS AND COMPETENCE

Informed Consent

As I suggested previously, it is important that we realize that the requirement of informed consent is much more of a *moral* than an epistemological demand. The information or knowledge involved is not that which would be required in order to allow a rational agent to make some probabalistic judgment concerning outcomes with a high degree of accuracy. This kind of information can be lacking (*e.g.*, in many experimental situations) and the consent can still, in the important moral sense, be informed. What is this moral sense? I suggest the following: The information required for informed consent is that level of information which is necessary in order to eliminate or at least radically reduce the possibility of the subject's being *manipulated* by the physician. It is not the *amount* of information *per se* available to the subject that matters; what is of primary importance is that relevant information *differentials* between the subject and the physician be minimized or (ideally) eliminated. This will eliminate what I shall call "informational vulnerability" on the part of the subject *vis-a-vis* the physician — a vulnerability which can, in obvious ways, give the physician an unfair advantage to be exploited in the manipulation of the subject toward the physician's desired end. Thus the proper requirement for informed consent is easy to state: *All* relevant information known in the medical-scientific community concerning the procedure (however little this may be) must be conveyed to the subject.[12] There are, so far as I can see, only three problems with this, two practical and one theoretical.

First, it might seem difficult to state in a very precise way what information is relevant, *i.e.*, how the concept of relevance is to be analyzed in this context. Surely the physician must not be required to tell the subject *everything* that is known about the procedure, *e.g.*, that the surgery used to be closed up with green bandages but that now blue ones are used. This piece of information clearly is not relevant to making a responsible choice concerning agreement to the procedure. On the other hand, other pieces of information (*e.g.*, 25% of persons undergoing the surgery die) clearly are relevant. The problem, however, may seem to be what to do, not with these obvious and clear cases, but with any borderline cases that might arise. But the answer to this strikes me as quite simple: When in doubt, tell the subject.

Second, there is the problem of the *language* in which the information must be conveyed to the subject. It obviously will not do to communicate the information in highly technical language which only trained physicians can understand. It must, rather, be translated into ordinary language which any normally competent person can understand. Two questions, of course, remain: (1) *Can* all relevant information be conveyed in non-technical language? and (2) How do we know when a proper communication − *i.e.*, one in non-technical language which can be understood by any normally competent person − is likely to take place?

My bet is that the answer to the first question is *yes*. If, contrary to my bet, it turns out to be *No* in some cases, then we simply have a case where informed consent in the relevant sense is *not* possible to secure. The second question, how do we know if the communication is likely to be successful, involves both a practical and a theoretical aspect. The practical aspect simply involves the creation of an environment which makes it likely that the right questions will be asked by the subject or posed by the physician and that these questions will be answered in a useful way − *i.e.*, an environment which is conducive to calm, reflective, comfortable discussion and deliberation. It should not be too difficult to devise mechanisms whereby these requirements are likely to be satisfied. One obvious way it might be attempted is to include non-professional, non-educated persons of normal competence on the review panels which typically oversee these cases. These persons could examine the setting for the questions and answers and the language used to pose the questions and provide the answers. If it all seemed proper and perfectly intelligible to them, this would at least be some good (if not conclusive) evidence that proper communication is likely to take place.

So much for the practical problem. The theoretical problem, and the third basic problem with the nature and justification of the informed consent requirement, is that talk of informed consent makes sense only on the assumption that the subject is *competent*. All of the information in the world is useless if directed toward an incompetent subject, *e.g.*, someone of radically subnormal intelligence or involved in some complex psychotic delusion. In the latter kind of case, the "risk" the subject may be worried about is whether his legs, since they are after all made of glass, are going to break on the operating table. What this suggests is that the concept of informed consent depends upon an adequate analysis of the concept of competent consent. I agree with this and shall discuss competence later. At present, however, I simply want to insist on the following: If an inmate of a total institution *is* competent, there is no reason to suppose that he is necessarily incapable of giving informed consent as I have characterized it above.

Voluntary Consent

One of my main objections to the opinion in *Kaimowitz* is the apparent inclination on the part of the court to maintain that when any factor (*e.g.*, the prospect of release) is introduced which makes a course of action more eligible or attractive for a subject, then that subject, if he chooses the course of action, has been *coerced* and thus that his choice or consent has not been voluntary. This cannot be correct, since it would make all sorts of behavior count as coercive (*e.g.*, my offering to sell you my six thousand dollar car for two thousand dollars) which we typically would not want to regard as coercive. My very strongly tempting you is simply not the same as my coercing you or putting you under duress.

Neither, however, do we want to go to the other extreme and argue that a person has not been coerced or put under duress unless it was *impossible* for him to act otherwise given some factor which was introduced into his deliberations. For example, it is certainly *possible* for a person to let his family be tortured to death rather than give in to the demands of some bandit who is using this as a threat. Even given this possibility, however, we should surely want to say that the person — if he gives in to the demand — has been coerced or put under duress and that, in some sense, what he did was not fully voluntary.

What this suggests is that the core of the concept of duress or coercion, like that of the concept of informed consent, is *moral*, not psychological. What we are concerned with primarily in avoiding coercion or duress is avoiding, not psychological pressure *per se* (that is not avoidable), but psychological pressure which is *unfair*, which involves taking an unfair advantage of some vulnerability in the subject. The case of the person whose family is threatened is a case of duress, not because he could not conceivably bring himself to let his family die, but because it is unfair to impose such a burden of choice upon him. What about the case of offering to sell my car? Most of us probably do not see anything unfair or immoral in such commercial transactions, and so we are not inclined to regard this as a case of coercion. However, if my offer is to sell you medical care, or food for your family, or essential clothing for a very high price, we would at least be *inclined* to speak of coercion or duress, not because you could not do without these things, but because it is unfair that you should do without them or make unreasonable sacrifices for them. Coercion (or duress) is a morally loaded concept; a coercive offer must be an immoral offer.

Professor Vinit Haksar has argued for the necessary connection between coercion and immorality and has introduced the useful concept of what he calls the potential coercer's "unilateral plan of action," *i.e.*, what he proposes to do if the subject does not do what is desired of him.[13] According to Haksar, coercion occurs only when the unilateral plan of action is immoral; this claim does accord with our previous cases. The offer to sell you my car is not coercive (no matter how much the car tempts you) because my unilateral plan of action is to keep the car if you do not pay me what I want, and surely my keeping my own car is not wrong. Withholding medical care, food or clothing at least seems to involve an immoral element, and these are cases which at least *tempt* us to talk of coercion. Killing your family is clearly immoral, and we have here a clear case of coercion.

Summing all of this up, then, I suggest the following: Coercion of a subject involves taking an unfair advantage of his vulnerability by proposing, unless he accepts a certain offer, to treat him in a way that is unfair and in a way which he has no power to prevent.[14]

What about an offer of psychosurgery (or some other organic therapy) to an inmate of a total institution? Such inmates are certainly vulnerable, *i.e.*, powerless to prevent things we might do to them. But there are ways of treating vulnerable people that do not involve taking an unfair advantage of their vulnerability, and this must be the focus of our concern. Let us then return to the two cases I discussed in connection with *Kaimowitz*.[15]

I have suggested that case (1) involves coercion whereas case (2) does not, and now I am in a position to elaborate why this is so. In both cases, we are dealing with vulnerable subjects. But only in the first case are we talking unfair advantage of the subject's vulnerability. In the first case, the unilateral plan of action is to leave the subject in the institution regardless of any change in the condition which presumably justified his incarceration in the first place. And that is surely unfair to him. If he is there because he is dangerous, it is only fair that he be released when he is non-dangerous. It is unfair to let his release depend upon something quite irrelevant to what justifies his being there, *e.g.*, the irrelevant consideration of his willingness to be an experimental subject.

In the second case, however, this unfair element is not present. Though he *may* be experimented on, the point of the experiment is, if possible, to render him non-dangerous and thus eligible for release for the *correct* reason. Though his consent will be contingently related to his improvement, he will be released *because of the improvement* (if it comes) and not without the improvement, no matter how willing the consent. The unilateral plan of action here is to keep the subject confined until he is better; this plan (assuming that we accept the rules of the commitment "game") is fair. Notice how different "until he is better" is from "until he plays ball with the researchers." The former renders the unilateral plan of keeping the subject morally acceptable; the latter renders it morally objectionable and the situation unfairly coercive.

From this I tentaively conclude the following: Case (2) involves no unfair coercion. Cases of this sort can arise in total institutions. Therefore, it is not impossible that inmates in total institutions give voluntary consent to psychosurgery and other organic therapies, just as it is not impossible that they give voluntary consent to consitions for parole.

But this conclusion is only tentative. Let me complicate matters a bit and introduce a line of reasoning which undermines the conclusion. The line of reasoning goes as follows: It can be agreed that there is one perfectly clear sense in which the choice between staying in a total institution or electing psychosurgery (or conditions of parole) is voluntary or non-coerced. But this sense does not go deep enough. The real moral pinch — to use the language of the court in *Kaimowitz* — is that the whole *background situation* is "inherently coercive." What might this phrase mean? I suppose that one might regard the following case, though involving a certain degree of voluntary choice, as still a case of inherent coercion: A gunman threatens to kill me unless I give him either my watch or my money. He is not overly greedy, so he will not make me give up both. My choice between giving him the money or giving him the watch is surely voluntary, not a case of coercion of duress. He has, after all, left *that much* utterly up to me. However, it is not fair that I be put in this position in the first place, because the gunman *has no right* to either my watch or my money. Though the choice is itself uncoerced, my having to make that choice is coerced. Borrowing the language of the court, then, we could say that this situation is unfair or immoral because "inherently coercive." But, if this is the kind of case the court has in mind (or is the only way to give sense to the phrase "inherent coercion"), it has a very interesting consequence, namely, that it is as much an argument against the legitimacy of incarceration (the analogue of the watch) as it is an argument against the legitimacy of psychosurgery (the analogue of the money)! Political radicals (who are inclined to argue, for example, that conditions of parole are attempts to coerce them into adopting white, middle-class values) will certainly not be upset by this conclusion,[16] but it is surely much more extreme than anything the court would want to support. For the court, in opposing psychosurgery in the terms of this model of unfair coercion, will find itself making an attack against incarceration or instutionalization itself.

Competent Consent

At this point, we should move to a careful examination of the concept of competence. Competence is a necessary condition for informed and voluntary consent, and its absence carries with it, at least *prima facie*, a very serious consequence, namely, that we are dealing with a person with respect to whom large scale *paternalistic* intervention is justified. We have here, then, a very important concept. I shall not explore this concept in detail here.[17] For present purposes, let me give just the barest summary of my views.

Incompetent people are, as the slang goes, "really out of it"; they are *devoid of reason*. Of course, a person's incompetence does not have to be across the board; it can be limited to certain areas of choice and decision. In those areas where a person is incompetent or devoid of reason, however, he is not simply eccentric or unusual. Rather he is radically out of touch with the common standards and shared judgments which make social life (and even communication) possible. There are various ways in which a person might reveal that his loss of contact is of such a radical nature. In the most extreme and least controversial case, we shall find persons who are in trances or comas, persons who are, like objects, *non*-rational. In other cases, we shall find various kinds of radical *ir*rationality, *e.g.*, the person will not be able to weigh the evidence relevant to making a reasonable judgment or, even more striking, will not even recognize what *counts* as relevant to making the judgment.[18] Of course, as we are all now well aware from the writings of Thomas Szasz and others, it is very difficult as a matter of practice to distinguish cases of genuine incompetence from cases of merely eccentric or nonconformist behavior; there is always the danger that our moral and ideological prejudices will cloud our judgment. But surely we can at least *sometimes* be on fairly safe ground, can *sometimes* be confronted with a case so clear that the noted dangers might be avoided.

Consider the case (drawn from fact) of a person who for years has spoken and continues to speak *only* the following sentence: "Jake is at the corner of 5th and Congress." This is the *only* sentence he ever utters, and it presumably exhausts his entire mental life. One can hardly imagine sitting down with this person and trying to inform him about some therapeutic procedure and getting his voluntary consent to it. Conversation with such a person is not just eccentric; it is *impossible*. Surely he is a paradigm case of an incompetent person, as are autistic children and many (though certainly not all) psychotics.

Given these cases, I find irresponsible those liberals who argue against commitment and therapy for such people by rhapsodizing incoherently about their "autonomy." Thomas Szasz and others have usefully inveighed against the dangers of "madness mongering," *i.e.*, regarding as sick those persons who may merely be unconventional or ideologically objectionable. But Szasz and his followers, as Professor Herbert Morris has noted, run the risk of doing comparable damage by "responsibility" or "autonomy mongering".[19] If the kinds of persons described above are going to count as autonomous and responsible persons, then the concepts of autonomy and responsibility lose whatever sense and moral force they might legitimately have enjoyed. It is astounding, for example, the extent to which traditional liberals have failed to appreciate the subtlety of Anthony Burgess's novel, *A Clockwork Orange*[20] (a novel which always comes up in these discussions), by viewing it simply as an unambiguous attack on the way in which behavioral technology can destroy the autonomy of subjects like Alex, the central character. They give this interpretation without explaining — or even without seeing that they might have a *problem* in explaining — exactly in what sense this psychopathic character was supposed to be autonomous *before* the therapeutic intervention![21]

How can the concept of competence be related to the main issue explored in this paper? Given the quite extreme conditions which (in my judgment) have to be satisfied before one can properly be called incompetent or devoid of reason, it seems fairly certain that not every (even long-term) inmate of a total institution will be incompetent, and it seems highly unlikely that even the majority of them will be. Given this, it is not reasonable to suppose (as the *Kaimowitz* court did) that inmates of total institutions are not competent to consent to organic therapies such as psychosurgery.

CONCLUSION

In closing, I want to re-emphasize that the argument of this article has very limited objectives. It was primarily the examination of a certain case against psychosurgery and the judgment that this case is a failure. I have not argued that inmates should be offered psychosurgery, only that it is possible that they could give informed, voluntary, and competent consent to it. And the mere claim that inmates can properly consent to X does not entail either that they have a right to X or that X ought to be offered to them. My belief, for example, that it is possible for inmates to give informed, voluntary, and competent consent to the use of copper bracelets for arthritis is perfectly compatible with my belief that the state should not (for both moral and prudential reasons) purchase, offer, and make available these items of medical quackery to inmates. Thus everything that I have said is quite compatible with my being — as I am — opposed to psychosurgery on inmates, at least at the present time.[22]

NOTES

*   Earlier versions of this article were presented at a symposium on 'Behavior Control and the Law,' American Philosophical Association, Pacific Division, March 28, 1975, and at the "Conference on Medical Ethics," University of Illinois at Chicago Circle, May 23, 1975. I am grateful to David Wexler and Keith Lehrer for their helpful comments on earlier drafts.

[1]   Shapiro,' Legislating the Control of Behavior Control: Autonomy and Coercive Use of Organic Therapies', 47 *So. Cal. L. Rev.* 237, 244 n.8 (1974) (original emphasis).

[2]   Civ. No. 73–19434–AW (Wayne County C. C., Mich., July 10, 1973).

[3]   E. Goffman, *Asylums* (New York, Doubleday, 1961).

[4]   Shapiro, *supra* note 1, at 280–81 (footnotes omitted).

[5]   Cal. A. B. 2296, § 2672(a), qoted in Shapiro, *supra* note 1, at 341.

[6]   See Murphy, 'Incompetence and Paternalism,' 60 *Archiv Für Rechts und Sozialphilosophie* 465 (1974); see also *Punishment and Rehabilitation* (Belmont, Calif.: Wadsworth Publishing Co., 1973).

[7]   Note 2 *supra*.

[8]   I. Kant, *Fundamental Principles of the Metaphysics of Morals*, trans. L. W. Beck (Indianapolis: Bobbs-Merrill, 1959), pp. 46–49.

[9]   Note 2 *supra*.

[10] I say "some of the reasons" because the inmate's becoming a more socially acceptable person clearly will not be sufficient to remove any retributive reasons that might have entered into the justification of his incarceration.

[11] Of course, if we had adequate evidence for the claims that the bad effects of psychosurgery are irreversible and that the bad effects of long term incarceration in total institutions are reversible, then it would be plausible to claim that psychosurgery represents a much worse option. I suspect, however, that we do not have such evidence. (Of course there is an uninteresting sense in which psychosurgery is irreversible: when n number of brain cells are gone, then they are gone for good. But this does not demonstrate that the bad effects of psychosurgery are permanently irreversible, *e.g.*, some physicians talk of parts of the brain being "retrained" to "take over" for damaged parts.)

[12] I use the phrase "known in the medical-scientific community" rather than "known to the physician" for the following reason: Although I think the primary goal of a requirement of informed consent is to prevent manipulation by the physician, another important goal is surely to protect the subject against a well-meaning but ignorant or negligent physician.

13 V. Haksar, 'Civil Disobedience, Threats and Offers', (unpublished paper). The relevant part has now been published as 'Coercive Proposals' in *Political Theory* 4, No. 1 (Feb. 1976), pp. 65–79. I now realize that Haksar's views, as presented in my paper, are somewhat misinterpreted. He distinguishes between coercive *threats* and coercive *offers* and argues that the nature of the immorality involved in the former is different from the nature of the immorality involved in the latter. His more complex analysis, however, can still be used in support of the basic claims of my essay.

14 Blackmail poses a problem for this analysis, since the blackmailer's unilateral plan of action (e.g. to tell what he knows) may be something he has a rights to do. Yet he is surely a coercer. See my 'Blackmail,' forthcoming in *The Monist.*

15 See text at pp. *supra.*

16 Indeed, some limited support for it can be found in Murphy, 'Marxism and Retribution,' 2 Philosophy and Public Affairs 217 (1973). (Reprinted in the present collection).

17 I have written extensively on the concept of competence in 'Incompetence and Paternalism,' *supra* note 6. (Reprinted in the present collection).

18 In 'Incompetence and Paternalism,' *supra* note 6, I expanded these notions in the following way:

Incompetent people may be people who are in a certain sense devoid of reason. What does this mean? I suggest that "Jones is devoid of reason" can mean any of the following:

(1) Jones is nonrational – i.e., like a stone or any other object Jones is such that it makes no sense even to attribute choice or decision power to him at all – e.g. Jones is in a deep coma, is catatonic, etc.

(2) Jones is irrational. This notion can be broken down as follows:

(a) Jones believes things that are *intrinsically* irrational – i.e. believes propositions which, by their very nature, no rational man could believe.

(b) Jones is *systematically wrong* in his judgments – i.e. he systematically weighs available evidence incorrectly.

(c) Jones *does not even appreciate what is relevant* to forming a judgment on the issue in question – i.e. he does not even *consider* relevant evidence.

Though these various kinds of irrationality have a tendency to merge into each other in actual cases, we can perhaps imagine cases where they may be isolated. (2a) is easiest: Suppose Jones literally believes that he is an insect. We would not have to know anything else about Jones at all to correctly conclude that he is irrational.

Let us try to construct a case to illustrate (2b). Suppose Jones is trying to determine the molecular structure of a certain substance. He draws upon some old, badly documented work by the late scientist Smith. It is the best work available, and worth considering, but it leaves a great deal to be desired. Suppose Jones now sets up an excellent modern laboratory, staffs it with the best experts available, and begins to perform elaborate x-ray defraction crystallographic analysis on the substance. Smith had said that the structure of the substance was A, Jones's carefully controlled experiments show not-A, and Jones publishes a paper in which he defends A and cites Smith's work as his main justification. And his whole scientific career (as long as it lasts) has a similar pattern. Here he knows what is relevant, and yet he seems unable to weigh it correctly – i.e. he gives a greater weight to old, badly documented studies than to controlled experiments carried out under the best conditions. Granting agencies, knowing this about him, would surely be reasonable in regarding him as incompetent to engage in this sort of research and correctly speak of him as irrational. Compare the case of the paranoid who agrees that certain compassionate behavior on the part of people is evidence that not everyone is out to get him but who systematically downplays and reinterprets that evidence in the light of anything, however slight, that seems persecutory in nature.

Let us move to case (2c). Jones wants to discover the cure for a certain disease. He has access to the best available scientific findings concerning the disease and its cure — findings that strongly indicate that the disease can be cured by administration of drug *D*. Indifferent to all this, however, Jones visits a local guru. The guru touches him on the head, mumbles a few beatitudes of doubtful intelligibility, and then loudly proclaims that God has revealed to him in a vision that the disease is not to be cured by drug *D*. It is rather to be cured by having the patient stand on his head and recite his astrological chart backwards in Greek. Jones, not even surprised that God would concern himself with such matters, immediately believes all that he has been told by the guru. Here we do not have a case of weighing relevant evidence badly, but a case where the individual involved reveals that he does not have the slightest idea of what counts as relevant to determining the question at issue. This kind of case, unfortunately, is not at all unreal — e.g., it parallels almost exactly the recently publicized case of a child allowed to die of diabetes because his parents, in trying to determine how best to control their son's diabetes, accepted the counsel of a faith healer over that of expert doctors who had prescribed insulin. This is a clear case of grotesque inattention to what is non-controversially relevant.

[19]   Morris, Book Review, 18 *U.C.L.A. Rev.* **1164**, 1166 (1971).

[20]   A. Burgess, *A Clockwork Orange* (New York: Norton, 1963).

[21]   See Murphy, 'Moral Death: A Kantian Essay on Psychopathy', 82 *Ethics* 284 (1972). (Reprinted in the present collection).

[22]   In my judgment, the main points to be made against psychosurgery are the following: (i) It has been persuasively argued that the claim that psychosurgery can in fact cure "brain diseases" which cause violence is in part incoherent and in part supported by evidence that is grotesquely inadequate. See John Hodson, 'Reflections Concerning Violence and the Brain,' 9 *Crim. L. Bull.* 684 (1973), review of V. Mark & F. Ervin, *Violence and the Brain* (New York: Harper and Row, 1970). If this is true, then psychosurgical interventions as a response to social deviance border upon charlatanism and medical quackery. As such, they would hardly deserve (either morally or prudentially) public funding or serious consideration as posible solutions to the problem of controlling crime. (Recall my analogy: My belief that it is possible for inmates to give informed, competent and voluntary consent to the use of copper bracelets for arthritis is perfectly consistent with my belief that the state should not purchase, offer, and make available these items of medical superstition to inmates). (ii) It is my belief that many (perhaps most) people incarcerated in prisons and mental hospitals are there for reasons that are largely suspect. Bad laws, bad criteria for such concepts as "dangerous" and "violent" and "disease," economic exploitation, and the occupance of crucial positions of power by evil, ignorant, and ideologically-biased persons have, in my judgment, a prominent part in the explanation of the incarceration of inmates in America. I am greatly opposed to having this venal aspect of the American system of "justice" further hidden with a strengthening of the already too prevalent illusion that social deviance, rather than frequently being a normal understandable response to certain intolerable social conditions, is primarily a result of individual pathology or disease. This illusion causes us to look for quick and simple solutions in all the wrong places. (iii) Finally, and closely

related to the above, I am extremely skeptical that procedures and mechanisms could be designed that would prevent the administration of psychosurgery to those who are *not* capable of informed, voluntary ad competent consent. Though, as I have argued, I believe that it is possible for some inmates to give such consent in total institutions, I am inclined to suspect that cases of correct use (*i.e.*, cases of type (2)) are likely to be greatly outnumbered by cases of abuse (*i.e.*, cases of type (1)). The burden of proof is surely upon the advocates of psychosurgery to come up with the proper safeguards. Until they do, I should continue to oppose psychosurgery on inmates even if all my other objections to it could somehow be met.

PART FOUR

DEATH AND THE SUPREME COURT

Primitive man saw someone who belonged to him die
— his wife, his child, his friend, whom assuredly he
loved as we love ours, for love cannot be much younger
than the lust to kill. Then, in his pain, he had to learn
that one can indeed die oneself, an admission against
which his whole being revolted; for each of these loved
ones was, in very truth, a part of his own beloved ego.
But even so, on the other hand, such deaths had a
rightfulness for him, since in each of the loved persons
something of the hostile stranger had resided. . . . The
death of the stranger he had no objection to; it meant
the annihilation of a creature hated, and primitive man
had no scruples about bringing it about.

Sigmund Freud
Thoughts on War and Death

RATIONALITY AND THE FEAR OF DEATH

> Cowards die many times before their deaths;
> The valiant never taste of death but once.
> Of all the wonders that I yet have heard,
> It seems to me most strange that men should fear;
> Seeing that death, a necessary end,
> Will come when it will come.

> Shakespeare, *Julius Caesar*

I

"To philosophize," writes Montaigne, "is to learn to die,"[1] This remark forms part of a long-standing tradition in philosophy which teaches that a truly wise or rational man will not fear death; and this tradition has found its way into our ordinary language — e.g. it is common to describe a person who accepts a terminal illness with patience as "philosophical" about his death. And most people would, I think, so describe the attitude expressed in the quoted remark given to Caesar — a remark particularly interesting because, in addition to telling us a great deal about the kind of person Shakespeare conceived Caesar to be, it appears to contain what has often been offered as an *argument* that one is irrational in fearing death. The argument is that death is necessary or inevitable in the natural order of things and that, once one sees this, one will also see that fearing death is irrational.[2] Such an idea is found in the Stoics and the Epicureans among others and is, in many respects, interestingly different from the way of thinking about death that Christianity introduced into our civilization. The most illustrious and systematic defender of the pagan conception, of course, is Spinoza:

A free man, that is to say, a man who lives according to the dictates of reason alone, is not led by fear of death, but directly desires the good, that is to say, desires to act, to live, and to preserve his being in accordance with the principle of seeking his own profit. He thinks, therefore, of nothing less than death, and his wisdom is a meditation upon life (*Ethics*, Four, LXVII).[3]

From Spinoza we get the idea, not merely that it is irrational to fear death, but that the absence of such irrational fearing is the mark of a kind of freedom or human liberation – the only kind of freedom or liberation possible in the realm of necessity. This idea of freedom as rational understanding, though a part of earlier philosophical traditions, is at the heart of Spinoza's philosophy.

My primary purpose in this paper is sympathetically to develop this pagan way of thinking about death – a way of thinking which many writers (e.g. Carl Jung)[4] regard as excessively rationalistic. This charge of excessive rationalism in part no doubt grows out of a desire to be as obscurantist as possible on important matters – a desire to convince ourselves, as J. L. Austin once remarked, of how clever we are by showing how obscure everything is. But part of the charge I suspect (particularly when it comes from psychiatrists and psychoanalysts) is based on the belief that rational thinking about death can ultimately provide no genuine solace or comfort to those troubled about the matter. (Why, for example, should the fact that death is a "necessary end" ease our minds? It might, if anything, seem to make matters worse, since inevitability precludes hope.) As the continued prevalence of sexual guilt and neurosis in a supposedly "sexually enlightened" age seems to indicate, intellectual understanding does not guarantee emotional peace.

I should certainly agree that there are no guarantees here. But surely there is evidence that rational thinking sometimes provides solace for some people – e.g. witness the lives and deaths of Spinoza, Hume, and Freud. It is not to be expected that all men will derive comfort from the same source, but this is no reason unjustly to discriminate against those who might find comfort in being reasonable. The primary goal of philosophy, of course, is not comfort but understanding; and understanding does not necessarily comfort. However, I am convinced that it is a fact that judging a fear to be irrational can sometimes be instrumental either in directly extinguishing that fear or in prodding a person to gain help (e.g. through therapy) in extinguishing that fear. For this reason, it will perhaps be of some practical use if it can be shown that it is irrational to fear death. I should not, of course, want to overestimate the probability here – something which "rationalists" are indeed perhaps inclined to do.

Judging the rational status of the fear of death has its most obvious practical utility, however, not in providing immediate comfort to people experiencing the fear, but rather in coming to terms with such issues as recommending therapy for others or in planning programs of education for children. Should we try to desensitize children to a certain degree by, for example, exposing them to the deaths of others rather than, as is our present practice, shielding them from such unpleasantness?[5] I take it that we cannot properly answer this sort of question unless we first make a judgment concerning the rationality (i.e. the appropriateness and utility) of this fear and the role it may play in human life. The fear of death makes people "feel bad," but not all feelings which are unpleasant to those who experience them are to be extinguished. Neurotic feelings of guilt or shame (i.e. feeling guilty or ashamed when one has really done nothing wrong), for example, should surely be extinguished. They are inappropriate and harmful. However, genuine moral feelings (e.g. outrage over unjust treatment of self or others, guilt over *real* injury or wrongdoing to others, etc.) are appropriate and moreover probably produce good consequences — e.g. action against injustice, restitution for injury, etc. And yet these feelings, though perfectly rational, are just as unpleasant to feel as those which are irrational. Thus the question of what feelings to extinguish is not to be answered solely by a consideration of whether they make the person feeling them suffer. Some suffering is appropriate and beneficial. This is not to say that suffering is irrelevant to rationality; for it is irrational to approve of suffering, either for oneself or others, for no good reason. My only point is that, since in some cases there may be good reasons, the appropriateness or desirability or rationality of a feeling is not solely a function of that feeling's hedonic tone.

Before beginning my development of the argument that (in a certain sense) it is irrational to fear death, it is necessary that I indicate what I mean to include, for purposes of this paper, under the expression "the fear of death." This phrase is used in ordinary language to cover a very heterogeneous group of phenomena; and it is obviously not true that all feelings that could be characterized by the phrase "fear of death" are irrational. When Spinoza, for example, claimed that it is irrational to fear death, he surely did not mean to suggest that it is irrational to do such things as look both ways before crossing a street — i.e. he surely wanted to distinguish a reasonably prudent concern for one's safety from that fear of death which he regarded as contrary to reason. It is presumably not irrational to fear a *permature* death and thus take certain steps — e.g. give up smoking cigarettes, reduce cholesterol intake, exercise, etc. — in order to prolong life as long as possible. Thus these concerns, even if they are properly characterized as involving a fear of death, are not directly my concern in this paper. I am rather concerned simply with the fear that one will die *simpliciter*, the fear based on the certain fact of human mortality — not the fear that one might die early (perhaps avoidable) but the fear that one will die sometime (certainly unavoidable). Thus my concern lies in assessing the rationality of fearing death in the sense in which death is *unavoidable*. Unavoidability is dramatically illustrated for the man who knows that he has a terminal illness, but the certainty of death is no greater for such a person than for the rest of us. He simply has a better guess as to the time. My subject, then, is man's necessary mortality as an object of fear and of the kind of self-deception that fear induces.

The syllogism he had learnt from Kiesewetter's Logic: 'Caius is a man, men are mortal, therefore Caius is mortal,' had always seemed to him correct as applied to Caius, but certainly not as applied to himself. That Caius — man in the abstract — was mortal, was perfectly correct, but he was not Caius, not an abstract man, but a creature quite, quite separate from all others. He had been little Vanya, with a mamma and papa, afterwards with Katenka and with all the joys, griefs, and delights of childhood, boyhood, and youth. What did Caius know of the smell of that striped leather ball Vanya had been so fond of? Had Caius kissed his mother's hand like that, and did the silk of her dress rustle so for Caius? Had he rioted like that at school when the pastry was bad? Had Caius been in love like that? Could Caius preside at a session as he did? 'Caius really was mortal and it was right for him to die; but for me, little Vanya, Ivan Ilych, with all my thoughts and emotions, it's altogether a different matter. It cannot be that I ought to die. That would be too terrible.' Such was his feeling.

Leo Tolstoy, *The Death of Ivan Ilych*

I shall now proceed by arguing in the following stages. First, I shall develop a general account of the concepts "rational fearing" and "irrational fearing." Second, I shall attempt to analyze the concept of *death* — what is it and why do people tend to regard it as a terrible and thus fearful thing? Finally, I shall apply the general account of rational fearing to the topic of death.

II

I should like to develop a general account of the distinction between rational fearing and irrational fearing in the hope that this account may ultimately be used to illuminate the fear of death. The account that I shall offer purports to capture and distinguish between some intuitively acceptable cases of fearings that are clearly rational and fearings that are clearly irrational. If the account looks correct for the clear cases, then we may have some confidence that it will help us come to terms with the rational status of the fear of death — a case where pretheoretical convictions no doubt are in conflict.

Now at the outset, it is important to realize that the expression "Jones is irrational in fearing" is crucially ambiguous. On the one hand, we can mean that the *fear itself* is irrational — i.e. inappropriate or not fitting to its object. On the other hand, we can mean that the *person* is irrational in the *role* that he allows his fears (however rational in the first sense) to have in his life.

Spinoza, remember, does not say that the fear of death is itself irrational. What he says is that a rational man will not let himself be *led* by the fear of death. There is a sense in which fear of death is obviously rational — i.e. obviously fitting or appropriate. Indeed, as I shall later suggest, one's own death and suffering in part define the concept of the fearful. However, just because fear is rational in this sense, it does not follow that a person is rational in being led by this fear. This sense of "rational," characterizing persons, involves more than fittingness or appropriateness and requires a consideration of *utility*. (Again we have a parallel with the moral feeling of guilt. Are Dostoevskiian characters — e.g. Stavrogin — who live a life dominated by guilt for their wrongdoings to be judged rational or irrational? In one sense, I should argue, they are rational; for guilt is the appropriate or fitting feeling for moral wrongdoing toward others. They are not like persons who feel guilt when they have really done nothing wrong, and thus they are not irrational in that sense. However, though their guilt feelings may not themselves be irrational, the *characters* seem irrational because they allow themselves to be dominated and destroyed by those feelings.) In this paper, I am interested primarily in the question "When is a *person* rational in fearing?" and am interested in the rationality of feelings themselves only insofar as this issue is relevant to the rationality of persons.[6]

My controlling assumption throughout is that Spinoza is fundamentally correct, at least in this context, in his attempt to analyze the concept of rationality (for persons) in such a way as to give a central place to concepts of self-interest or self-realization — what he calls "profit".[7] The basic idea in some ways anticipates Darwin and Freud in claiming that man is basically an animal whose reason functions, as instincts function in other animals, primarily for self-preservation and self-enrichment. A similar concept of rationality is found in Hobbes, who argues that no rational man could knowingly frustrate his own long-range self-interest. And Philippa Foot has recently reiterated this view: "Irrational actions are those in which a man in some way defeats his own purposes, doing what is calculated to be disadvantageous or to frustrate his ends".[8] This "egoistic" analysis of rationality might be challenged by philosophers of Kantian sympathies who believe (as I am inclined to) that *moral* rationality involves something different. However, since I do not see the problem of the rationality of fearing death as a moral problem, I do not think that Kantian scruples need detain us on this particular issue. Fear, after all, is not a likely candidate for a moral feeling. Its primary significance, unlike that of such genuine moral feelings as guilt and shame, lies simply in the avoidance of danger.

Having laid my controlling assumption on the table, I shall now offer the following as an account of the distinction between rational and irrational fearing:

It is rational for a person P to fear some state of affairs S if and only if:

(1) P holds the reasonable belief that S obtains or is likely to obtain,

(2) P holds the reasonable belief that S (a) is not easily avoided and (b) is very undesirable, bad, or evil for P,

(3) the fear of S could be instrumental in bringing about some behavior or action that would allow P to avoid S, and

(4) the fear of S is compatible, at least in the long run, with the satisfaction of the other important desires of P.[9]

If conditions (1) and (2) obtain, the fear is rational in the sense of being fitting or appropriate to its object. Conditions (3) and (4) have to obtain, however, in order for the *person* to be rational in his fearing.

Since this general account is probably not intuitively obvious, I shall comment upon each of the four conditions separately.

(1) *P holds the reasonable belief that S obtains or is likely to obtain*. This, I take it, is the least controversial of the conditions I have put forth. Perhaps paradigm examples of people who suffer fears we regard as irrational are those who suffer from psychotic delusions. Paranoids, or alcoholics experiencing delirium tremens, for example, may fear the demons in the water faucets, the Martians in the closet, or the pink spiders on the wall. The best reason we have for thinking that these fears are irrational is the absence of any grounds or evidence that there might be demons in the water faucets, Martians in the closet, or pink spiders on the wall.

(2) *P holds the reasonable belief that S (a) is not easily avoided and (b) is very undesirable, bad, or evil for P*. Except for one problem to be noted shortly, this condition also seems fairly noncontroversial. Phobias, I take it, are acceptable examples of irrational fears. We should tend to characterize as irrational persons who are "scared to death" of (nonpoisonous) snakes or of high places. This is not because, as was the case in (1) above, there are no snakes or high places, but is rather because snakes and high places are normally harmless. Typically we pass these fears off as "silly" and would not regard a person experiencing them as seriously irrational unless they had other harmful effects — a point to be explored when I discuss (4) below.

Now what may appear to some as a problem with the condition is the claim that S must be bad *for P*. This may strike some as too egoistic; and they might argue that it is perfectly rational to fear that something bad will happen to another. On this point I am inclined to argue as follows: One can certainly care deeply (perhaps on moral grounds) that others not die; but this caring typically is not, in my judgment, to be explicated as a kind of *fearing*. Wanting others in general not to die is, I suppose, simply part of what it means to be a morally sensitive person placing a high value on human life. One's own fear of dying, however, is hardly to be understood in this way. Fear is a very personal (self-regarding) feeling, and thus it seems to be tautological that one can literally fear only that which deeply involves oneself. The following conversation, for example, would be extremely odd: "I am terribly afraid." "Why"? "Because people are continuing to die in Bangladesh." One's own suffering and death, it could be said, *define* the concept of the fearful.

Thus I am inclined to think that one can literally *fear* evil happening to another only if that other is so close to one (a wife or child perhaps) that what happens to the other in a sense happens to oneself. As Freud says about the death of a child: "*Our* hopes, *our* pride, *our* happiness, lie in the grave with him, we will not be consoled, we will not fill the loved one's place."[10] For reasons that will become apparent when I later analyze the nature of death, I think there is a sense in which it is true (at least for some parents) that a part of them would die in the death of their child.

It is perhaps morally regrettable that most of us do not identify a very wide range of persons (perhaps the whole human race) with ourselves to such an extent that we could fear their deaths. It is surely not psychologically regrettable, of course, since if we did make such an identification we could probably not stand the emotional damage that would result. However, regrettable or not, it is false that very many people would sincerely agree with John Donne's observation that each man's death diminishes me. We may not be islands, but neither are we continents or worlds.

(3) *The fear of S could be instrumental in bringing about some behaviour or action that would allow P to avoid S*. This condition is at the heart of Spinoza's concept of rationality as involving self-preservation, as securing a "profit" in one's life. One way to characterize an activity as rational is to see that it has a point or purpose — that it at least appears to accomplish something. And surely it is avoidance behavior that gives fearing its significance. Suppose we imagined ourselves to be in a position of a Creator giving man the instinct of fear. What could this be except giving man the general capacity to make self-protective responses to danger? Fear's primary biological function is found in self-defensive behavior — what physiologists call the "fight or flight" reflex. And surely such fear, in addition to being biologically functional, is a part of what we understand by a rational approach to danger. If one discovers a hungry and aggressive tiger in the room, a state of affairs

which surely satisfies conditions (1) and (2), who would doubt that the result-ing fear is appropriate and that a person is rational in being "led" by the fear to the extent that he attempts to get out of the room as quickly as possible?

Since this condition will (not surprisingly) play a role in my later argument that it is irrational to fear death, I shall defer further discussion of it until later.

(4) *The fear of S is compatible, at least in the long run, with the satisfac-tion of the other important desires of P.* If the first three conditions are unsatisfied, we can perhaps, some may argue, conclude nothing more than that in such fearing the person is *non*rational. The present condition, how-ever, surely gives us a test for genuine *ir*rationality with respect to fearing; and indeed its nonsatisfaction is a mark of fearings which we should call *neurotic*. A phobia, for example, becomes clearly a neurotic symptom, and not just something silly or eccentric, when it so pervades the life of the per-son who experiences it that he is rendered incapable of leading a successful and satisfying life. A person who merely shudders when he sees a spider, for example, is perhaps just a little silly. A person who is so afraid that he might see a spider that he never leaves his home and has that home visited by a pest exterminator several times a week is something more than silly. He is pathetic and is in need of help.

Even fearings which would normally be quite rational become irrational when this condition is unsatisfied. A certain fear of germs, for example, is certainly rational. There are germs, many germs are very harmful, and a fear of them can prompt a person to take reasonable precautions against disease. However, a person who is so afraid of germs that he washes twenty times a day, sprays all items in his house with germicide, refuses to leave his sanitized bedroom, etc., has crossed the boundary between reasonable prudence and irrational fearing.

As with condition (3), this condition will play an important role in my later discussion of the fear of death.

III

The conditions I have outlined above provide a very rough way of distinguish-ing two very different ways of attempting to come to terms with death — what I shall call the "other-worldly" and the "naturalistic." Otherworldly Christians, for example, who counsel that at least certain persons (the saved) should not fear death, tend to argue that the fear of death fails to satisfy conditions (1) or (2) — i.e. they argue either that there is no such thing as death or that death is a good thing. In practice, of course, these two claims — insofar as they are intelligible at all — tend to be collapsed together. Naturalistic writers, such as Spinoza, tend to argue that a rational person will not be led by the fear of death because such fearing fails to satisfy conditions (3) or (4) — i.e. they argue that the fear of death is pointless (since it cannot help us to avoid death) or harmful (because it interferes with the satisfactions that life offers).

Though my primary purpose is to develop the pagan naturalistic tradition represented by Spinoza, it might be worth pausing a few moments over the obvious weaknesses in the other-worldly tradition. First, and most obvious, the set of beliefs that underlie that tradition (distinction between soul and body, immortality of the soul, etc.) are not very likely candidates for reasonable beliefs. Indeed, if they are held in a literal or "fundamentalist" sense, they might better be offered as candidates for obscurantist superstition. Second, and more important for our present purposes however, is the following: Even if these beliefs are accepted, there is an important sense in which they really do not provide answers to the question "How are we to come to terms with death?" For they are, after all, *denials* that there is such a thing as genuine death. Socrates (at least according to Plato) seemed to have this kind of other-worldly outlook — e.g. he says in *Apology* that, after his body passes away, it is not unlikely that his soul (his true person) will pass to a kind of heaven where he will converse with such departed luminaries as Hesiod and Homer. This seems to me to be a way of *not* facing death and certainly does not deserve to be characterized, as many people have characterized it, as facing death with *courage*. For what is courageous about accepting the fact that one will move to a place where one will be better off than ever before? And what is intellectually commendable about believing such things in the absence of any shred of evidence? [11]

There is one other argument that condition (2) is not satisfied which, though also found in naturalistic writers (e.g. Lucretius [12] and Hobbes), shares a common feebleness with the arguments noted above. It is, very generally the argument that the death of P is not bad for P because it cannot *hurt* P. Hobbes puts the argument in the following way:

There be few lingeringe diseases or sudden paynes that be not more sensible and paynefull then death, and therefore I see little reason why a man that lives well should feare death more then sicknesse.

"Of Death"

Even more comforting thoughts are expressed by the Christian poet John Donne:

> From rest and sleep, which but thy picture be,
> Much pleasure; then from thee much more must flow.
>
> "Death, Be Not Proud"

These arguments are so far beside the point that they at most demonstrate only one thing — namely, that the fear of death must be very terrible indeed for some people if they are willing to grab at such small straws and take comfort in such inanity. Though it is natural that some people might confuse a fear of death with a fear of pain (or, in our own day, with a fear of winding up one's days being treated as a nonperson in one of our contemporary hospitals), it is quite obvious on reflection that the fear of death and the fear of pain are quite distinct. It should also be clear on reflection that all things bad for us (e.g. loss of reputation) do not necessarily have to "hurt" in any literal sense. If the fear of death just was the fear of pain, then there would indeed be little reason why anyone should fear death. For death is not always a painful affair; and, in most of those cases where it might be, we have drugs or (if it comes to it) suicide. Thus Hobbes and Donne have perhaps provided us with reasons why we should not fear a *painful* death, but these are not reasons why we should not fear death *simpliciter*. They have not given us reasons why death itself, independent of suffering, is not a very undesirable, bad, or evil thing for a person.

IV

What, then, is death such that it is a very undesirable, bad, or evil thing for a person? *That* it is bad is, I take it, obvious; for death, along with suffering, in part define the very concept of what is a bad thing for a person and (as I suggested earlier) the very concept of the fearful. Thus, I should argue, explaining what is bad or fearful about death is part of explaining what death itself is.

The death of a *person*, unlike the death of a beast, represents not merely the extinction of an organism. It also represents the end of a conscious history which transcends itself in thought. All I mean by this high-sounding phrase is that, to use the language of Sartre, persons define themselves in large measure in terms of their future-oriented *projects*. What I am is in large measure what I want to accomplish. This is perhaps a very "bourgeois" conception of personality, for it is a definition in terms of individual agency. In more collectivist societies the conception of a person might well (for better or worse) be different and the fear of death correspondingly different.[13] However, the analysis I am offering does seem to me true of at least a great many persons in society as we now find it. Our self-identifying projects may be bound up with persons very close to us; and this explains why we sometimes, as I noted earlier, see the deaths of our children or wives as a partial death of our own persons. But it is rare (and perhaps regrettable) that the range of such persons included in self-identification is anything but quite narrow.

If I am correct that a person is self-defined largely in terms of certain projects — e.g. the desire to accomplish something in one's profession, to provide for one's family, to achieve certain satisfactions, to redress moral injuries done, etc. — then we can see wherein much of the badness of death lies: Death represents *lost opportunity*. My death might prevent me from finishing a book, from getting my children through school, from rendering aid to those who have a claim on my benevolence, from making amends for moral wrongs against others. It is this idea that death means *no more chances* which tormented Ivan Ilych — a man who had already thrown away the chances he had to live the right sort of life.

His mental sufferings were due to the fact that that night, as he looked at Gerasim's sleepy, good-natured face with its prominent cheekbones, the question suddenly occurred to him: 'What if my whole life has been wrong?' It occurred to him that what had appeared perfectly impossible before, namely that he had not spent his life as he should have done, might after all be true. It occurred to him that his scarcely perceptible attempts to struggle against what was considered good by the most highly placed people, those scarcely noticeable impulses which he had immediately suppressed, might have been the real thing, and all the rest false. . . . 'But if that is so,' he said to himself, 'and I am leaving this life with the consciousness that I have lost all that was given me and it is impossible to rectify it — what then?'

Mary Mothersill has put the point in the following way:

Death is the deadline for all my assignments. . . . To know what it is like to hope that one will not be interrupted is to know something about (one sort) of fear of death. We may think of death (rather grandiosely) as the person from Porlock but for whose untimely visit, *Kubla Khan*, or so Coleridge claimed, would have been much, much longer than it is.[14]

At this point, I should like to raise the following query: Would one fear death more than (or in a way different from) the fear of permanent coma resulting from massive brain damage? If, as I suspect, most people would answer *no*, then this is support for the account I have been offering.

Now one thing we can learn from this account is in keeping with the Christian message that we should (within reason of course) live each day as though it may be our last. Knowing that death will come, we can make an effort to accomplish what we feel we need to accomplish — realizing that there will not always be chances to "do it later." There are, of course, those unfortunate and generally neurotic individuals who have no sense of self-worth, who feel that they never can accomplish anything that matters, who feel that their very existence is an injury to others. These persons, unless they are helped by therapy, really lack self-defining projects and thus really lack a strong sense of themselves as persons. Not surprisingly, such individuals tend to fear death with the greatest intensity of all. For they fear, not simply that they will not finish, but that they will never even get started.[15]

Even if we are fortunate and are not plagued by neurotic self-doubts, and even if we make a prudent effort to accomplish what we think important with some sense of urgency in order to "beat death," we shall never be completely successful. Not only will we always fail to get something done which we think we ought to have done, but we shall also (as long as we remain persons) continue to generate new self-defining projects as we grow older. Thus, though with diligence we can perhaps prevent death from being as bad as it might be, for most of us it will, when it comes, be bad enough.

V

What does all of this tell us about the rationality of fearing death? Applying conditions (3) and (4) of the previously developed analysis, conditions which I regard as perhaps doing little more than formalizing Spinoza's general account of the fear of death, I should conclude that a prudent fear of death is perfectly rational. By a prudent fear of death I mean simply (a) one which provokes people into maintaining a reasonable (though not neurotic compulsive) diligence with respect to living the kind of life they regard as proper or meaningful (e.g. maintaining their health, not making the mistake of Ivan Ilych, etc.) and (b) one which is kept in its proper place — i.e. does not sour all the good things in one's life. If the fear of death, even if initially inspired by the desire to accomplish important things in time, becomes a neurotic compulsion, then the saying "In the midst of life we are in death" is exemplified.

Fear of death is irrational and properly extinguished, then, when it can serve no legitimate purpose in our lives — i.e. when it cannot aid us in avoiding bad things (e.g. failed assignments) in a way which is consistent with the successful and satisfying integration and functioning of our person. As Spinoza would put it, the fear of death is irrational when it redounds, not to our profit, but to our loss. For, other things (especially moral things) being equal, the pursuit of loss rather than profit could not be the goal of any rational man.[16]

To call the fear of death irrational is not, of course, moralistically to *condemn* those who feel it. A man is fairly to be blamed only for that which is in his control, and typically feelings are not in our control — at least not in our direct control. The irrational fear of death, if it pervades the life of a person, becomes a kind of neurosis; and normally the proper response to a fearful neurotic is not blame but is rather a suggestion that he seek therapeutic help in extinguishing his fears.[17]

If a person can extinguish or have extinguished such irrational fears of death he will move toward being, in Spinoza's sense, liberated or free. To fear irrationally is to be a kind of prisoner to one's pointless passions, in bondage to feelings that preclude the enjoyment of what is now valued and the pursuit of what is wanted for the future. The meaningfulness of the present and the future are destroyed, and one is put in the pitiful position, described by Socrates, of caring so much about simply living that one loses whatever it is that makes life *worth* living. To quote Montaigne again:

The thing I fear most is fear. . . . He who has learned how to die has unlearned how to be a slave. . . . For as it is impossible for the soul to be at rest when she fears death, so, if she can gain assurance against it, she can boast of a thing as it were beyond man's estate: that it is impossible for worry, torment, fear, or even the slightest displeasure to dwell in her. . . . She is made mistress of her passions and lusts, mistress over indigence, shame, poverty, and all other wounds of fortune. Let us gain this advantage, those of us who can; this is the true and sovereign liberty, which enables us to thumb our noses at force and injustice and to laugh at prisons and chains.[18]

VI

I am not sure how much comfort or solace, if any, can be derived from the way of thinking about death that I have outlined. One small comfort, at least to me, is that this way of thinking about death under some circumstances renders *suicide* a reasonable option, not merely for coming to terms with such misfortunes as pain, but also as a way of fulfilling (or at least not compromising) one's conception of oneself as a person. For if what one really values is the preservation of oneself as a certain *kind* of person (e.g. one who does not become a vegetable as a result of a debilitating illness, one who does not dishonor oneself and betray one's friends under torture, etc.) one can see, in voluntary death, at least this comfort — that one will end as the person one is and perhaps admires, not as another person that one perhaps would despise. What this shows is that the general reasons we have for not wanting to die may, in a particular case, constitute reasons for wanting to die. An American journalist, Charles Wertenbaker, wrote the following before his own suicide:

Problem with death is to recognize the point at which you can die with all your faculties, take a healthy look at the world and people as you go out of it. Let them get you in bed, drug you or cut you, and you become sick and afraid and disgusting, and everybody will be glad to get rid of you. It shouldn't be such a problem if you can remember how it was when you were young. You wouldn't give up something for instance to add ten years to your life. All right, don't ask for them now. You wouldn't give up drinking and love-making and eating — and why should you have given them up? Nothing is ever lost that has been experienced and it can all be there at the moment of death — if you don't wait too long.[19]

In a case like this, it is possible to see suicide, not merely as reasonable, but even as noble. This way of thinking, found in Greek, Roman and some Oriental civilizations, and eloquently defended by David Hume (*Of Suicide*), provides the man who accepts it with an ultimate "out". And having an out is having a certain kind of limited freedom. For at least one's bondage is not total.

In closing, I must admit that even the above provides precious little in the way of comfort. The universe is impersonal, and is thus not kind. And it is just false that there is to be found, even by the exercise of our reason, a comfort for every sorrow. Even a man who clearly recognizes the irrationality of fearing death will sometimes, I am sure, be tormented by that fear anyway; and I make no pretense that I am any different. However, I am confident of one thing: that any occasional comfort, however little, that may be derived from rational understanding, unlike that which may flow from various forms of superstitious obscurantism, is at least consistent with human dignity and intellectual integrity.[20] And that, I think, is something.[21]

NOTES

[1] *Montaigne's Essays* trans. by Donald Frame (Stanford: Stanford University Press, 1958) p. 56. Montaigne is here paraphrasing a remark made by Cicero. The thought, of course, goes back much further — at least to Socrates.

[2] There is also an element of superstitious fatalism in this remark which I shall not pursue.

[3] Spinoza agrees with the Stoics and Epicureans that the fear of death is irrational. He disagrees with them, however, on the question of how the fear is to be extinguished. The

Stoics and Epicureans counsel that we should desensitize ourselves to death by thinking of it constantly (a thought shared by Montaigne). Spinoza, on the other hand, suggests that we should try to avoid thinking of death entirely, to forget about death in the pursuit of the values of life. As Woody Allen has remarked, "It is impossible to experience one's own death objectively and still carry a tune" (*Getting Even* [New York: Random House, 1972], p. 31.)

4   "The Soul and Death," in *The Meaning of Death*, ed. Herman Feifel (New York: McGraw-Hill, 1959), pp. 3–15.

5   Psychiatrist Elisabeth Kübler-Ross raises this question in her book *On Death and Dying* (New York: Macmillan Co., 1969).

6   I am grateful to Barbara Levenbook for forcing me to see the importance of drawing a distinction between two senses in which a fearing may be irrational.

7   This concept of profit, of course, is not to be understood in any monetary sense, or even necessarily in terms of any external accomplishments. It is meant to include such things as personal satisfaction and feelings of self-worth, self-respect, and integrity.

8   'Morality as a System of Hypothetical Imperatives,' *Philosophical Review* 81, no. 3 (July 1972): 310.

9   A few comments about this analysis, not worth making in the text, are perhaps worth making in a footnote: (i) The phrase "state of affairs" is here meant to include both things and events. Normally persons fear future events, bad happenings to them, but it is possible to fear things (e.g. nonpoisonous spiders now in the room) quite independently of any belief that these things will *do* anything at all. (It could plausibly be argued that all fears of the latter sort are intrinsically irrational.) (ii) The concept of "reasonable belief" is introduced into the first two conditions for the following reason: It is obvious that a fear of S can be rational even if it is false that S obtains or is harmful so long as P believes that S obtains or is harmful and provided that this belief is reasonable. If a neighbor, for a joke, comes to my door disguised as a bandit and pretends he is going to shoot me, my fear is rational if I have no grounds for believing that it is my neighbor or that I am being fooled. (iii) By "reasonable belief" I simply mean a belief for which one has good grounds or evidence. (iv) The second condition stipulates P must believe that S is not easily avoided and is *very* undesirable, etc. This is because it would be absurd for P to claim that he feared S and then admit that he believed that S was nothing but a very minor inconvenience or that he could avoid S with no trouble at all. (v) Finally, it should be noted that, though P must himself hold the beliefs included in the first two conditions, P does not have to hold a belief in conditions (3) or (4). Typically, a person who is really afraid would not be in a position to entertain complex propositions of this nature. It is enough that (3) and (4) be true or at least reasonable for someone (e.g. the person evaluating the fears of P) to believe them.

10   'Thoughts on War and Death,' *Collected Papers*, vol. 4, trans. Joan Riviere (New York: *Basic Books*, 1959), p. 306 [italics mine].

11   It is possible that Socrates may not have literally accepted such beliefs but was rather simply using certain traditional and metaphorical language as his way of evincing courage.

12   Lucretius, following Epicurus, writes as follows: "It does not concern you dead or alive: alive, because you are; dead, because you are no more. . . . Where death is, I am not." In addition to making the point that death is not necessarily painful, he also seems to be raising the conceptual puzzle noted by Wittgenstein: "Death is not an event in life"

(*Tractatus*, 6.4311). The difficulty here is the following: If death is a misfortune, how is it to be assigned to a *subject* at all? When a person is alive, he has not died; when he has died, he no longer exists as a subject to which any attributes (including misfortunes) can be assigned. Lucretius also raises a temporal puzzle about the fear of death — namely, we regard as bad a future in which we will not exist, but none of us lament the fact that there was a time before our birth when we did not exist. These puzzles are interestingly discussed in an exchange between Thomas Nagel and Mary Mothersill, and I do not want to go over this ground again here. See 'Death,' by Thomas Nagel, *Nous* 4, No. 1 (February 1970): 73–80; and 'Death,' by Mary Mothersill, in *Moral Problems*, ed. James Rachels, (New York: Harper & Row, 1971), pp. 372–83. (The Rachels anthology also contains a reprinting of the Nagel essay.)

[13] "Are there great variations in the awareness or fear of death from person to person, from epoch to epoch, from culture to culture? If so, how are these variations to be explained? Surprisingly, very little attention has been given to these questions. The most interesting and almost the only hypothesis on the topic is that of Huizinga and Paul-Louis Landsberg. According to these authors, the consciousness of death has been most acute in periods of social disorganization, when individual choice tends to replace automatic conformity to social values; they point especially to classical society after the disintegration of the city-states; to the early Renaissance, after the breakdown of feudalism; and to the twentieth century. This hypothesis has yet to be confirmed or disconfirmed by careful historical and anthropological study. However, it is true that late antiquity, the early Renaissance, and the twentieth century have made unusually great contributions to the literature on death" (Robert G. Olson, 'Death,' *Encyclopedia of Philosophy*. ed. Paul Edwards, vol. 2 [New York: Macmillan Co., 1967], pp. 307–9). Freud, *Collected Papers*, thought that major wars were the primary historical stimulus to reflection on death, and the breakdown of traditional religion and its comforts is also probably a factor.

[14] *Op. cit.*, I suspect that Mothersill is correct when she says that this way of thinking captures only *one sort* of fear of death. Many writers have traced at least part of the fear to the supposed impossibility of imagining one's own death and the resulting fear of "the void" or "nothingness." I do not feel competent to discuss this possible aspect of the fear of death and simply refer the reader to the following: 'My Death' by Paul Edwards, *Encyclopedia of Philosophy*. vol. 5, pp. 416–19; and 'On Death as a Limit,' by James van Evra, *Analysis* 31, No. 5 (April 1971) 170–76.

Though I cannot pursue the point at any length here, I believe that the account I am offering of the death of a person and the fear of such death (i.e. the fear of death as the fear that self-defining projects will be aborted) provides a partial explanation for the analogy that seems to obtain between death and sex — e.g. the common and rather convincing literary and poetic characterization of sexuality (particularly orgasm) in metaphors of death and dying. (Thomas Mann's *Death in Venice* is just one of many obvious examples that could be given.) Sexual orgasm involves a total immersion in the present and a corresponding loss of that future-orientation required for self-defining projects. There are, of course, obvious differences: "Loss of self" in sexual orgasm is temporary and is typically surrounded by intense sensual pleasure — both features, alas, missing in death. In spite of this, however, the analogy is provocative. The analogy of sex with death may explain why the prospect of intense sexual intimacy contains (at least for some persons) an element of fear. Also, the analogy may help to explain why death is not just fearful but is (again, at least for some persons) seductive. For surely it must sometimes appear attractive and tempting to be freed from all those elaborate projects which define us, freed from all the responsibilities they impose, and freed from the enormous effort involved in carrying them through – attracted and tempted, in other words, by that "letting go" so seductively characterized by Emily Dickinson ('After Great Pain a Formal Feeling Comes').

[15] "Paradoxically bit understandably," writes psychiatrist Theodore Lidz, "it is those who have never been able to live, either because others have restricted them or because of their own neurotic limitations, who may fear death the most" (*The Person*, [New York: Basic Books, 1968], p. 502).

[16] On this analysis, Caesar's attitude (as portrayed by Shakespeare) might not be so purely "philosophical" after all. It could be argued that Caesar (because of his "tragic flaw" of pride) *recklessly* risked his life (i.e. stepped into danger that was both physically and morally avoidable) and thus revealed himself as more imprudent than courageous. His attitude of *che sarà sarà* was perhaps inappropriate to the actual circumstances in which he expressed it. This, at any rate, is one possible interpretation; and I mention it here to point out that a complete analysis of the rationality of fearing death would have to consider the following question: For the fear of death to be rational or prudent, do the as yet unfulfilled projects themselves have to be rational – i.e. is *any* projection of oneself into the future (however irrational) enough to make rational or prudent the fear of death aborting it? Suppose one of my uncompleted projects is to play a full length golf course with a score of less than seventy-five. In addition to the high probability that I could never do this, the project might seem irrational for another reason – namely, the triviality of such an achievement. One could also regard as trivial Caesar's desire to play to the hilt the role of fearless general and heard of state. One wants to be as tolerant as possible, of course, with respect to differences in human desires and projects; but there are perhaps limiting cases. I am grateful to Anthony D. Woozley for pointing out this complexity to me.

[17] There is a sense in which the person who (a) sees that his fears are irrational, (b) lacks the capacity to overcome them on his own, but (c) has the capacity to seek out therapeutic help, may legitimately be blamed if he does not seek out such help and praised if he does. Successful psychotherapy is often a long and painful process, requiring a kind of close self-examination that most people would prefer to avoid. Seeking it out when needed can thus be a moral achievement for which moral praise is merited. It could, of course, be suggested that the fear of death is far too common, too "normal," to be characterized as neurotic; contrary to what Caesar says, the fear does not seem "strange" at all. There are two responses that can be made to this suggestion: (1) Though a certain fear of death is indeed common (not to mention prudentially desirable), the extreme and self-damaging forms of this fear (the only forms properly called neurotic) are not. (2) Extreme and self-damaging attitudes are properly called neurotic no matter how common or "normal" they are. For example: It is not implausible to suggest that most living Americans experience deep neurotic conflicts with respect to their sexual behavior.

[18] *Montaigne's Essays*, pp. 53, 60–64.

[19] Lael Tucker Wertenbaker, *Death of a Man* (New York: Random House, 1950), p. 10. Quoted in R. F. Holland, 'Suicide,' in *Moral Problems*, ed. Rachels, p. 358. For a more philosophically grandiose elaboration of a similar view, see Sec. 36 'Morality for

Physicians,' of Friedrich Nietzsche's *Twilight of the Idols*.

[20] It is frequently suggested that some people are too weak to face death honestly and it is better that these people derive some support and happiness from comforting illusions. This is perhaps true. But those who make this suggestion should do so with a certain sense of regret; for the suggestion, even if benevolently motivated, involves a patronizing and degrading response to those people for whose benefit it is made. Would anyone want this said of *himself*?

[21] I wish to thank Lewis W. Beck, Peter Laska, Barbara Levenbook, Ronald D. Milo, George Panichas, and Anthony D. Woozley for their kindness in commenting on an earlier draft of this paper. I am particularly grateful to Lars Hertzberg for commenting on several previous drafts and for prolonged and instructive conversations on the issues involved.

CRUEL AND UNUSUAL PUNISHMENTS

> Excessive bail shall not be required, nor excessive fines
> imposed, nor cruel and unusual punishments inflicted.
>
> Amendment VIII
> *The Constitution of The United States of America*

This constitutional statement of right, like that of the English Bill of Rights (1689) from which its language was drawn, should be viewed as placing an absolute ban on certain punitive practices.[1] Indeed, this is an instructive way (at least initially and primarily) to view all bans contained in the Bill of Rights — as side constraints on permissible legislative enactment.[2] In the language of moral theory, one can say that a constitutional bill of rights is the attempt to formulate reasonable deontological restrictions (restrictions of principle) on the pursuit of social utility.[3] The constitutional provisions tell citizens what their rights are, and it is wrong in principle (not just bad policy) to pursue even laudable social goals in violation of such rights. As Ronald Dworkin has suggested, "The Constitution ... injects an extraordinary amount of our political morality into the issue of whether a law is valid".[4] Thus if one can mount a good argument that to treat a person in a certain way is gravely unjust or would violate some basic human right of his, this is also and necessarily a good argument that it is unconstitutional to treat him in this way. The Constitution is a document of moral principle and is in this sense anti-democratic.

This essentially deontological or principled conception of constitutional rights (as absolute bans on certain means a majority might be tempted to employ to maximize social utility) will be presupposed in the following discussion of cruel and unusual punishments.[5] In other words, my basic questions will be the following: Are there certain punishments which one would want to oppose in principle, as unjust violations of the rights of the person being punished, regardless of the social utility (e.g. deterrence) which might flow from such punishments? Since I believe that the answer to this question obviously is *yes* (will anyone stand up for torture and mutilation?), another and much more difficult question must next be confronted – namely, what is it about such punishments which make them cruel and unusual in the sense of being wrong in principle? When an answer to this question has been developed, I shall turn to the final question I wish to explore in this essay: Is there any good reason for believing that *death* is cruel and unusual, that capital punishment should be opposed in principle? Attempting to answer this final question will require a consideration of recent Supreme Court cases in which the death penalty has been discussed in terms of the Eighth Amendment.

What does it mean to say that the infliction of some punishment *P* is wrong *in principle*? Getting at this question is, as I have suggested, to get at the core of the Eighth Amendment ban on cruel and unusual punishments. I shall argue that the best way to explicate the concept of a punishment's being wrong in principle is through a *retributive* conception and justification of punishment – i.e. a conception and justification resting upon the concepts of justice, rights and desert (and *not* social utility). Before arguing positively for this, however, let me first briefly suggest why other ways of proceeding (other conceptions of cruel and unusual) will not work.

(1) *Literalism.* The only punishments banned are those which cause great physical suffering and which happen with statistical infrequency – i.e. punishments which satisfy the literal meaning of the words "cruel" and "unusual".[6]

This analysis, of course, is absurd. Would anyone seriously maintain that radical mutilation or disfigurement will become acceptable as a punishment if we do it under anesthetic and several times a week? Surely not. And does anyone seriously maintain that we can meet all the reasonable objections of those who believe that the death penalty violates the Eighth Amendment by suggesting that we execute painlessly and with great frequency? Physical suffering is a relevant factor and, if severe enough, may even be a sufficient condition for calling a punishment cruel. It is not, however, reasonable to regard it as a *necessary* condition – as the case of anesthetized mutilation demonstrates. (Psychological suffering poses interesting problems because it is present in many punishments – e.g. long term imprisonment – which most persons would be reluctant to regard as cruel and unusual. The extent to which, if at all, this reluctance is justified is a question I shall explore later in the essay).

(2) *Historical Authority.* The only punishments banned are those which the Founding Fathers regarded as cruel and unusual at the time the Constitution was enacted.[7]

Surely this will not do either. Suppose that the Founding Fathers banned punishment *P1* because of their realization that *P1* had horrendous property *Q*. Suppose further that punishment *P2* also has horrendous property *Q* but that the Founding Fathers did not realize this. Are we then to be prohibited from attacking *P2* on constitutional grounds even though we realize that it has the very same property the Founding Fathers most wanted to oppose? This would be a strange kind of historical piety indeed. (For this reason it seems to me incorrect to suppose that the issue of whether the death penalty is cruel and unusual punishment is closed merely because the Founding Fathers did not explicitly ban it.) In my view of constitutional intent, the Founding Fathers should be viewed as intending to formulate reasonable deontological side constraints or restrictions of principle on the pursuit of majoritarian utilitarianism. Thus, whenever we can mount a good argument for a principled restriction, we are at least not wildly far afield of their intent — as we would clearly be if we tried to interpret the Constitution in terms, not of principle, but of some notion of wise or useful or efficient social policy. The Bill of Rights is not a document of policy; it is a document attempting to give us just or fair ground rules for the pursuit of policy.

(3) *Consensus.* The only punishments to be banned are those which would be rejected as inconsistent with the moral conscience of the citizens of the society at a certain time in history — namely, the time at which the Court is actually considering the constitutional permissibility of a certain punishment. This is at least part of what it means to claim that the Clause "must draw its meaning from the evolving standards of decency that mark the progress of a maturing society".[8]

This consensus test is open to two interpretations. On one, it is irrational; on the other, it is redundant. First, let us suppose that the consensus is the sort one could discover by taking a random sample of citizen preferences — e.g. an opinion poll. It is, of course, ludicrous to regard the Constitution as sanctifying this kind of consensus. Probably the best test of what the citizens will find morally tolerable is that which is enacted by their representatives. But to say that a punishment passes the Eighth Amendment test if it has been enacted into law by a legislature is simply to abandon constitutional review of legislative enactments — i.e. to abandon the very point of having a Bill of Rights. One cannot use a right to check majoritarian excess if that right is interpreted in terms of majoritarian preference or tolerance. If tomorrow an opinion poll reveals (as I fear it might if such a poll were taken) that Americans are tolerant or even in favor of tortune and mutilation, the Eighth Amendment will not have to be reinterpreted in light of that fact. Thus this kind of appeal to consensus is irrational.

A second interpretation of the consensus test is the following: A punishment will be rejected as cruel and unusual if it would be rejected as shocking the conscience, not of a majority of people selected at random, but of those citizens who are truly informed, educated, and morally sensitive.[9] These are two problems with this elitist consensus. First, it is very likely that the characterization of the elite will be circular and question-begging — i.e. we shall count as members of the relevant elite only those persons who hold the view we want to appeal to consensus to defend (opposition to the death penalty, perhaps).[10] Second, and more important, is the following problem: If genuinely enlightened persons all agree that some punishment P is evil and shocking to the conscience, it must be because of some property Q (pain, unfairness, degradation, etc.) which they have found in P. But then P is wrong because of property Q, not because of a consensus of enlightened judges. P is not wrong because there is a consensus against it; there is a consensus against it because it is wrong and can be demonstrated to be so by argument (the showing that P contains Q).[11] This reveals that the consensus is morally redundant. We can go directly to P and condemn it as wrong because we can see that it bears morally obnoxious property Q — i.e. we can be brought to see whatever it is about P that the elite sees which makes them form a consensus against it.[12]

(4) *Utilitarianism.* A punishment is to be banned as cruel and unusual only if it is more extreme than that required for the pursuit of a legitimate state end or goal. As Bentham might put it, the purpose of punishment is to cause pain to the criminal as a means of deterring him and others from engaging in anti-social conduct, conduct which undermines the general welfare. Any pain inflicted beyond what is required for these goals is simply the gratuitous infliction of suffering and constitutes cruelty.[13]

In American law, the utilitarian interpretation of the cruel and unusual punishment clause has taken the form of the so-called "least restrictive alternative" test — i.e. a punishment is cruel and unusual (in the sense of being "excessive" — a crucial word in the total language of the Eighth Amendment) if it is more restrictive or intrusive than necessary to accomplish a legitimate state purpose.[14] For example: Capital punishment will be cruel and unusual if the same legitimate state purpose (deterrence of murder, say) could be accomplished with a less restrictive or intrusive punishment — e.g. long term imprisonment.

There is insight in this test, and it can be reformulated in retributive language so as to represent a demand of justice rather than utility. For example, I shall later suggest that "excessive" can be interpreted as "lacking a reasonable *proportionality* to the seriousness of the offense" — where the legitimate state purpose is conceived to be, not simply deterring murder, but also insuring that the punishment for murder will be of a gravity justly proportional to the gravity of murder. And so too for other crimes and punishments.[15] When interpreted in a strictly utilitarian manner, however, the test simply will not work as an interpretation of the Eighth Amendment — and this for one very simple reason: It will not account for the paradigms, for the cases of punishments which everyone would agree are cruel and unusual: torture and mutilation. The Eighth Amendment does not tell us that torture and mutilation may be used only when required by a legitimate state purpose; it tells us rather that torture and mutilation may never be used *at all*, regardless of the state's purpose. It is this absolute or side constraint nature of a constitutional ban which no utilitarian outlook can capture. Constitutional bans are not policies; they are constraints on policies. Thus they cannot be explicated in terms of policy considerations.

The above comments have been far too sketchy, but I hope that they have at least provided grounds for suspicion against some common and initially tempting analyses of the Eighth Amendment ban on cruel and unusual punishments. I now wish to move to more positive considerations. I wish to develop a retributive account of the concepts of cruel and unusual punishment which will account for why the ban on such punishments must be regarded as a side constraint or principled restriction on policy. A retributive theory of punishment is one which characterizes punishment primarily in terms of the concepts of justice, rights and desert — i.e. is concerned with the just punishment, the punishment the criminal deserves, the punishment society has a right to inflict (and the criminal has the right to expect). In this way the theory makes central the special moral status of persons — unique individuals who, because they are autonomous and responsible creatures, must not be used for the benefit of others (as we use objects or animals) but who must be regarded as inviolate. Human persons have that special value which Kant (the most illustrious defender of retributivism) called *dignity* — a value which we respect when we address ourselves to them in terms of their unique characters and acts (i.e. what those characters and acts *deserve*) and not in terms of the general usefulness of treating them in certain ways.[16] The retributivist obviously does not want to ignore such utilitarian matters as deterrence and rehabilitation and incapacitation, but he insists that these values be pursued only after the values he regards as primary (rights, justice, and desert) have been secured. The intuitive idea, then, is that a cruel and unusual punishment is among the class of unjust punishments, of undeserved punishments, of punishments we have no right to inflict — regardless of utility. A general theory of the *just punishment* is thus what is required. For reasons I have already suggested, such a theory will have a strong bearing upon constitutional interpretation. But, given that every reasonable person of every nationality must care about the restrictions demanded by justice on the pursuit of utility, it should also be of interest to those with no particular concern for American constitutional law.

Worries about the justification of particular kinds of punishment normally presuppose, of course, a belief that punishment in general is justified. Though I do not hold that this belief is obviously correct,[17] I shall assume its correctness for purposes of the present discussion. Otherwise, the discussion of the nature of certain punishments (torture, mutilation, and other cruel and unusual punishments) might be boringly brief — i.e. one might argue that these are wrong simply in virtue of their being punishments at all. Of course, even if one thought this, one might still want to argue that certain punishments have *something else* wrong with them. Just because one believes that all members of a series of acts $A1 \ldots An$ are bad, one is not committed to believing that they are *equally* bad. So even the person who thinks that all punishments are evil might still reasonably believe that torture is a worse instance of this kind of evil than, say, a small fine.

Thus our basic worry is not whether punishment of any kind is ever justified, but is rather the following: Given that we are going to punish in some way, are there certain *kinds* of punishment or certain *amounts* of punishment or certain *procedures* surrounding punishment which are so objectionable as to be banned outright or severely limited for reasons other than utilitarian deterrence? All of these worries — kind, amount, procedure — may plausibly be regarded as covered in the Eighth Amendment — a claim (controversial with respect to procedure) for which I shall argue later in the paper. P is intrinsically the sort of thing (torture perhaps) which we simply should not do to a person. P is not intrinsically evil but this amount of P (30 years in prison for possession of one marijuana cigarette, perhaps) is too much of P for this sort of conduct. P is the kind of punishment which is likely to be adminstered in an arbitrary and capricious way.[18] These are the three primary ways we are inclined to object to a particular punishment on grounds of justice (and thus oppose it in principle) and thus are the primary ingredients of the Eighth Amendment ban on cruel and unusual punishments.

Stating all this, of course, is not to solve anything — but is only to set the problems for discussion. *Why* are certain punishments intrinsically objectionable? *How much* punishment is too much (or too little)? All punishments certainly can be administered in an arbitary and capricious way, so what is it about certain punishments which make such administration more likely?

Here traditional retributive theories are not as precisely helpful as one would like though they do give us a start in the right direction. Retributivism, as a general justification for punishment, proceeds in the following way — a way drawn from the theory of Immanuel Kant:[19] Punishment is justified primarily by backward looking considerations — i.e. the criminal, having engaged in wrongful conduct in the past, *deserves* his punishment. It would be unjust for him not to receive it. In receiving it, he pays a kind of *debt* to his fellow citizens — to those other members of the community who, unlike him, have satisfied the social obligation of reciprocity, have made the sacrifice of obedience that is required for any just legal system to work. Since all persons benefit from the operation of a just legal system, and since such systems require general obedience to work, it is only fair or just that each person so benefiting make the sacrifice (obedience or self-restraint) required and thereby do his part. Those who do not must pay in some other way (receive punishment) because it would be unfair to those who have been obedient if the criminal were allowed to profit from his own wrongdoing. (In this view a certain kind of profit — not bearing the burden of self-restraint — is intrinsic to criminal wrongdoing.) Hegel, who elaborated this Kantian retributive theory, argued that the criminal, who as a rational person could see that even he derived benefits from participation in a community of law, could be regarded as rationally willing (though not empirically desiring) his own punishment.[20] This being so, he deserves it in the sense that he has a *right* to it.[21] It is important to see that this theory grounds punishment on justice or fairness (i.e. justice demands that we inflict the punishment deserved, that we have the right to inflict, that the criminal has the right to receive), *not* on utility. The basic principle is that no person should profit from his own wrongdoing, and retribution keeps this from happening. If a person does profit from his own wrongdoing, from his disobedience, this is *unfair* or *unjust*, not merely to his victim, but to all members of the community who have been obedient — one reason why crime is an offense against the *state*. Now it may be, as the utilitarian might argue, that such unfairness — if widespread — would have socially undesirable consequences. But this is is not Kant's argument. His argument is that the *injustice or unfairness itself*, regardless of consequences, demands retribution. As H. L. A. Hart has argued, "a theory of punishment which disregarded these moral convictions [about justice] or viewed them simply as factors, frustration of which made for socially undesirable excitement, is a different kind of theory from one which *out of deference to those convictions themselves* [justifies] punishment".[22] Kant's theory is clearly of this latter sort.

I have attempted to defend this retributive outlook in detail in other essays, and I shall not go over this ground again here except to mention three general points in an attempt to counter the bad press the theory usually gets:[23] (1) The theory is not an attempt to give approval to such barbaric motives as a desire for vengeance or vindictiveness. The only motive behind it is the desire to do justice. Thus retributivism is not an irrational cry for more and nastier punishments. Indeed, if retributivism were followed consistently, we should probably punish less and in more decent ways; for we now treat many criminals in ways harsher than, in justice, they deserve. (2) Retributivism is built around a rather attractive (if controversial) model of human beings as free or autonomous creatures, as enjoying rights, and responsible for what they do. Surely this is more attractive than the "you are sick and helpless or like a child" model behind a therapeutic response to crime or the "you can be used and manipulated for the common good" model behind utilitarian deterrence theory.[24] (3) Even many people who do not like the *name* "retributivist" are persuaded by considerations that are clearly retributive in nature. Suppose it was suggested that we punish negligent vehicular homicide with life imprisonment and first degree murder with a couple of years in jail, and suppose this suggestion was justified with the following utilitarian reason: Conduct of the first sort is much more common and dangerous than conduct of the latter sort (we are much more likely to be killed by a negligent driver than by someone who kills us with the primary object of killing us), and thus we should use the most severe deterrents against those who are genuinely dangerous. If we object to this suggestion, as most of us would want to, that this would be unjust or unfair because it would not be apportioning punishment to fault or desert, we should be making a retributive argument. Thus even if the label "retributivist" repels most people, many of the actual doctrines of the theory do not.

Let us grant for present purposes, then, that the retributive outlook sketched above can provide a reasonable general justification of punishment in terms of its being unjust or unfair to allow criminals to be free-riders or parasites on schemes of social cooperation — something which would occur if they were not made to sacrifice in some way for not having made the required sacrifice of self-restraint. How will this help us in determining the *kinds* or *amounts* of punishment which will be tolerable — i.e. what alternative methods of sacrifice will be allowed, and which ones will be prohibited?

Here the guidance provided by the retributive theory is not as clear as one would like. Some version of the *jus talionis* ("like for like") principle seems initially tempting; but even Kant — one of its staunchist defenders — cannot consistently maintain it to the end. One immediate problem is that the principle cannot with sense be taken literally in all cases. Hegel observes "It is easy enough ... to exhibit the retributive character of punishment as an absurdity (theft for theft, robbery for robbery, an eye for an eye, a tooth for a tooth — and then you can go on to suppose that the criminal has only one eye or no teeth)".[25] Kant also sees that there is a problem in applying *jus talionis* to "punishments that do not allow reciprocation because they are either impossible in themselves or would themselves be punishable crimes against humanity in general".[26] With respect to rape, pederasty and bestiality, for example, Kant believes that imprisonment is inadequate as a punishment but that a literal return of like for like would either be immoral (e.g. the rape of the rapist) or impossible (e.g. we cannot by definition commit bestiality upon a human criminal). Thus he proposes castration for the former two offenses and expulsion from society for the latter. He admits, however, that this is not a literal application of *jus talionis* but only in some sense captures the intuitive "spirit" of the principle.

What is it to capture the "spirit" of the principle? Perhaps something like the following: The principle of *jus talionis*, though requiring likeness of punishment, does not require *exact* likeness in all respects. There is no reason in principle (though there are practical difficulties) against trying to specify in a general way what the costs in life and labor of certain kinds of crime might be, and how the costs of punishment might be calculated, so that retribution could be understood as preventing criminal profit.[27]

There are still serious difficulties here, however — the chief being that, once a literal reading of *jus talionis* is abandoned, its application "in spirit" seems to be largely a matter of intuition unguided by any systematic theory. Kant's favorite example of *jus talionis* is the penalty of death for the crime of murder — this in spite of the fact that the punishment for *almost everything else* is imprisonment, a punishment which can literally satisfy "like for like" only for the offenses of false imprisonment or kidnapping. And speaking explicitly of the death penalty, Kant argues that this punishment must be "kept entirely free from any maltreatment that would make an abomination of the humanity residing in the person suffering it".[28] The criminals "innate personality," he claims, protects the criminal against any morally indecent treatment.[29] In suggesting that the state should never do anything to a criminal that humiliates and degrades his dignity as a person, Kant seems to be working toward a ban on those punishments that have been described as cruel and unusual — i.e. a principled ban on certain punishments (torture and mutilation?) even when the "like for like" principle would seem to require them. There is insight here, but how the insight is to be squared with his support of castration as a punishment is a mystery to me.

The principle of *jus talionis* has thus produced a bit of a muddle, and the explanation for this is the following: Though a conception of reciprocity explains why the guilty should be punished, it is not clear that this same principle will explain why like should be returned for like or even that the evil inflicted on the criminal should be of equal gravity with that which the criminal has inflicted on his victim. The criminal has acted unfairly and that is why he must be punished. But unfairness is unfairness, murder being no more *unfair* than robbery. Thus if murder if worse than robbery (and thus deserves a worse punishment), this cannot be shown on the basis of purely formal considerations. Consider, again, the punishment for rape if the "like for like" position is adopted. If it be argued that the position does not entail that we rape the rapist but only do to him something of *equal* evil, it can be replied that the question "What evils *are* equal?" does not admit of a purely formal answer. Thus a retributivism grounded on fairness can at most demand a kind of *proportionality* between crime and punishment — i.e. demand that we rank acceptable punishments on a scale of seriousness, rank criminal offenses on a scale of seriousness, and then guarantee that the most serious punishments will be matched with the most serious crimes, the next most serious punishments with the next most serious crimes, and so on. This ranking must be reasonable, of course, but there is no reason to suppose that it will be determined solely or even primarily by considerations of fairness — i.e. no reason to suppose that seriousness can be totally analyzed in terms of fairness. In particular, considerations of fairness alone will not answer the question of which punishments will be allowed as the most serious. There will be substantive reasons for not allowing certain punishments (e.g. torture) even if these would satisfy a fairness principle of proportionality.

Let me say one other thing at this point about the concept of proportionality as applied to punishment. It can mean either (a) doing to the criminal something of equal gravity to what he has done to his victim or (b) making sure that the most serious punishments are applied to the most serious offenses, etc. So if the most serious punishment in a particular legal system in 20 years in prison and if this punishment is applied to the crime of murder, it could plausibly be argued that the proportionality demand stated in (b) has been satisfied, but not that stated in (a). And my argument thus far has been that (b), but not (a), can reasonably be derived from Kant's theory. At most a constrained variant of (a) might be derivable: (a*) do to the criminal something of equal gravity to what he has done to his victim unless this would require our doing something (e.g. torturing) to which there are serious substantive moral objections. If we allow such substantive restrictions, however, we shall be forced to admit that the decision to allow or not to allow *death* to remain as a system's most severe punishment cannot — contrary to Kant — be based simply on considerations of fairness or proportionality. We must at least reflect upon the possibility that our choice of this as a punishment will be constrained by other morally relevant properties of death.[30]

So far, then, we can get this much from Kant's theory: A punishment will be unjust (and thus banned on principle) if it is of such a nature as to be degrading or dehumanizing (inconsistent with human dignity). The values of justice, rights and desert make sense, after all, only on the assumption that we are dealing with creatures who are autonomous, responsible, and deserving of the special kind of treatment due that status. This is why animals can be treated wrongly but cannot be wronged, cannot be treated unjustly, cannot have their rights violated. A theory of the just punishment, then, must keep this special status of persons and the respect it deserves at the center of attention. And there are at least two ways suggested by Kant whereby, in punishing, we can fail to do this: First, we can employ a punishment which is in itself degrading, which treats the prisoner as an animal instead of a human being, which perhaps even is an attempt to *reduce* him to an animal or a mere thing. Torture is of this nature. Using Kantian language, one might say that torture is addressed exclusively to the sentient or heteronomous — i.e. *animal* — nature of a person. Sending painful voltage through a man's testicles to which electrodes have been attached, or boiling him in oil, or eviscerating him, or gouging out his eyes — these are not *human* ways of relating to another person. He could not be expected to understand this while it goes on, have a view about it, enter into discourse about it, or conduct any other characteristically human activities during the process — a process whose very point is to reduce him to a terrified, deficating, urinating, screaming animal. I cannot, of course, *prove* that it is wrong to treat people in this way; for the wrongness of doing this is more obvious than any premises which could be given to justify its being wrong. Anyone who did not see this could not be made to understand anything else about morality. For we have here a paradigm of not treating a person as a person — and thus an undermining of that very value (autonomous human personhood) upon which any conception of justice must rest.[31] It is unjust to be tortured, everyone has a right not to be tortured, no one has a right to torture, no one deserves torture – all these claims flow from a theory of punishment (such as retributivism) which takes seriously and makes central the special status of persons.

A second way in which a punishment can fail to show respect for the status of autonomous persons is through radical lack of proportionality.[32] An autonomous person has a right that his punishment be *addressed* to that status – to those unique features of his individual, responsible conduct which occasion the punishment. A punishment radically disproportionate to the seriousness of the offense is not addressed to that for which he is responsible and blameworthy and deserving of punishment but is necessarily addressed to something else – e.g. society's mere *dislike* of him or his conduct.[33] This, in my view, is how the concept of "excessive" found in the Eighth Amendment should be interpreted.[34] To the degree that a person is being punished out of reasonable proportion to the seriousness of his offense, then to that degree is he being *used* – not being punished as justice would demand.

But is not the amount of punishment prescribed for an offense a criterion for how serious the offense is? That is, is it not almost true by definition that the most serious offenses will carry the most serious punishments – the prescription of the punishment by society being an index of how seriously society deplores the conduct? This challenge, in my judgment, is to be met in the following way: A just society cannot criminalize conduct simply because in deplores that conduct; its grounds for deploring the conduct must be *reasonable*. Conduct such as homosexuality does not cease to be morally trivial and become morally serious simply because a majority of people *think* it is morally serious and deplore it. As the Supreme Court correctly held in the *Robinson* case: if narcotic addiction is a disease, then no reasonable society may criminalize it – no matter how much it may represent a status detested and deplored by many persons.[35] In a just society, therefore, punishment must be proportional to the *objective* seriousness of the conduct, not to its subjective seriousness – i.e. the degree to which it is held in disapproval by the society at large.

A present, of course, we lack a coherent theory of objective seriousness. Thus, except in extreme cases, it will be practically difficult if not impossible to guarantee just proportionality in punishing. For one who cares about justice, however, this lack will stimulate research and thinking in order that a reasonable theory on these matters may be developed. The alternative is simply to stop caring about doing justice – hardly an acceptable outcome.[36]

As I indicated previously, a theory of justice alone may not be able to tell us which offenses are most serious; it may require supplementation by a consideration of the substantive or intrinsic character of certain kinds of conduct. A theory of justice, however, can at least demand the following: that everyone has the right to have offenses graded in terms of individual fault or blameworthiness (i.e. desert) and not mere social utility, that other even substantive bases for grading be reasonable,[37] that punishments be graded on a comparable basis, and that there be a matching between seriousness of punishment and seriousness of offense. A theory of justice may not be able to supply all the details for ranking, but it can supply the framework.

Thus (by a process of deduction, variation, and free association) I have extracted the following from a generally Kantian account of retributive sentencing: A punishment will be banned in principle if (1) it represents a direct assult on the dignity of persons or (2) it is radically disproportional to the seriousness (the *objective* seriousness) of the conduct criminalized. Consideration (1) is, of course, more basic than (2) — i.e. certain punishments might pass the proportionality test but would still be rejected because they fail what might be called the "respect for persons" test. Thus the punishment of torture by an act of torture could hardly be faulted on grounds of proportionality, but it would still be rejected as an intrinsically inhuman method of punishment.

Both of the above notions — intrinsic heinousness and radical lack of proportionality — have a secure place in the interpretation of the Eighth Amendment. A ban on the first is clearly a part of the original meaning.[38] and a ban on the second has been prominent in twentieth century Eighth Amendment cases — including the recent *Coker* case where it was held (incorrectly in my judgment) that death was too severe a penalty for the crime of rape.[39]

Now what has gone on so far, even if one does not agree with the theoretical background, has probably done nothing more than produce *conclusions* which almost everyone would regard as non-controversially reasonable — namely, that justice demands absolute side constraints against punishments which are intrinsically heinous or radically disproportionate. This is required if we are to respond to criminals as *people* — as individuals with unique characters and degrees of responsibility. (We are not to think of them simply in terms of dangerousness — as on a par with wild animals, or such natural disasters as earthquakes, or even madmen.[40])

What I wish to do now is to move this general account I have been giving into an area of genuine controversy — namely, the penalty of *death*. Given the above sketch of the concepts of cruel and unusual punishments, is it reasonable to regard the punishment of death as falling under this description? That is, are there good reasons why, on grounds of justice or respect for rights (rather than utility), we should accept an absolute ban or principled restriction against the penalty of death? Does it belong, in other words, in the same camp as torture, mutilation, or punishments of radical disproportionality? We have the right not to be treated as animals — in a dehumanizing way. We have the right to be punished with sanctions proportional to our offenses. Do we also have the right not to be punished with death? If so, is this because death is necessarily a dehumanizing punishment or because it necessarily lacks proportionality with all possible offenses (or both) — or for some new reason entirely?

It should be obvious at the outset that there is no reason to believe that a punishment of death will always fail to satisfy the proportionality requirement. It would, of course, fail to satisfy this requirement for many offenses — but surely not for at least some acts of *murder*. (Kant's intuition seems correct here.) It is often said that, by making the criminal wait for a long time in terror and uncertainty before execution, we do something worse to him than any murderer does to a victim.[41] But this is just not so. What about the killers of Moro? Or suppose Patty Hearst's abductors had finally killed her? Are these acts not quite proportional to capital punishment? (It is also perhaps worth noting that much of the waiting is *chosen by the prisoner* while he files appeals.) Or what if the murderer tortured and mutilated his victim before the murder? We think of these activities as so horrible that we shall not even allow them as punishments, so surely their horribleness plus killing could be proportional to capital punishment — if anything, capital punishment might seem disproportionally *little* here. (A query: If torture and mutilation are so terrible that we will not allow them as punishments even when we do allow death, why then do we rank murder as an offense as *more serious* than torture and mutilation?)[42] Thus, if the concept of proportionality can be worked out at all, it seems that it should be possible to work it out for some acts of murder punishable by death.

Even when proportionality is satisfied, however, we shall not use a certain punishment if it is intrinsically degrading to the humanity of the criminal — e.g. we shall not torture the torturer. Is there perhaps, then, something intrinsically degrading, showing lack of respect for persons as persons, in the punishment of death — so that it too could be banned even in cases where it satisfies the proportionality demand?[43]

Now it is easy to think that capital punishment is intrinsically degrading if we allow ourselves to be dominated by a certain picture of what capital punishment is like − e.g. the final part of Truman Capote's *In Cold Blood.*[44] But all that this may show is that brutalization may preceed and may accompany (as surrounding circumstances) the punishment of death.[45] This would be a reason for objecting to and changing those circumstances. But it would not be an objection to death *simpliciter* as a punishment. For suppose we consider another picture: the final scene of Plato's dialogue *Phaedo*, depicting the execution of Socrates by self-administered painless poison amid discourse with friends and family − all those around, even the jailer, showing great respect. This seems, at least intuitively, to depict a humanized death − a civilized execution. In this way, thus, does death seem to differ from torture. Is it conceptually possible to depict Socrates at a civilized torture session, a humanized case of evisceration of Socrates, a way of sending high voltage through Socrates's testicles which shows respect for him as a person? The answer seems *no.*[46] In a variety of social contexts (e.g. euthanasia) people are now rallying around the slogan "Death with Dignity." This suggests that they intuitively grasp some distinction between death *simpliciter* (which is surely bad) and circumstances which could surround death which would make it, not just bad, but degrading. But can we imagine anyone, who understands language and knows how to think, suggesting the slogan "Torture with Dignity" as part of a campaign against the excesses of certain political regimes? Death may be brought about in a degrading way; torture *must* be brought about in a degrading way. Thus we could imagine devising ways to humanize executions, to design them so that respect for the criminal would be shown. We cannot (*logically* cannot) imagine devising humanized or civilized torture sessions.[47]

Thus it seems to me that it is by no means obvious that exectuion *in itself* is necessarily − like torture − a way of showing lack of respect for a person, a way of treating hin as or reducing him to an animal. Thus death may pass both the proportionality test and the respect for persons test. If so does this then show that the punishment of death cannot legitimately be opposed in principle, that we have no general right not to be executed by the state, and that opposition to the death penalty on principle is, at best, a kind of well-meaning sentimentality or, at worst, merely an illegitimate attempt to legislate our preferences for policy through the vehicle of constitutional law?[48]

In the remaining part of this essay, I shall present a defense for an answer *no* to this question. That is, I shall argue that a basic right of citizens in just societies is compromised by the death penalty and thus that there are grounds for a side constraint or principled restriction against it. My argument will support, in broad outline, a primary portion of the majority reasoning in *Furman v. Georgia* and later capital punishment cases.[49]

In what way did the court hold capital punishment to the unconstitutional? Many arguments were given, but the one which comes through most clearly is the following: The death penalty is applied in an *arbitrary* and *capricious* way[50] – e.g. it tends to be used upon the poor and blacks and on almost no one else. Thus we are required on constitutional grounds to do *one* of the following: (a) devise ways to keep capital punishment from being applied in an arbitrary and capricious manner or (b) ban it outright.[51] Against the general thrust of this argument, two charges are immediately to be made: (1) *All* punishments (including imprisonment) are arbitrary and capricious in the way noted, but it is absurd to say that all punishments are unconstitutional. And yet the court decision might seem to commit us to this absurd conclusion.[52] (2) To call capital punishment arbitrary and capricious is to make a *procedural* objection to it, one which could best be expressed by the Fourteenth Amendment "due process of law" or "equal protection" clauses. Why then drag in the Eighth Amendment, as the court did, in support of its decision? The Eighth Amendment, in banning cruel and unusual punishments, is surely *substantive* and not procedural in nature; and bringing it in simply muddies the waters.[53]

What I should like to do now is the following: Develop a principle relevant to the capital punishment issue which (a) breaks down a sharp substance-procedure distinction and thus renders the Eighth Amendment relevant and (b) distinguishes death from other punishments – especially imprisonment. That is, I want to meet both of the above objections and thus vindicate the major thrusts of the Court's reasoning.

What will the principle be? Recall that I am concerned with principles which rest on *rights* (i.e. with principles proper) and not with useful social policies. And what possible rights could be relevant to the kinds of punishment permissible other than the ones already mentioned (right not to be dehumanized; right to proportionality) and tentatively rejected for the death penalty? I shall suggest the following: *the right not to be dealt with negligently by one's government*, the right not to have one's basic interests threatened in casual and irresponsible ways by the state.[54] But is this not simply a statement of procedure; and, as such, how can it bridge the substance-procedure gap? To answer this objection, we can do no better than to turn to the writings of Judge Learned Hand whose discussion of negligence in tort law will be useful for our present purposes:

The degree of care demanded of a person by an occasion is the resultant of three factors:

the likelihood that his conduct will injure others, taken with the seriousness of the injury if it happens, and balanced against the interest which he must sacrifice to avoid the risk.[55]

In other words, there is no such thing as negligence *per se* or in the abstract. Whether the steps I take to reduce risk (the *procedures* of my acting) are negligent or not will depend in part on the (*substantive*) gravity of the harm that might result. Thus what constitutes due care as a precaution against my hurting your mailbox may not come close to what constitutes due care as a precaution against hurting your eyes. And, in the criminal area, what constitutes due process with respect to a parking fine may not come close to what constitutes due process for a long jail term.[56]

How does this apply to capital punishment? In the following way: All trial, conviction, and sentencing procedures are subject to *error* — to the possibility that they will convict the innocent. And there are two kinds of innocence at stake here: those totally innocent of any wrongdoing and those whose conduct, though meriting convicting of something (e.g. manslaughter), does not merit conviction of an offense of supreme gravity (e.g. murder in the first degree). Due process is an attempt to guard against both sorts of error. And what will be responsible (i.e. non-arbitrary and non-capricious) principles of due process for various criminal sanctions? How is the state to exercise due care instead of negligence in dealing with its citizens in terms of penal sanctions? Obviously, if Hand is correct, this question can be answered sensibly only if we have a reasonable view of the gravity of the (substantive) *harm* that might result from the error. Thus we have broken down the sharp line which supposedly separated substance and procedure, and the Eighth Amendment at least has a foot in the door. One objection to the Court's reasoning is thus met. But what about the other objection — that the Court's condemning of capital punishment as cruel and unusual because arbitrary and capricious logically must condemn *all* punishments in our society (even imprisonment) as cruel and unusual? Obviously, the objection can be met in only one way — namely, by showing that death is a *graver harm* than loss of liberty and that, therefore, higher standards of due care (due process) must surround the former sanction.

Can this be shown? Perhaps not in all cases — particularly in the case of life or extremely long-term imprisonment. Studies on the effects of long-term incarceration in "total institutions" indicate that long-term confinement develops in persons an "institutional personality" — i.e. a personality with diminished affect, neurotic dependencies, loss of autonomy and mental competence generally: in short, a kind of death (of personhood).[57] If these studies are correct, then long-term incarceration will be a kind of slow torture and psychic mutilation and *should* no doubt be banned on Eighth Amendment grounds (something the courts may be moving toward in declaring whole prison systems in violation of the Eighth Amendment).[58] This being so, it is a *virtue* of the Court's analysis that its arguments against death also apply to long-term incarceration. If they applied to all incarceration (or even to long-term incarceration if it does not have the above consequence), however, this would indeed be an absurdity. So what is it about death *simpliciter* which makes it a graver harm than loss of liberty *simpliciter*? Is it that people *fear* death more? — surely not, since many people fear death less than loss of liberty ("Give me liberty or give me death!") because they value liberty as a primary good of greater value than life.[59] Is it because death must entail intolerable suffering or degradation? No. As I have previously argued, certain manners of death may have this defect, but not necessarily death itself. What then?

One of the most common claims made in defense of the claim that death is worse than loss of liberty is the claim that death is *irrevocable*. But this will not do. Everything that is past is irrevocable. If I kill you in error, I have indeed done you an irrevocable injury. But so too if I imprison you falsely for five years. Margaret Radin, in her excellent discussion of capital punishment, attempts to meet this worry in the following way:

Of course, even one day in prison is irrevocable in the sense that all past events and their resultant effects on human beings are irrevocable. Yet, although it might be difficult to articulate, most people intuitively recognize a distinction between the irrevocability of everything and the irrevocability of death or mutilation. The latter is the strong sense of irrevocability referred to here. It encompasses irreversible deprivations of attributes or capacities essential to, or at least closely connected with, complete personhood.[60]

This will not work. Radin is trying to show that death is a greater evil than loss of liberty because death is irrevocable — that is, she is supposed to be analyzing "grave harm" in terms of "irrevocability". But she is actually reasoning quite the other way around — i.e. analyzing irrevocability (in the "strong sense") in terms of grave harm. But if we already know the harm of death is greater than the harm of loss of liberty, we do not need the concept of irrevocability at all. One suspects that her analysis is unhelpfully circular — a suspicion reinforced when we notice that a synonym for "irrevocable" ("irreversible") is used in the analysis.

Let me then simply step in at this point and offer my own suggestion:

Death is a greater harm than loss of liberty because it is (a) totally *incompensable* and (b) represents *lost opportunity* of a morally crucial kind. First, the concept of incompensability.[61] This is a concept which obviously admits of degrees. Some harms which we do to people are of such a nature — e.g. damage to their property or income — that it makes sense to speak of totally compensating them for their loss. For other harms, we cannot totally compensate; but we can at least make a reasonable attempt. Loss of liberty seems to me of this nature. In a culture such as ours, we know what it is like — and it intuitively seems reasonable and acceptable — to set a monetary value on my time and labor. Indeed, I can reasonably *bargain* these away for money — as when I work for a living. Thus if I am imprisoned by the state in error, it is at least not intuitively absurd to suggest that damages be paid as a way of compensating for the resulting harm. (We cannot totally compensate, of course, but we can in some sense make a reasonable stab at it.) But what would it be like to be paid anything even resembling adequate compensation for being tortured, radically mutilated, or debased in some other way — for being deprived of my status of honor or dignity as a person? If these have a price, this means that in a very real sense I do not have them to begin with — a man whose honor has a price simply being a man without honor. Suits in tort law may be brought and won here, of course, but how many winners would really believe that they had been even close to adequately compensated? How many would have bargained for this "price" in advance? Let us now move to death: On a scale of incompensability, death does indeed seem at the top. It is both logically and empirically impossible to compensate me if I am executed in error. (A wrongful death action may pay off someone, but necessarily *not me*). In contract law, we do not even *allow* people to bargain away for money their life or their personal integrity against torture and mutilation; but we do allow them to bargain away almost totally their personal liberty — e.g. by joining a volunteer army.[62] Should we punish people by doing S to them when we shall not even allow them to do S to themselves — even for pay?

The question, of course, is rhetorical; and I shall move from it to present the upshot of what I have been saying thus far. I have argued that death is like torture and mutilation (and unlike loss of liberty) in at least one important respect: that when we injure someone by killing him in error, we have done him an injury which is incompensable. Not so with imprisonment in error; for this is at least compensable to a significant degree. Thus in at least this one respect death is a graver harm than loss of liberty, and thus it is reasonable to require greater standards of due care or due process to prevent error in its application as a punishment. The Court was thus correct: the procedures which surround the punishment of death may properly be called arbitrary and capricious even if those same procedures are adequate for imprisonment.

But is this all? Is the only reason that death is worse than loss of liberty the fact that the former (when done in error) is totally incompensable and the latter (when done is error) is only partially incompensable? This does not seem correct — not as the *whole* story. Surely death is a worse injury than loss of liberty even when the punishment is *correctly* administered (i.e. not in error) — this being the very point, after all, of having death as the most severe sanction in one's arsenal of responses to crime. What this shows is that the person in favor of the death penalty for the most serious crimes (and reserving imprisonment for lesser crimes) *cannot consistently oppose the Court's reasoning in Furman v. Georgia*! For by his own admission, the death penalty *is* more serious than imprisonment; and thus, unless he wants (unreasonably) to quarrel with the claim that standards of due care or due process are in part a function of gravity of harm, he must agree with the Court that higher standards of review are required for the death penalty than for any other.

Why, then, might death reasonably be regarded as substantively more serious than loss of liberty? An answer to this question might help provide an interesting reason for why death is an incompensable injury — i.e. a reason more interesting than "You cannot compensate Jones if Jones is no longer around to be compensated".

Thus I shall now turn to the second point I want to make about death — that it represents *lost opportunity* of a morally crucial kind.[63] What I shall say here will be very brief; and it may also seem rather old-fashioned and romantically sentimental. Be that as it may, here it is: the most important thing within a human life (something stressed by philosophers from Socrates through Kant and by such other admirable and insightful individuals as Jesus and Tolstoy) is the *development of one's own moral character*, the development of oneself in such a way that one's life can honestly be said to be coherent, meaningful, and perhaps even admirable. To use the language of Plato and Socrates, one might say that what is most important in a human life is not what happens when the *body* is confined but is rather any harm that may come to the *soul* — or, to use less metaphysically provocative language, harm that may come to those crucial attributes of moral character and integrity which are most essential to personhood. The development of a morally coherent personality is the most crucial task or project of any human life —

a project which we all muddle through with various degrees of success or failure (mostly failure) for our lifetimes. To block or interrupt this project (or to preclude one's ever having an opportunity to have a change of heart, reflect on one's life, and *start* such a project) is, in my judgment, the gravest harm that one can do to a person. Imprisonment (unless of such a nature or duration as to have profound effects on the inmate's mental health) will not do an individual this kind of harm — witness the number of inmates who in a very real sense have become "new people" while serving prison terms. But death, alas, provides no such opportunities and thus can certainly harm a person in this highly significant (one could say spiritual) way.[64] For death is the *loss* of significant opportunity (the opportunity to accomplish certain things, to treat people differently, to become a new person); and for many persons this must be the most terrifying thing about it.

His mental sufferings were due to the fact that that night, as he looked at Gerasim's sleepy, good-natured face with its prominent cheekbones, the question suddenly occurred to him: 'What if my whole life has been wrong?' It occurred to him that what had appeared perfectly impossible before, namely that he had not spent his life as he should have done, might after all be true. It occurred to him that his scarcely perceptible attempts to struggle against what was considered good by the most highly placed people, those scarcely noticeable impulses which he had immediately suppressed, might have been the real thing, and all the rest false . . . . 'But if that is so,' he said to himself, 'and I am leaving this life with the consciousness that I have lost all that was given me and it is impossible to rectify it — what then?' (Leo Tolstoy, *The Death of Ivan Ilych*)

Given the exceptional moral gravity of having one's prospects for a morally significant and meaningful life interrupted, one might well want to deny the state any right to do this — i.e. one might adopt a direct absolute ban on the penalty of death. For it is by no means clear that one can show repect for the dignity of a person as a person if one is willing to interrupt and end his most uniquely human capacities and projects. Thus, contrary to initial and plausible impressions of the kind sketched previously, there is perhaps a case to be made that the punishment of death is degrading after all. Even if one does not buy this, however, one must at the very least — given the considerations I have noted — have strong sympathy with the disjunctive position articulated by the Court — namely, that granting the supreme gravity of the penalty of death, the Constitution requires either (a) significantly more stringent standards of review for this penalty than for any other or (b) an outright ban on the penalty. Recent Court decisions requiring an elaborate consideration of mitigating and aggravating circumstances before a sentence of death may be imposed are an attempt to work with (a).[65] If this attempt fails — i.e. if it turns out that the standards of review surrounding imprisonment are really the best we can do — then we may be led indirectly into an outright ban on the death penalty. I am hoping for failure.

I have no pleasure in the death of the wicked; but that the wicked turn from his way and live.

Ezekiel **XXXIII**, 11

NOTES

[1] The best general treatment of the constitutional issues surrounding an application of the Eighth Amendment — with special focus on the death penalty — will be found in Margaret Jane Radin, 'The Jurisprudence of Death: Evolving Standards for the Cruel and Unusual Punishments Clause,' *University of Pennsylvania Law Review*, Volume 126, No. 5, May, 1978, pp. 989–1064. My own treatment of this topic has been enormously influenced by her essay.

[2] The notion of side constraints (as opposed to patterns or end results) as basic in moral theory has been developed by Robert Nozick, *Anarchy, State and Utopia* (New York: Basic Books, 1974), Chapter 3.

[3] See John Rawls, *A Theory of Justice* (Cambridge: Harvard University Press, 1971), all references under the headings 'Constitution' and 'Constitutional convention' on 591 of Index.

[4] Ronald Dworkin, *Taking Rights Seriously* (Cambridge: Harvard University Press, 1977), p. 215.

[5] I realize that these matters are more complex than I am suggesting here. What I wish to explore in this essay, however, is how far one can go with a purely deontological conception of constitutional restrictions and a purely retributive conception of punishment. It turns out, I think, that one can go pretty far.

[6] See Chief Justice Burger's discussion (with respect to cruelty) in *Furman v. Georgia*, 408 U.S. 238, 392 (1972) (Burger, C.J., dissenting).

[7] *Furman v. Georgia*, 408 U.S. 238, 418 (Powell, J., dissenting).

[8] *Trop v. Dulles*, 356 U.S. 86, 101 (1958) (plurality opinion) (Warren, C.J.).

[9] *Furman v. Georgia*, 408 U.S. 360 ff. (Marshall, J., concurring). Justice Marshall considers and rejects the opinion poll model and adopts a version of an elitist model involving a prediction of what people would deplore if fully informed.

[10] One is reminded of John Stuart Mill's "competent judge" test in *Utilitarianism* (Chapter 2). Mill attempts to show that contemplative pleasures are superior to sensual pleasures because persons who have experienced both (competent judges) prefer the former to the latter. Any person who has experienced both and does *not* judge in this way, however, would obviously pose a problem for Mill's test. How does he deal with this? In the following circular way: such persons reveal that they have lost their capacities for finer feelings and thus lose their status of competence.

[11] This, of course, is logically similar to Socrates's puzzle in Plato's dialogue *Euthyphro*: Is that which is pious pious because the gods approve of it; or do the gods approve of it because it is pious?

[12] The elite, of course, may be *epistemologically* relevant – i.e. they may get us to see or appreciate some morally relevant feature which we otherwise might have missed but for their insight. Their attitude toward the feature is not what *makes* it relevant, however.

[13] Jeremy Bentham, *The Principles of Morals and Legislation* (1789), especially Chapter XIV.

[14] "There is no reason to believe that [capital punishment] serves any penal purpose more effectively than the less severe punishment of imprisonment" (*Furman v. Georgia*, 408 U.S. 305) (Brennan, J., concurring). The general constitutional notion of the least restrictive alternative is articulated in *Shelton v. Tucker*, 364 U.S. 479.

[15] Consider persons in an "original position" of the kind described by John Rawls. *supra* note 3. It seems reasonable to suppose that they would chose a system in which penalties were no more severe than necessary to accomplish whatever purpose they set as reasonable. If Rawls is correct in claiming that choices in such a constrained setting yield principles of justice, then we have a non-utilitarian foundation for a least restrictive alternative principle.

[16] For more on this, see my 'Rights and Borderline Cases,' *Arizona Law Review* 19, Number 1 (1977) 228–241.

[17] See my 'Marxism and Retribution,' *Philosophy and Public Affairs* 2 Number 3 (Spring 1973) 217–243.

[18] It has been argued, for example, that capital cases bring out the worst and the most irrational in juries and judges. See Charles L. Black, Jr., *Capital Punishment: The Inevitability of Caprice and Mistake* (New York: Norton, 1974).

[19] I have elaborated this Kantian account more fully in my 'Marxism and Retribution,' *supra* Note 17. See also my *Kant: The Philosophy of Right* (London: Macmillan, 1970).

[20] See my 'Marxism and Retribution,' *supra* note 17.

[21] For more on punishment as a *right* of the criminal, see Herbert Morris, 'Persons and Punishment,' *The Monist,* 52, No. 4 (1968) 475–501. This is reprinted in my *Punishment and Rehabilitation* (Belmont, Calif.: Wadsworth, 1973).

[22] "Murder and the Principles of Punishment," *Punishment and Responsibility* (Oxford: Oxford University Press, 1968), p. 79.

[23] The retributive theory of punishment is, fortunately in my judgment, undergoing a bit of a renaissance at the moment. For a careful discussion which generally deplores this, see Hugo Bedau's essay in the 'Symposium: The New Retributivism,' *The Journal of Philosophy* LXXV, Number 11 (November 1978) 601 ff.

[24] For an argument that utilitarianism also tends to treat persons as children, see Adrian M. S. Piper, 'Utility, Publicity, and Manipulation,' *Ethics,* 88, No. 3 (April 1978) 189–206.

[25] *Philosophy of Right*, translated by T. M. Knox (Oxford: Oxford University Press, 1952), p. 72.

[26] *The Metaphysical Elements of Justice*, translated by John Ladd (Indianapolis: Bobbs-Merrill, 1965), p. 132.

[27] One interesting attempt to work something like this out may be found in Claudia Card, 'Retributive Penal Liability,' *American Philosophical Quarterly Monographs*, No. 7, 1973. According to Card, a retributively just punishment exposes the offender to

hardship that is comparable to the worst that anyone could reasonably expect to suffer from such conduct were it to become general in the community. As Andrew von Hirsch has pointed out, however, this will not do "because it gives disproportionate emphasis to the potential harmfulness of the conduct, and relegates culpability to the role of a limiting principle" ('Symposium: The New Retributivism,' *supra* note 23). Von Hirsch's essay is a reply to Bedau.

[28]   *Supra* note 26, p. 102.

[29]   *Supra* note 26, p. 100.

[30]   As I shall later argue, the mere fact (if it is a fact) that people tend to *believe* that death is horrendous is not a morally relevant property of death. (What people believe about death is surely not a property of death at all.) Such beliefs about death, however, might be relevant in a Rawlsian "original position" (*supra* note 15) in that they might prompt the rational choosers to place special constraints on its intentional causation.

[31]   For an expansion of this sort of argument (or of a defense for not giving an argument), see my 'The Killing of the Innocent,' *The Monist* 57, No. 4, (October 1973) 527–550. (Reprinted in the present collection.)

[32]   I say *radical* for the following reason: Any departure from proportionality is less than ideal justice would demand, but it may be impossible to grade these matters in a very fine way. We should still want to condemn, however, cases where the gap in seriousness between punishment and offense is clearly too wide.

[33]   Obvious examples here are severe punishment for drug use, or consensual homosexual activity among adults, or any other "victimless crimes."

[34]   See *Lockett v. Ohio*, 98 S. Ct. 2981 (1978) (White, J. dissenting in part and concurring in part). Justice White articulates both the utilitarian and the retributive analyses of "excessive".

[35]   *Robinson v. California*, 370 U.S. 660 (1962).

[36]   Andrew von Hirsh has made a start toward developing a framework for a theory of objective seriousness. See *supra* note 27 and his *Doing Justice: The Choice of Punishments* (New York: Hill and Wang, 1976). Though von Hirsch believes that such devices as the Sellin-Wolfgang survey technique for measuring degrees of seriousness have a use, he sees clearly that objective criteria for seriousness cannot be ultimately based on popular judgments. Von Hirsch has not (as I believe he would be the first to admit) given us very much, but he has given us a start – and a start in the *right direction* (toward just retribution).

[37]   "Reasonable" may equal "would be chosen by parties in a Rawlsian original position." See *supra* note 15.

[38]   For an excellent survey of the history of the Eighth Amendment and its interpretation, see *Furman v. Georgia*, 408 U.S. 314 (Marshall, J., concurring).

[39]   *Coker v. Georgia*, 433 U.S. 584 (1977). In my judgment, the Court erred in not considering *degrees* of rape and aggravating circumstances which might render a punishment of death proportional – a point well made by Justice Powell in the dissenting part of his judgment.

[40]   Some criminals (e.g. the psychopathic killer) are perhaps best regarded as wild animals or other non-responsible natural forces of destruction. Such a way of looking at them is not to regard them as persons; but this is all right because, from the moral point of view, *they are not persons*. If drastic steps (e.g. execution) are advocated for them, this cannot coherently be regarded as capital punishment (since they are not

responsible and thus not legitimately open to *punishment*) but must be regarded simply as painless extermination – something done in the same spirit in which we destroy a mad dog. I see nothing *intrinsically* wrong about such steps (i.e. see no reason for believing that psychopaths have a moral right to life); but the *practical* dangers of acting in this way (i.e. letting legal authorities – as in Nazi Germany – decide who is and who is not a person) are so grave that it is irresponsible even to consider this as a legal option. For more on this, see my 'Moral Death: A Kantian Essay on Psychopathy,' *Ethics* 82, Number 4 (July 1972) 284–298.

[41] Albert Camus argued in this way in his essay 'Reflections on the Guillotine.' One other serious problem about long delays is the following: during the delay a prisoner can in a very real sense become a "new person" by morally transforming himself. Is it fair that this new person be executed for a crime committed by a different and previous self? As I shall argue later in the paper, the possibility of self-transformation is a very good reason against the penalty of death.

[42] There is, of course, the utilitarian reason: we wish to give the torturer an incentive for not killing his victim after the torture session is over.

[43] There are three bad arguments (addressed to me in various public discussions) that the infliction of the death penalty is intrinsically wrong which – since they may be widely used – are perhaps worth a brief attack. (1) Punishing people by killing them *degrades us* – *we* are demeaned in the process. But we shall be demeaned by doing this only if doing it is wrong; it cannot be wrong *because* it demeans us. This begs the question. (2) "Two wrongs do not make a right" – a favorite cliché of Americans, particularly undergraduate students. This, of course, begs the question also. The very point at issue is whether capital punishment is a wrong. (3) We must defend the value of the "sanctity of human life" – a value compromised when we execute. This bare slogan is of little help, because it can plausibly cut both ways on the capital punishment issue. Looking at the condemned person, we shall cite sanctity of life as a reason for not killing him. If we look at the *victim* (of murder), however, we could just as well cite sanctity of life as a reason *for* capital punishment – i.e. our use of a punishment this serious is our way of expressing how seriously we take the crime of murder. With analysis, however, this slogan can be turned into an argument – one which I shall develop later in the paper. Even analyzed, however, it will rest on a controversial assumption – namely that killing is morally worse than letting die. For a defense of this assumption, see my 'The Killing of the Innocent,' *supra* note 31.

[44] This book (based on a factual murder and execution) was made into a successful Hollywood movie. Both the book and the movie depict two marginal human beings of unclear responsibility who, after being convicted of murder and sentenced to death, arouse our pity and compassion as they reveal both their humanity and animality in touching ways. Their route to death (except for their contact with Capote) is cold and impersonal.

[45] For more on the distinction between death and the terrible circumstances which may surround death, see my 'Rationality and the Fear of Death,' *The Monist* 59, Number 2 (April 1976) 187–203.

[46] This is not to say that some persons – e.g. Church martyrs, soldiers who will not betray comrades under torture, etc. – cannot rise above the inherent degradation of what is being done to them. Their animal nature is being addressed, but they hold out for a very long time (perhaps until death) before allowing that nature to answer. I am

grateful to Merrilee Salmon for discussing these matters with me.

[47] We would be more inclined to regard as insane a person who voluntarily tortured himself than a person who voluntarily took his own life.

[48] This is the suspicion expressed by Justice Rehnquist in his dissent in *Furman v. Georgia* – a suspicion shared by some of the other dissenting Justices.

[49] The major relevant cases, other than *Furman v. Georgia*, are: *Gregg v. Georgia*, 428 U.S. 153 (1976); *Woodson v. North Carolina*, 428 U.S. 280 (1976); *Roberts v. Louisiana*, 428 U.S. 325 (1976); *Jurek v. Texas*, 428 U.S. 276 (1976); *Coker v. Georgia*, *supra* note 39; and *Lockett v. Ohio, supra* note 34.

[50] This is also the central argument of Charles Black's widely read book on capital punishment, *supra* note 18.

[51] The Justices are clearly divided on which alternative is preferable.

[52] Again, see Black (*supra* note 18) for a clear statement of and an attempt to meet this objection.

[53] "The Eighth Amendment was included in the Bill of Rights to assure that certain types of punishments would never be imposed, not to channelize the sentencing process. The approach of these concurring opinions has no antecedent in the Eighth Amendment cases. It is essentially and exclusively a procedural due process argument [dealt with and dismissed in *McGautha v. California*, 402 U.S. 207] . . . and it would be disingenuous to suggest that today's ruling has done anything less than overrule *McGautha* in the guise of an Eighth Amendment adjudication" (*Furman v. Georgia*, 408 U.S. 399 and 400) (Burger, C.J., dissenting).

[54] Again, it is perhaps worth noting (for those who are impressed, as I am, by his theoretical machinery) that Rawls's contractors (*supra* note 3) would surely adopt such a principle in the original position.

[55] *Conway v. O'Brien* (2 Cir. 1940) 111 F. 2d 611, 612. See Also *United States v. Carroll Towing Co.* (2 Cir. 1947) 159 F. 2d 169.

[56] Mr. Justice Harlan wrote: "I do not concede that whatever process is 'due' an offender faced with a fine or a prison sentence necessarily satisfies the requirements of the Constitution in a capital case" (*Reid v. Covert*, 354 U.S. 1) (1957).

[57] See Erving Goffman, *Asylums* (New York: Doubleday, 1961). See also my 'Rationality and the Fear of Death,' *supra* note 45.

[58] It is not uncommon for federal court to declare the prison systems of entire states (e.g. Arizona) to be in violation of the Eighth Amendment – the primary reason usually being overcrowding. But what is the matter with overcrowding? Presumably the effects it has on prisoners. But what if long-term incarceration has the same or similar effects?

[59] As noted above (*supra* note 30) attitudes toward death as opposed to other punishments could be relevant in the Rawlsian original position; but, unless these attitudes are absolutely uniform for all persons, it is hard to see how the application of the punishment could be fair – i.e. some will be more hurt by it than others. Again, one needs an objective account.

[60] Radin, *supra* note 1, p. 1022. Irrevocability is probably the most frequently cited reason in defense of the claim that death is more serious than loss of liberty. See Black, *supra* note 18. And Justice Marshall: "Death is irrevocable; life imprisonment is not" (*Furman v. Georgia*, 408 U.S. 346).

[61] For an excellent discussion of the distinction between compensable and incompensable injuries, see Nozick, *supra* note 2, Chapter 4.

[62] We do, of course, have the concept of a Faustian contract. But we also take these to be perverse.

[63] I have elaborated this point in great detail in my "Rationality and the Fear of Death," *supra* note 45. I am very grateful to Ellen Canacakos for discussion of this closing portion of the paper.

[64] I say *can* instead of *must* because some persons (e.g. Socrates and other exceptionally rare individuals) seem to have attained personal excellence prior to their execution. The Justices in *Furman v. Georgia* who seem to me closest to the view I am here articulating are Marshall and Brennan. Marshall (at 346) writes "Death, of course, makes rehabilitation impossible." And Brennan (at 272,273) writes: "When we consider why [certain punishments] have been condemned, however, we realize that the pain involved is not the only reason. The true significance of these punishments is that they treat members of the human race as nonhumans, as objects to be toyed with and discarded."

[65] *Lockett v. Ohio, supra* note 34. There is, of course, a social cost of having stricter procedures to prevent error — Hand's third factor in his algebra of negligence. The primary social costs for criminal due process will be expense, court time, and — of course — the greater possibility that guilty and dangerous persons will be freed to prey again upon innocent victims and that others will be less effectively deterred from crime. I have had little to say about these matters — not because I think they are unimportant but because (as indicated in note 5) I wanted to see how far one could go via a different route. On the capital punishment question, however, this issue will not be too central for the following reason: Probably no one would want to grant *less* due process than existed prior to *Furman*. But, even with that amount, executions had become so infrequent as to have (probably) very insignificant deterrence value. Studies seem to indicate that it is *certainty* of punishment (and not severity) which tends to deter. See Jack R. Gibbs, *Crime, Punishment, and Deterrence* (New York: Elsevier, 1975).

LEGAL CASES CITED

Coker v. Georgia, 235, 246, 248
Conway v. O'Brien, 248
Furman v. Georgia, 238 ff., 242, 244, 245, 246, 248, 249
in re Gault, 155, 158, 163
Gillette v. United States, 22
Gregg v. Georgia, 248
Jurek v. Texas, 248
Kaimowitz v. Department of Mental Health, xv, 184, 185 ff.
Lambert v. California, 127
Lockett v. Ohio, 246, 248, 249
McGautha v. California, 248
Morisette v. United States, 126
Olmstead v. United States, 147
People v. Decina, 116
People v. Wells, 158
People of Athens v. Socrates, 40–57
Reid v. Covert, 248
Roberts v. Louisiana, 248
Robinson v. California, 234, 246
Shelton v. Tucker, 245
Trop v. Dulles, 244
United States v. Carroll Towing Company, 248
United States v. Falcone, 22
Woodson v. North Carolina, 248

NAME INDEX

Abrahamsen, David 157
Acton, H. B. 111
Adkins, W. D. 54
Alexander, Franz 156
Allen, Woody 219
Anscombe, G. E. M. 10 ff., 15, 20, 22, 127
Aristotle 140
Austin, John 117 ff., 126
Austin, J. L. 62, 72, 206

Barry, Brian 24, 37
Bay, Christian 61
Beck, Lewis White xii, xx, 20, 142, 222
Bedau, Hugo 245
Beethoven, Ludwig van 163
Bennett, Jonathan 15, 20, 22, 23
Bentham, Jeremy 94, 226, 245
Black, Charles L. 245, 248
Bleibtreu, Herman xvi
Bonger, Willem Adriaan 104 ff., 112
Bosanquet, Bernard 96
Brakel, S. 178
Brandeis, Louis D. 147
Brandt, Richard 21
Brennan, William J., Jr. 245, 249
Burger, Warren E. 244, 248
Burgess, Anthony 135, 163, 182, 197, 200

Campbell, G. A. 131, 141
Camus, Albert 14, 132, 139, 247
Canacakos, Ellen 249
Capote, Truman 237
Capron, A. M. 180
Card, Claudia 245
Cleaver, Eldridge 164
Cleckley, Hervey 128, 130, 140
Coleridge, Samuel Taylor 215
Cook, Walter Wheeler 126

Creighton, Bishop 92

Daniels, Norman 37
Darrow, Clarence 131
Darwin, Charles 61, 113, 209
Davidson, Donald 127
Dershowitz, Alan 157, 160
Dickey, James 19, 24
Dickinson, Emily 221
Dilman, Ilham 142
Donne, John 214
Douglas, William O. 127
Duerrenmatt, Friedrich 141
Dworkin, Gerald 181
Dworkin, Ronald 56, 71, 73, 223, 244

Edwards, Paul 220
Eliot, George 72
Epicurus 219
Erhard, J. B. 91
Ervin, Frank 200
Evra, James van 220
Ezekiel 244

Fagothey, Austin 20, 22
Falk, Richard A. 20
Feinberg, Joel 26 ff., 33, 36, 39, 91, 179, 181
Fingarette, Herbert 142, 180
Fitzgerald, P. J. 119, 126
Foot, Philippa 23, 209
Fortas, Abe 155
Freeman, M. D. A xx
Freud, Sigmund 113, 123, 203, 206, 209, 211

Gandhi, Mohandas K. 132
Gass, William H. 22
Gerstein, Robert 81
Gibbs, Jack R. 249

251

Glueck, Sheldon 157
Goffman, Erving 198, 248
Green, Thomas Hill 96, 111
Grossman, S. 178

Haksar, Vinit 140, 194, 199
Hand, Learned 11, 238, 239, 249
Hare, R. M. 22, 37, 130, 140
Harlan, John M. 248
Harnish, Robert M. 110
Harrison, Bernard 95, 111
Hart, H. L. A. 21, 22, 51, 78, 84, 96, 111, 112, 118, 119, 125, 126, 127, 132, 141, 229
Hartmann, Nicolai 141
Hayek, F. A. 61, 72
Hearst, Patty 236
Hegel, G. W. F. 40, 77, 79, 84–85, 93, 95, 96, 101, 110, 141, 229
Hertzberg, Lars 222
Hirsch, Andrew von 246
Hitler, Adolf 6, 13
Hobbes, Thomas 40, 49, 66, 103, 136, 209, 213, 214
Hodson, John D. 179, 200
Holland, R. F 221
Hollingshead, August B. 114
Holmes, Oliver Wendell 56, 117, 119, 126
Holmes, Robert L. 20
Hubin, D. Clayton 39
Huizinga, Johan 220
Hume, David xi, 58–73, 108, 132, 206, 218

Jaspers, Karl 143
Jesus 92, 242
Jorden, Samuel 114
Jowett, Benjamin 55
Jung, Carl 206

Kant, Immanuel xii, xiii, 1, 10 ff., 15, 16, 17, 18, 23, 24, 28, 29, 37, 38, 40, 49, 58–73, 75, 77, 78, 79–80, 82–92, 93, 96 ff., 128 ff., 141, 186, 198, 209, 227, 229 ff., 242
Kesey, Ken 135
King, Martin Luther, Jr. 132, 153–154, 162
Klein, M. 178
Kolko, Gabriel 20
Kübler-Ross, Elisabeth 219

Landsberg, Paul-Louis 220
Laska, Peter 222
Lehrer, Keith 198
Levenbook, Barbara 219, 222
Lidz, Theodore 221
Lifton, Robert J. 20
Livermore, Joseph 178
Locke, John xiii, 28, 36, 49, 54, 58, 66
Lucretius 213, 219
Lukacs, Georg 114
Lukes, Steven 111

Maclagen, W. G. 143
Macpherson, C. B. 112
Malmquist, Carl 178
Mann, Thomas 114, 220
Mark, Vernon 220
Marshall, Thurgood 244, 246, 248, 249
Marx, Karl xiii, 40, 54, 79, 80, 86, 87, 93–115
Matthews, Gareth 20, 81
McCord, William and Joan 130, 140
Meehl, Paul 178
Melden, A. I. 123, 127, 141
Melville, Herman 10
Menninger, Karl xiv, 147–158, 159
Mill, John Stuart 29, 30, 36, 99, 139, 165, 166, 178, 244
Milo, Ronald D. xvii, 20, 23, 54, 222
Mitchell, John 159
M'Naghten, Daniel 154
Montaigne 205, 217, 218, 219
Moro, Aldo 236
Morris, Herbert 81, 112, 114, 141, 157, 178, 197, 200, 245
Mothersill, Mary 215, 220

Nagel, Thomas 8, 21, 24, 39, 72, 127, 181, 220
Narveson, Jan 24
Newton, Isaac 58
Nietzsche, Friedrich 222

Nozick, Robert 25, 26, 28, 29, 35, 36, 38, 39, 72, 73, 244, 248

Olson, Robert G. 220

Packer, Herbert L. 157
Panichas, George 222
Paton, H. J. 129
Perkins, Rollin M. 21
Peters, R. S. 123, 127
Pfeiffer, Eric 180
Philips, D. Z. 142
Piper, Adrian M. S. 245
Plato 55, 213, 237, 245
Powell, Lewis F., Jr. 246

Raab, Francis V. 110
Rabinowitz, Joshua 37
Radin, Margaret Jane 240, 244, 248
Rawls, John xii, xiii, xvii, 10, 22, 25, 26, 30, 31, 32, 36, 37, 38, 39, 49, 59, 73, 77, 80, 83, 91, 98, 101, 106, 112, 114, 134, 141, 175, 181, 244, 245, 248
Redlich, Frederick C. 114
Rehnquist, William H. 248
Rock, R. 178
Rosenblatt, Paul xvi
Roth, Philip 168
Rousseau, Jean Jacques 49, 98
Russell, Bertrand 109, 145
Ryle, Gilbert 117, 123, 124, 126

Salmon, Merrilee 248
Salmond, John 117, 126
Sartre, Jean Paul 214
Schaefer, John Paul xvi
Scoville, Stanley E. 178
Sellars, Wilfrid 128
Shakespeare, William 92, 205, 221

Shapiro, Michael 183, 184, 198
Socrates 40–57, 213, 219, 237, 242, 245
Spinoza, Benedict de 205, 206, 209, 213, 216, 217, 219
Staub, H 156
Stevenson, C. L. 55
Stone, Alan A. 39
Suárez 3
Szasz, Thomas 157, 164, 166, 178, 197

Tarde, Gabriel de 113, 131 ff., 141
Thoreau, Henry David 54
Tolstoy, Leo 142, 208, 242, 243
Turk, Austin J. 105, 113

Wald, Patricia M. 114
Wallraff, Charles F. 143
Walzer, Michael 22, 25
Warnock, G. J. 23
Warren, Earl 244
Wasserstrom, Richard 20, 21, 111, 127, 182
Weaver, Albert xvi
Weiss, Peter 3
Wertenbaker, Charles 218
Wertenbaker, Lael Tucker 221
Wertham, F. 157
Wexler, David xvii, 39, 178, 179, 182, 198
White, Byron R. 246
Wittgenstein, Ludwig 117, 219
Wolff, Robert Paul 37, 54, 69, 96
Wolin, Sheldon 59
Wood, Allen W. 113
Wootton, Barbara 129–130
Woozley, Anthony D. 20, 41, 43, 53, 54, 56, 81, 110, 221, 222

Zinn, Howard 14, 22

SUBJECT INDEX

act, defined 116 ff.
act, Austin's analysis 117 ff.
act, Hart's analysis 118 ff.
anarchism 69 ff.
attempt 7 ff.
autonomy 28, 165 ff., 183 ff.
autonomy rights 28–29, 31 ff.

Bhagavad-Gita 116
Billy Budd 10

capital punishment 223 ff.
Cartesianism 123
children, their rights 33 ff.
christianity, its account of death 212 ff.
civil disobedience 40 ff.
combatants 6 ff.
competent consent 196 ff.
compulsion 168 ff.
consensus, role in constitutional interpretation 225 ff.
consent
    competent 196 ff.
    informed 191 ff.
    voluntary 193 ff.
constitution, as document of deontological moral principle 223 ff.

death, as lost opportunity 214 ff.
death, as a punishment 223 ff.
death, as graver harm than imprisonment 239 ff.
desert, in punishment 223 ff.
deterrence theory 152 ff.
devoid of reason, as mark of incompetence 170 ff.
double effect 4, 15, 25
due process 151

fear, when rational 210 ff.

God 15, 19, 59, 95, 180, 211

harm, Socratic account 43 ff.
history, role in constitutional interpretation 225
homicidal diabetic 22, n. 15
hypocrisy, in punishment 92

ignorance 167 ff.
imprisonment, may be cruel and unusual punishment 239 ff.
incompensable injuries 241 ff.
incompetence, defined 166 ff.
informed consent 191 ff.
innocence, concept analysed 4–9

Julius Caesar 205, 221
Jus talionis 77, 79, 231, 232
justice, theories of 26 ff.
justice and utility 148 ff.

least restrictive alternative test 226 ff.
legal realism 51 ff.
let him who is without sin cast the first stone 87 ff.

mutilation, as punishment 233 ff.

natural rights 135 ff.
Nazi "medicine," 19
negligence 238 ff.
noncombatants 6 ff.

Odysseus 72
omission/commission distinction 14 ff.

paternalism, defined 165 ff.
preventive detention, problems of prediction 160
proportionality, as requirement of just

254

punishment 227, 232 ff., 234
psychopath, defined 129 ff.
psychosurgery 183 ff.

rational choice 106
reciprocity, in punishment 77 ff., 83
   as presupposition of rights 131 ff.
retarded persons, their rights 34 ff.
retribution, in Kant's theory 82–92
   in Kant and Rawls 93–102
   defined 229 ff.
rights, as basic in morality 16 ff., 28 ff.
right to be punished 134

self defense, reasonable belief requirement
   8 ff.
shared guilt 89 ff.
social contract, argument for fidelity in
   Socrates 46–53
   Hume's criticism of 59–64
   Kant's and Rawls's use as model of
      rational choice in theory of justice

65 ff.
   in justifying punishment 93–102
   in justifying paternalism 174 ff.
social contract rights 29–31
Stavrogin 209
strict liability 116, 125 ff.
suicide 218

therapy, as an alternative to punishment
   147 ff., 161
torture, as a punishment 233 ff.

utilitarianism, role in constitutional interpretation 226 ff.
   grounds for rejection as moral theory
      16 ff., 29 ff., 71 ff., 94 ff.
utility and justice 148 ff.

voluntary consent 193 ff.

war and war crimes 3–20